THE ART OF
ARMED ROBBERY

THE ART OF
ARMED
ROBBERY

MEMOIRS OF AN ARMED ROBBER

by Terence George Michael Smith

metro

Published by John Blake Publishing Ltd,
3, Bramber Court, 2 Bramber Road,
London W14 9PB, England

www.blake.co.uk

First published in paperback in 2005

ISBN 1 84454 130 4

British Library Cataloguing-in-Publication Data:

A catalogue record for this book is available from the British Library.

Design by www.envydesign.co.uk

Printed in Great Britain by Bookmarque

1 3 5 7 9 10 8 6 4 2

Papers used by John Blake Publishing are natural, recyclable products made
from wood grown in sustainable forests. The manufacturing processes conform
to the environmental regulations of the country of origin.

Every attempt has been made to contact the relevant copyright-holders,
but some were unobtainable. We would be grateful if the appropriate
people could contact us.

*In memory of my niece, Ava Smith, who passed away
at the tender age of 17 months. Sleep tight, little princess,
for we are always with you.*

Author's Note

The idea to write a book began while I was in prison awaiting trial for a crime in which I'd been blatantly and ruthlessly set up by both the police and criminals. During a legal conference with my counsel, James Scobie, he said that he had read the defence material that I had written and that he was so impressed by its style and content, he suggested that I should seriously consider using my time constructively while I was in prison and write a book.

I took this advice and began to scribble away and, before long, I was flying through the chapters. I always knew that I had a decent book or story to tell in me, but it would always be difficult, because how can a former professional criminal write a detailed book about his past without doing others and himself some harm?

I sat and thought about this long and hard in my prison cell and felt that with a little imagination and careful selection it would be possible, particularly as most of the protagonists have sadly passed away. As for those who are still alive, I have used either their nicknames or a pseudonym.

I hope and pray that most readers will view this book as more than just a personal account of crime and adventure in the East End during the latter part of the last century. I hope that social historians, criminologists and even members of the criminal justice system may benefit from the book, so that it may help them to understand the birth and development of the criminal mind, and how it evolves and matures over time.

Most of all, although it is very difficult to avoid, I hope that this book does not sensationalise or glamorise crime, as it not my intention to promote or encourage criminal behaviour. You will discover a whole range of personal, social and criminal topics and issues throughout the course of this book, some that I had to force myself to recall and commit to paper. I felt that this had to be done, though, so that future criminals might realise that a life of crime is not all strawberries and champagne. In essence, this book charts a roller-coaster ride of criminal life and behaviour, and I pray that it makes future blaggers think twice before they pick up a gun and start robbing.

Terry Smith
July 2003

Contents

Acknowledgements

I would like to thank John Blake and his team for giving me the chance to see my story in print. Also Cass Pennant for his excellent advice and support in the publishing of this book.

A bone-deep thanks to my beautiful wife Tracey and our family Terence, Bradley, Jade and Sonny for being simply the best.

Thanks also to my loyal and devoted extended family, Dolly Smith (RIP), Nanny Ada Harris (RIP), Pat and Iris Etherden, Suzy Etherden, Linda Redwood, Iris, Paul, Alec, Thomas and Olivia Woollard. And the funky Freeman family, Patsy, Boozie, Jonathan, Jessica and Maisie who all travelled the length and breadth of the country to visit me in many a remote and hostile prison. God bless you all.

Special thanks also to Mark and Annette Blake, John and Gina Laveve, Tony, Martin and Jack Bowers, Peter Welch, Dean, Christine and family, Tony and Janice Smith. The Old family, Audrey, Ray, Billy, Carly. My brother Lenny and little Len.

Ultimate respect and gratitude to my staunch and remarkable friends who helped me to escape from the prison van in November 1984. Every time I look at my beautiful daughter Jade – now 17 years old – I think of you all and how you did me proud.

Special appreciation to Mr Nick Paul, Mr Atherton, Ray Hill, Monica and Josephine Trustcott, formerly of the psychology department at Long Lartin Prison, and Ericka Calvo of the University of East London for having faith in me and giving me a chance to reform.

Thanks to Dr Mizra, orthopaedic consultant at Central Middlesex Hospital and his medical team for saving my leg. Also Dr Chang of Wandsworth Prison hospital for thinking of my plight when you did not have to!

Strength and honour to Jon Patty (solicitor), James Scobie (counsel) and David Nathan QC (The God of Strategy and Tactics) for helping me defeat the forces of evil.

Special thanks to all the good gravy guys whom I met in the trenches. We had some inexorably tough times, but we made the best of the situation and got through it. I hope that I helped you all 'get through your bird' as you helped me conquer mine. As the old adage says, 'Nothing lasts for ever!' Not even the slamming of the cell door. Still rooting for you all.

Finally, supreme respect to all those who are no longer with us. In alphabetical order: Tony Ash, Dezzy Cunningham, Lenny Carter, Paul Edmonds, Nicky Gerard, Kevin Gregory (The Soldier), Rocky Harty, Old Tommy Hole, Young Tommy Hole (The Best), Jarrot, Lionel Jefferies, Reggie Kray, Charlie McGhee, Darren Pearman, Steve Pearson, Alex Sears, Pat Tomlin and Johnny Wickes.

Foreword

'I did ask if you were going to do the foreword, didn't I?' That was how Terry Smith asked me to write an foreword to this book. I had several reactions – Why me? How come? I felt honoured, as I'd revoked his parole licence back in 1995. Then I thought about the background and history that went into writing this book.

As a fairly new Probation Officer in Canning Town, myself and one or two other Probation Officers were involved with the youngsters, as well as adults. Some evenings, we would go to the Mayflower Centre Youth Club on club nights. We also went to the Rumpus Room, which was a youth club established by Tony and Martin Bowers in some garages attached to Dunlop and Cranbrook Point in Silvertown, now Britannia Village. The negotiation skills of those two, who, at the time, were no more than 14 years old, put many adults to shame in their dealing with the local council and officials.

The Mayflower was a vibrant, exciting place and was always packed. It had as its members some of the Snipers and the Mini-Snipers, many of the people who are described in more detail later in this book. One of the activities I took part in was playing football in 'the cage'. Well, to be honest, I was not that skilful, which you needed to be in the cage, but at least I could tackle when I got close to the players. Terry was among those who played. I recall the man in charge of the Mayflower, Pip Wilson, lovely, dedicated and enthusiastic. It was his enthusiasm and commitment that made the Mayflower the centre it was – for some, a haven; for others, a place to explore their early adolescence.

In the mid-1980s, Pip Wilson wrote a book about Canning Town and I know a few of the lads were not overpleased with one or two things mentioned in it. I remember saying to a couple of them, 'Well, perhaps you should write your own book one day ...' Well, here it is, written by one of those lads, warts and all.

Following his arrest at Kensal Rise, I visited Terry in the hospital wing at Wandsworth Prison and I remember how he left no stone unturned in researching treatment for his leg injury. As time went on, however, he started to walk and then run and play football. I have never heard him moan or whinge about what happened. He never blamed anyone else but himself.

I was pleased for him that during his long prison sentence he focused on education and began to discover the world of books, and particularly words. His joy was obvious at discovering that he could put words together in a creative and descriptive manner. His letters contained some beauties.

I am not here to judge or condone his actions over the years – I'll leave that to others. This book has been a task, in some respects a saviour of his sanity, and a journey through his life so far. It gives an insight into how an armed robber comes to be.

Something else that struck me strongly about this book is that it does not glorify robbery, but shows the waste of talent and life for all concerned. It has taken being locked up for all those years for Terry's story to be discovered.

Nick Paul
Probation Officer

Prologue

It was a beautiful summer morning and the sun was shining brightly. In a nearby cluster of trees, I could hear a turtle dove cooing softly in celebration of such a fine day. I took a deep breath and thought to myself, Mmmm, I feel good. At the mellow age of 42, I had kept my body hard and trim all my life and, whenever a subversive fold of loose skin would appear around the midriff, I would get down the gym and work out until the surplus tissue had been banished for good. Because, in my view, physical fitness and exercise had become synonymous with personal discipline and dependability; no one likes sloppy and unreliable people, more especially when your name and reputation depend on it.

Every weekday, my first mission of the day was to take my adolescent daughter to school. Dropping her off at the side entrance, I was oblivious to her warning mantra, 'Dad, I can't kiss you today,' as she pointed to the unusual gathering of teenage boys enjoying their pre-assembly rush of nicotine. 'It's OK,' I crooned, 'I understand.' The delicate embarrassment of kissing one's father goodbye in public no doubt would have led to an avalanche of ridicule at break time. Jade departed.

I returned home and then, in tune with my principles of keeping fit, I trundled off on a three-mile jog along the picturesque seafront of Canvey Island, Essex. I called it 'Dog-Shit Drive', due to the plethora of fecal waste that walkers and fellow joggers had to negotiate as they inhaled the salty breeze flowing down the Thames Estuary.

The month of June has always embodied a mystical element of ambivalence for me. On the merit side, I met, fell in love and married my beautiful fiancée in June. On the debit side, I was sentenced to 15 years' imprisonment for armed robbery and nearly lost my life during another robbery in June. Put bluntly, all manner of serious criminality, which included an erstwhile fascination for the contents of security vans, had come to an end a long, long time ago in the flaming month of June.

So how was it I ended up on this day, 5 June 2001, in the bizarre situation of having my vehicle forced to a standstill on a public road by the combined might of eight police vehicles? Not to mention the numerous police machine-guns and service pistols pointing menacingly at my head? And how had I managed to acquire an Uzi sub-machine-gun, 376 rounds of ammunition, shoulder stock and silencer, all nestling in the passenger footwell of my car? What the hell was happening? For surely this was hell, the beginning of my own personal nightmare.

Quite simply, I had been set up by a suspected Machiavellian crook collusion. An evil deed without a name, and I was the reluctant sucker. How was I to explain this one? With my hands held high in the air, I looked up to the clear blue sky and wondered when I would next see my beautiful newborn baby boy again. It was then that I realised that my only saviour would be the universal power of truth!

1

Tough Love

According to history or memory, it all began in a dark and dingy backroom of a grocer's shop in Canning Town, London E16. Amidst the makeshift bedroom-cum-stock room of cocoa, corned beef and conflakes, I poked my pretty little head into the world. Boy, if I'd only known what I had let myself in for, I would have quickly and quietly slipped back into the warmth and security of my mother's womb. By all accounts, however, nature and fate had other plans for me. Therefore, on the twelfth day of February 1959, Terence George Michael Smith, second son of Leonard Charles Smith, and the fourth child of Rosemary Gertrude Smith, née Lord, was born.

Whether there were sighs of relief, whelps of joy or unalloyed celebration by close family and friends, I was not to know. What was for sure, the seminal clock of human life and existence was ticking away and I was here to stay to face and confront all that this beautiful and brutal world could throw at me.

Although the provenance of the name 'Canning Town' is unrecorded, we learn that its origin can be traced back to a settlement on low-lying marshland in the 1840s. The subsequent development of a railway line, the docks, shipbuilding works and chemical factories in the mid-eighteenth century, not only created demand for housing in the area but, by the 1880s, Canning Town had evolved into a major centre of industry in the south.

In many respects, the availability of low-grade labour combined with cheap and sub-standard living accommodation made Canning Town a social and economic magnet for diverse immigrant populations. Over the past century or more, these have ranged from German, Italian, Jewish, Afro-Caribbean and, more recently, Pakistani, Somalian and African settlers.

By the 1900s, however, the sudden demise of the Thames Ironworks brought about widespread unemployment and distress. During this period of social upheaval, many voluntary organisations, such as hospitals, churches and charities, sought to alleviate the pervasive social ills of poor sanitation, health and poverty. Things did not improve, though, until after the World War II, when there was a concerted effort by West Ham Council to redevelop the south of Canning Town with modern housing and amenities in the form of the Keir Hardy Estate. This was bolstered by the earlier construction of Silvertown Way in 1934, which was afforded the grand title of 'the Road to the Empire'. Increased demand for low-paid and low- and semi-skilled labour by the Royal Docks, Beckton Gasworks, the Post Office and the sugar refineries in the 1950s and 1960s led to an ever-increasing shortage of housing.

Seemingly, the short-term solution to this recurring problem was the genesis and development of the tower blocks. At a most generous interpretation of this social experiment, it imprisoned and dehumanised its inhabitants. At it most damaging and soul-destroying, the collapse of Ronan Point in 1968 saw the tragic loss of five people.

On a very simplistic level, if concrete is associated with inflexibility and hardness and open spaces of green areas are associated with flexibility and softness, then surely there is a stark lesson to be learnt by the planners and architects of modern housing estates.

Put succinctly, I view myself as a product of Canning Town and, whether I like it or not, that is where my roots lie. This has partly made me what I am today, an individual who has voraciously sucked upon the nipple of E16 crime, culture and adventure. Somehow, us 'Towners', as we are often referred to, have had to drag ourselves out of the gutter and adopt and embrace social and economic improvement. I chose the tools of the professional armed robber, the mask and the gun. This is my story, the unvarnished truth of a cosmic struggle between good and evil, light and darkness and, finally, a long-awaited spiritual cleansing.

Looking back, 1959 was a period of uncertainty and change in England and around the world. It must have been a time of bone-deep concern and apprehension about where humanity was heading. At home, CND members and supporters marched from Aldermaston to Trafalgar Square in central London in order to stop the armaments race. West Indian immigrants were still travelling from their Caribbean homeland in search of work and security. Henry Cooper, the heavyweight boxer, won the Empire Championship and Manchester City beat Bolton Wanderers 2–1 in the FA Cup Final at Wembley.

On an international level, Fidel Castro seized power in Cuba and then denied that he was a Communist. The Dalai Lama fled Tibet to escape his Chinese oppressors and travelled to India. There was an attempted assassination of François Mitterand, the French politician, and astronauts sent a Rhesus monkey on a successful trip into space for 13 minutes.

Sadly, 1959 also saw the loss of the jazz singer Billie Holiday, the immensely gifted rock 'n' roll singer Buddy Holly, and the talented and debonair Hollywood actor Errol Flynn. To compensate for this, Hollywood presented us with the Roman epic *Ben Hur* starring Charlton Heston.

All this compressed into the space of 12 months suggests that the world was going through an uneasy process change in which anything could happen and, indeed, did happen. The only consolation we could grasp was that 1959 became the social and cultural springboard into the much more permissive and vibrant era of the 1960s.

There was, perhaps, one remarkable person whom I could say with my hand on my heart was overjoyed at my timely arrival in

1959, and that was my dear grandmother Dolly Smith. For, by pure coincidence or design, we not only shared the same birth sign of Aquarius, but also the same birth date.

Dolly was married to my grandfather Leonard Smith. Together, thay had raised three strong, healthy sons – Leonard (my father), Tony and Derek, the youngest. Apparently, my grandfather, who was a very principled and hard-working man, had a greengrocery stall in the old Rathbone Market in Barking Road, Canning Town. Evidently, he use to rise at 3.00am every day, except Sundays, to wheel his barrow to the Fruit and Vegetable Market at Spitalfields, near Aldgate, and then pull it all the way back to Rathbone Market to serve his local customers. Such was his dedication and commitment to his business, he was confronted by an aggressive mob on the Ironbridge at Canning Town during the General Strike of 1926, whereupon he was threatened that if he did not stop working, they would throw his barrow over the bridge and into the River Lea.

Later, my grandfather bought a corner greengrocer's shop in Clarence Road, Canning Town, where his sons were encouraged to help out and run the business. The eldest son, Leonard, my father, borrowed £500 from his parents and set up his own grocer's shop directly opposite the original greengrocery outlet. Part of the deal was that my father and his wife, Rose, would not sell any products or foodstuffs that would undermine the greengrocery business. But, within weeks, this unwritten family agreement was broken and the new grocery shop was selling, among other items, tins of potatoes, processed peas and carrots.

In spite of this inter-family disagreement, my grandmother Dolly was at the epicentre of the growing Smith clan. She possessed and expressed a natural ability to beam love and warmth upon everyone in equal measure. I always recall as a small child running to and from our shop to theirs across the road to play in the storerooms at the back of their premises. A natural lover of people and animals, my grandmother always had dogs, cats, ducks, geese, goats and the occasional horse. The intense joy and pleasure of being near my grandmother was perhaps compounded by the unique temporal coincidence of our birth dates. To some degree, this was to symbolise an umbilical cord of maternal love, warmth and togetherness that stretches even now beyond life itself.

All in all, the new Smith family at the grocery shop developed into a largish camp. Apart from my mother and father there were five siblings – my elder half-sister Carol and my elder half-brother Stephen were both the progeny of a previous marriage, and then there was Lenny junior, who was sixteen months older than me, and my younger sister Audrey.

To this day, I do not know whether my conception and attendant birth was a planned event or the dire consequence of rampant sex. All I do know was that I was slap bang right in the middle of a nepotistic alliance between my father and his favourite, Lenny junior, and my mother and her favourite, my younger sister Audrey. Relatively quickly, I realised that this was not going to be some fun-loving, leisurely stroll through the Utopian fields of childhood, but that this was going to be a veritable battle to reach the safety net of adulthood and independence.

To exacerbate matters, this belligerent and squawking nest of Smiths were all crammed into what was basically a squalid Victorian ground-floor lock-up shop. In theory, there was only one visible entry into the shop and this was directly from the street. Once you entered the self-service corner shop, which was, or supposed to be, our front living quarters, the rest of the diminutive dwelling consisted of the main stock bedroom, a very small living room, a grimy back bedroom with green, distempered walls, a scullery and a small yard that abutted a lock-up garage which was rented out to Puggy Ford, an amicable scrap-metal dealer. Above us lived a strange and mystical mother and adult daughter who punctiliously paid their rent and were as quiet as church mice in the dead of night.

In comparison with modern standards of living, 74 Clarence Road, Canning Town, was a grade 'A' piss-hole. We had one tin bath a week, no hot water, no method of heating save the traditional coal fire and an outside toilet. The décor was Spartan and the living space was being persistently encroached upon by the ever-increasing demands of the grocery business. If there was one silver lining to this cramped cloud, it was that we would never go hungry.

Anyone who has grown up with older brothers and sisters – and, more especially, if one of them is an aggressively competitive brother who is 16 months older – will tell you that life is going to be damned tough. So tough, in fact, that your life seemingly becomes one fraternal conflict in which violence becomes synonymous with survival. Even at an early age, I can always remember fighting with my brother Lenny. With him being significantly older than me, I was always on the back foot, constantly on my guard for the next test of strength and combat. We were two eggs in the nest – his hatched before mine, and was therefore appreciably bigger and stronger and able to dominate me, the weaker chick.

More interestingly, in psychology, there is a theory that puts forward the view that an ugly or less attractive infant or child will invariably be punished or penalised by a parent or guardian more frequently than an attractive or angelic-looking child. I am not saying that I was an ugly urchin, but the same principle must apply to the favourite son or daughter versus the runt of the litter. For as long as I can remember, I was always in trouble or being punished for some perceived slight or misdemeanour.

Alternatively, however, my existence could also be construed as a vulnerable principality encircled or beset by bellicose states of ill intent. For there was the omnipotent presence of a superpower, my towering father, who chastised and disciplined his subjects with all the might of an Orwellian dictator. All forms of persuasive democratic argument or debate were outlawed in our household. Quite simply, it was a matter of two parents good, five brats bad.

Put plainly, the superpower was a 6ft-plus, 17st brute of a man who dished out punishment with the broom handle or an aluminium hoover extension. To be fair to all the family, he was an uncouth thug who administered violent beatings so frequently that we had all become conditioned to this type of behaviour and, indeed, considered it a social norm which not only occurred in our family but also naturally in all other families. From what I can recall, the violence and intimidation was so pervasive in our household, if it was not the superpower venting his wrath and frustration, it was my equally punitive mother with her wooden clogs, or the inherent sadism of Stephen or the almost hourly head-to-heads with Lenny. Put quite bluntly, being situated at the end of the line, like modern-day Afghanistan, all the thumps stopped with me.

Admittedly, my younger sister Audrey was not impervious to physical violence and beatings which she occasionally received but, being a small girl, and a stunningly pretty girl at that, to some extent rendered her an exceedingly soft target of little worth or import. In short, the creation and distribution of physical violence behind the closed doors of the Smith household was a wretched disease which could flare up at any time. It took me a long time to decide that the only substantive antidote to this infectious and contagious malaise was to escape. And given the first opportunity, I would be gone.

Absurd as it seems, if there was one consolation to be taken from this, it is that one learns the value of fear and violence as an all-important mechanism for survival. For example, if I won one in ten fights against Lenny as a child, at least it would have had a deterrent effect to some degree. As he would not come back for any more until his confidence had risen for a fresh attack. Germany revisited.

On another level, being on the receiving end of regular beatings made one extremely streetwise, like the time when the superpower had come home from his traditional Sunday afternoon guzzle at The Durham Arms public house in Stephenson Street, Canning Town. I was fighting with Lenny as usual when I rather eloquently, for a child, blurted out, 'FUCK OFF, YOU CUNT!' to which the inebriated tyrant roared, 'WHO SAID THAT?'

Quick as a parliamentary heckler, I added, 'Him, Dad,' and pointed at Lenny with all the solemnity of a judge passing sentence. As the giant beer-snorting brute came menacingly towards us, I slipped away to the wailing cries of pain as poor Lenny was getting a good hiding. Of course, I am not proud of this, but our house was a battle zone and short-term guerrilla tactics were all part of the long-term survival strategy.

Sometimes the only way to prevent the superpower from inflicting brutal violence was to run for your life, rabbit-like, to the limited sanctuary of your bedroom or any available exit to beautiful freedom. The superpower wised up to this and used to corner us while he ordered a reluctant Audrey to go and fetch the broom. No doubt this was psychological and emotional torture for Audrey, who not only had to supply the bullets to the firing squad, but also had to witness the brutal execution of a loved one. I always recall her tearful face as she was forced to bring the broom and listen to those terrible beatings. In my view, there is nothing worse than to hear another human being or animal in severe pain, and being totally unable to help the victim in any shape or form. I cannot understand the mentality of such a father who would subject his own flesh and blood to such a violent and oppressive regime. Admittedly, every family or household in the world should adopt and embrace some workable code of discipline and order, but unwarranted physical abuse on this unacceptable scale is completely at odds with the healthy promotion and development of loving family relationships.

Little wonder then, as some criminologists proclaim, dysfunctional childhood development is often linked to a tendency towards criminal behaviour in adulthood. Please do not get me wrong; I am not seeking to lay the blame for my criminality squarely at the door of inadequate parental upbringing, but what I am trying to say is that an oppressed and brutalised child who is constantly physically abused by his or her peers is more likely to adopt and exhibit deviant adolescent behaviour than those who derive from a so-called 'normal' family background. One compelling argument suggests that, if you place a child in an abnormal social setting with abnormal rules and regulations, it follows that you must anticipate or expect an abnormal response or reaction. In my view, the intensely punitive social environment of the Smith household played a significant, though not entirely exclusive, role in the growth and development of my criminal behaviour and tendencies.

Therefore, even as a child, all manner of personal discourse and debate was constrained and repressed by an unhealthy dollop of rules and regulations, which were enforced by excessive punitive measures to keep me in check ... but I was having none of it. The comfortable path back to the warmth and security of the womb was cut off. I had to make allies and alliances with those outside the confines of Stalag 13, who were equally victimised and oppressed. Thank God for the saviour of school.

2

School of Hard Knocks

I first attended Star Lane Infants School aged five in 1964. In many respects, Star Lane School was the product of the Education Act of 1850 which expressed the need to provide basic education to children from the ages of five to eleven years. The general aims of primary schools during the 1960s were to teach children the three 'Rs' – reading, writing and arithmetic – and prepare them for the thoroughness of secondary school education.

Star Lane Primary School itself was built in 1893. It was, and still remains, a large, brick-built Victorian structure with some 30 or so spacious classrooms. Its main catchment area was that of Canning Town and, therefore, it had to contend with a multitude of social and economic problems which emanated from urban working-class life. Despite being a predominantly Christian-based school with its daily diet of religious assemblies of hymns, sermons and prayers, it did welcome and cater for other diverse religions and cultures. Although I was very reverential towards Christianity, with its pious and moral values, I was, however, totally against the way that it was spoon-fed on a daily basis, chanting archaic catechisms and singing sombre songs. Basically, I felt that the world of unrestrained adventure and excitement was nigh, and I had no need or desire for the spiritual enlightenment or restraints of the Christian faith.

As far as I can remember, my period at the Infants School was largely uneventful, save for a small role in a school play in which I played the part of a frog in green tights. There was also the time when my brother Lenny had a fight with a stronger boy, who had him in a tight headlock. I distinctly recall desperately ordering the boy to let him go and, when the boy did not comply, out of fraternal loyalty, I smashed an upper-cut into the boy's face only to hear the piercing scream of Lenny's voice as I misdirected the punch into Lenny's face. Whoops! It did the trick, though, as Lenny's screaming made the boy let him go.

As always, I was invariably up to mischief in the playground, either fighting, wrestling, swearing, climbing out of bounds or whatever. I must have driven our teacher Mrs Owen to the end of her tether, as she said to me, 'If you misbehave once again, I am going to pull your shorts down, put you over my knee and smack your bottom in front of the whole class.' I do not know if this threat was supposed to scare or humiliate me but, as sure as night follows day, the inevitable happened and I was caught misbehaving again. Mrs Owen reissued the threat and said that she was going to do it after playtime. After the break, on the way up to the classroom, I weighed up the situation and thought that I would front it out. Surely she didn't mean it!

Unfortunately, she kept her promise and smacked my bare bottom in front of the whole class. I was going to tell my parents but, fearing another wallop, I decided to turn the other cheek, and take the humiliation on the chin. I most probably deserved it anyway.

After two years in the Infants School, I was moved up to the Junior School and, no doubt, my reputation as a notorious troublemaker preceded me as I was placed in Mr (Percy) Dunlop's class. He was a very elderly, surly, sergeant major-type of teacher who abhorred any form of insolence or indiscipline. In his perceptive eyes, I was the living embodiment of mischievous devilment. There was not a day that passed where either me, Ossie Hassan or Mo Elliot did not receive the cane. It became such a daily ritual that it ceased to be an effective deterrent. Mr Dunlop, in his trembling fury, used to say to me 'Wipe that smirk off your face!' and I would do my best to change my facial expression, but to no avail. The smirk, if there ever was one, never left my mooey.

Despite the persistent corporal punishment, I had respect for Mr Dunlop as he made a special effort in teaching me the art of calligraphy. To this day, I still recall the little individual flourishes and quirks of his penmanship.

Moreover, Mr Dunlop was the school football manager and coach. He would take our school team all over the London Borough of Newham to play rival schools. On one occasion, we were to play Ranelagh School of Plaistow on our home turf and their coach was also the selector for the Newham District side. Eager to impress him, we beat them 3–0 with me scoring two identical volleys from outside the penalty box. It did not do me any good, though, as I did not reckon in the District coach's plans. Our best player at school was Barry Wallace, a brilliant left-winger with a dynamite left foot shot. I believe that he went on to play professional football and ended up making a living out of the game.

Perhaps the most memorable match took place on the day that my half-sister Carol was to marry her fiancé Steve Perryman. Seeing as the wedding was to be held on a Saturday, my father forced me to work down at the new Silvertown grocery shop which he had bought in 1965. I was desperate to play on this particular Saturday as we were facing Central Park School in the semi-final of the School's Cup at Flanders playing field, East Ham. Once at the Silvertown shop, my father dived into the toilet and I was gone. I crept out of the back door and, with three pence in my pocket, I had just enough money to catch a bus from either Silvertown to Canning Town or Canning Town to East Ham. I decided to run from the shop to Canning Town, some two miles in the pouring rain, and then catch the bus to East Ham. We played the match and lost 2–0.

Fearing greatly for my safety, I crept back to my mother's Clarence Road shop and, I suppose, due to the subsequent matrimonial merriment and mirth of the day, I was spared a copper-bottomed beating.

To my utmost surprise, during the school assembly the following Monday morning, Mrs Hood, the school's headmistress, was recounting a story or sermon with the theme of dedication and determination, when something occured to me – I was sure I knew the story she was droning on about. All of the sudden she said, 'And this boy, Terry Smith ... where is Terry Smith? Please come up here and stand in front of me.'

I thought, God, what have I done now? I am being dragged up in front of the whole school. Little did I know, someone had told the teacher about my running from Silvertown to Canning Town in the pouring rain and was extolling the virtues of dogged commitment to play football for the school.

The seasonal promotion and encouragement of inter-school boxing was also part of the sports curriculum at Star Lane. Naturally, seeing as I was enduring a lifelong boxing match with my elder brother nigh on every day, I enrolled as a potential candidate. Initially, I had two preliminary bouts at Credon Road School, Plaistow, and then went on to the grand final at Canning Town Town Hall. I was really proud of myself. The Town Hall was packed as I met my opponent. I recall sitting in a room before the fight, talking to a fellow boxer. I said, 'Who are you fighting?'

He replied, 'Someone called Smith from Star Lane School.'

'That's me,' I said, and we proudly pointed out each other's parents sitting in the hall while chatting to each other like gladiators before the battle of strength and skill in the Colosseum. I went on to win the fight and was awarded a heavy, inscribed bronze medal. For once, this really pleased my parents who, ironically, adored boxing.

The following year, I met the same boxer in the preliminary bouts and was disqualified for slapping. This annoyed me, as I was bashing the hell out of my opponent. I was so aggrieved by the perverse verdict, I retired unbeaten.

Due to the uncontrollable behaviour of a specific group of pupils at Star Lane and the adverse effect that it was having on the well-behaved, more studious members of the class, Mrs Hood decided to create a policy of segregation of trouble-makers. The school recruited a Mr Rose, a resolute West Indian teacher of strong character and principles who was put in charge of the newly formed sin-bin class. Along with myself, there was Gee Ashman, Gerald Fisher, Ossie Hassan, Boozy Freeman, Mo Elliot, Willie Russell and several others. On reflection, the creation and implementation of this special class signifies how unruly and mischievous we urchins really were. Having said that, Mr Rose won us over with his lifelong love of cricket. He would take us over to the nearby sports field during his dinner breaks and organise matches. In spite of the overall aims and objectives of the sin-bin class to isolate or segregate us rebels from the main body of the school, I cannot recall Mr Rose ever using corporal punishment on his pupils.

The headmistress Mrs Hood, Mr Rose and Mr Dunlop – who, in 1972, went on to become the oldest working teacher in the country – were all excellent teachers in their own right. These teachers were, to some degree, at the coalface of primary education. Year after year they prepared pupils for the 11-Plus examination, which, more often than not, determined the type of secondary education the children would be given and, by extension, what occupational path or career they might eventually pursue. Seeing as I never took the 11-Plus, there was only one port in the storm for me – the redoubtable Pretoria Road Secondary School.

As it turned out, a rather strange family event occurred to me during my education at Star Lane. During the school holidays, the Smith clan used to visit my grandparents who had a cosy retirement bungalow on two acres of ground near Maldon, Essex. Trips to Balmoral, as they were called, were always fabulous treats for us, as not only did it give us the opportunity to visit our warm-hearted grandmother, but it allowed us to explore and enjoy the countryside. This was, perhaps, the happiest period of my childhood, more specifically as, during one of our sporadic visits to Balmoral, I asked to stay longer and, to my amazement, this was granted and I even started to go to the local village school. I do not know if this occurred by accident or it was a pre-planned arrangement, but I was not complaining. It seemed like I had progressed or evolved from the urban hell-hole of Canning Town and its attendant conflict and upheaval to the sweet Utopia of the countryside. The cumulative effect of being surrounded by woods and wildlife, fields and trees and the close proximity of my affectionate grandmother made me feel like I was in paradise.

There was no pressure at the local village school. I was receiving private schooling from my grandmother and, more importantly, aged seven, I created my very own little private world of fantasy where I made a bow and arrow and set off into the fields to hunt for food. Perhaps the most striking recollection I have of this fine period is waking up on a bright sunny morning and realising that no one was inside the bungalow. In a seemingly sleepy reverie, I strolled out to the nearby apple orchard to see my grandmother up a ladder picking apples. It was like a surreal dream, all soft and unfocused, like I was cosseted in a cocoon of loveliness.

Then the inevitable occurred. One autumn day, I was walking home from school when I clumsily tumbled backwards down a ditch and muddied my jeans. On getting back to the bungalow, very uncharacteristically, my grandmother shouted at me and told me to get to bed. Her bizarre behaviour coupled with the fact that it was only 4.00pm shocked me. Bemused and confused, I refused and ran off up to the spinney. Later, my parents were summoned from London and at 2.00am they found me sleeping with the animals in the rabbit hutch. After approximately nine glorious months of my pastoral idyll, I was carted off back to the cultural depravity of Canning Town. Who knows how things would have turned out for me had I remained in the countryside? Whatever, that short snapshot of bone-deep peacefulness and contentment has remained the yardstick of happiness to which I aspire for the rest of my life. A tree, we are told, is known by its fruits. Well, if that is the case, I will return for another bite, that's for sure.

On my return to London, I was once again thrown into the ever-growing and tightening clutch of the Smith household. Only this time it was not back to the cramped and squalid lock-up shop in Clarence Road, Canning Town, but to a Victorian terraced house two miles away in Grange Road, Plaistow. The sleeping arrangements were split into three bedrooms. My parents, of course, monopolised the main bedroom. Audrey and Carol were dispatched to the small bedroom, while I was billeted with my two elder brothers, Lenny and Stephen. As always, once the novelty of a new face indoors had evaporated, we were invariably bickering, quarrelling or fighting over something inane or trivial.

By far the most fascinating aspect of the property for me, however, was that it backed on to the East London Cemetery, a seemingly massive burial ground that had all the mystery and intrigue of a dark continent. It was to become my very own Africa, a sacred place where I could lose myself and explore all the elusive mystery and imagery of death. Later, as I got older, it would become my very own playground, where I would spend hours and hours alone reading the tombstones of unknown people, wondering what they were like, how they lived, how they died and particularly where they were now. The more I thought about such obscure and unfathomable concepts, the more they both perturbed and fascinated me. Surely there was more to our mere existence than our physical presence? The deeper I thought, the darker the solutions became, to the extent that I would switch off and accept this existence as my lot and that I was to make the best of it.

Early in the mornings, my father would rise before us and set off for his grocery shop in Silvertown while the rest of us would walk to the other grocery shop at Clarence Road and open for business. On one specific occasion, I recall walking to the shop with the others and I was sucking a plastic compass that I had retrieved from a lucky jamboree bag. Somehow, the compass got lodged in my throat and I was too scared to tell anyone for fear of getting a good hiding. My elder sister Carol, who noticed that I was looking rather pale and unwell, suggested that I should have some Junior Aspirin which I gulped down ... and actually swallowed the entire compass. Years later, I told my grandmother and she reassured me that nature would have taken its course.

On another occasion, I came home from school to have dinner at the shop and I must have antagonised Carol as she thumped me in my abdomen and walked away. The next thing I recall, I was being woken up from a deep sleep by a seriously concerned Carol who must have knocked me unconscious.

Perhaps the scariest incident occurred at our house in Grange Road when every Saturday night my parents used to visit their favourite pub, The Dartmouth Arms in Bidder Street. Not surprisingly, the responsibility of managing your own business is a very stressful occupation, especially with added stresses and strains of raising a large family. Obviously, my parents needed some sort of social life to relieve all their pent-up tension and stress. Therefore, light ale and gin and tonic became their liquid panacea. During these, to a great degree, anodyne social events, we occasionally used to have a babysitter to mind us. But one night, we all fell asleep in the lounge while watching late-night television with the lounge door closed. Unbeknown to us, my electric blanket was smouldering away upstairs, sending thick, acrid smoke all round the house, except the room we were in. When my parents came home in the early hours of the morning, they opened the front door to the smoke. Full credit to my father, who ran upstairs and picked up the smouldering blankets and threw them out of the bedroom window. To a great extent, we were lucky that night as there were many cases in the 1960s of cheap and unsafe paraffin fires setting houses alight in the area; on one tragic occasion, three children perished.

As I have mentioned before, in about 1965 my father decided to expand the grocery business and purchase another lock-up shop in Barnwood Court, Silvertown. Essentially, Barnwood Court was situated midway between Canning Town and North Woolwich. It consisted of two tower blocks, Dunlop and Cranbrook Points, a semi-circular row of shops, a pub, a primary school, a small park and very little else. In my view, it was the last place on earth that I would want to live, as it appeared totally cut off from civilisation. In reality, it should have been called 'Greywood Court', as everything appeared to be imbued with greyness. The sky, the tower blocks, the vista, the future. I hated the place, and particularly the wretched grey confines of my prison, the Spar grocery shop. Invariably, my brother Lenny and I were forced to work in the shop stacking the shelves, mopping the floors or washing out the fridge freezers, but gradually, bit by bit, we managed to make contact with visitors to the shop and made some good friends. I emphasise 'good' friends as, in a world of impenetrable greyness, the likes of Tony and Martin Bowers, Trevor and Leon Shakes became veritable rays of light and hope.

Due to the isolated nature of Barnwood Court, we had to make do with the basic amenities and artefacts around us. For instance, within the dark bowels of the tower blocks were adjoining pram sheds, which were more like catacombs for the unsalvageable. These spooky surroundings, the source of many ghost stories, were perfect for playing run-outs, or we would venture over to the nearby Royal Docks and explore its vast loading bays and storage sheds. Later, Tony and Martin came up with the idea of our own youth club called 'The Rumpus Rooms'. Later still, through their drive and enthusiasm, this project evolved into The Peacock Gymnasium, a large multi-purpose gymnasium in East London that has become a credit to the local community and an equally renowned international boxing enterprise.

In the late 1990s, as if to confirm or underscore this unfavourable depiction of Barnwood Court, it was completely demolished and replaced with low-rise dockland accommodation. Someone, somewhere, like me, must have felt the same way about this grey monstrosity as it is now confined to the annals of East London history.

3

Ganging Up

After the cumulative experience of six years at Star Lane Infant and Primary School, in 1970 it was time to move on to the 'big school'. Despite the fact that the Smith clan had moved to Grange Road, we still came under the catchment area of Pretoria Road Secondary School for boys and girls. At this time, much to the annoyance of our bubbling and frothing testosterone, the school was split up along gender lines, which was supposed to promote concentration and excellence in the academic arena. The transfer from Star Lane to Pretoria Road, however, was like discovering and exploring a hidden continent, as Pretoria produced the golden opportunity for me to make and embrace new friends and new freedoms in a totally new social arena where older or more senior boys and girls set the standards in the three 'Ss' – style, sport and sex. It was, for me, like finding a cornucopia of exhilaration and excitement and, boy, was I going to have fun, fun, fun.

Duty and demands at home dictated that both Lenny and I were allotted the tasks of helping our father stack the shelves and wash and mop the surfaces and cabinets at the wretched Spar grocery shop at Silvertown. This was a significant burden, as by day we had to slave over the mysteries and demands of academia at school, and at night we had to endure the monotonous drudgery of restocking the shelves at the shop. This aggrieved us considerably, as there was little time to play and socialise with our new-found school friends. When classmates asked us if we had watched a particular cartoon on children's television, we would make pathetic excuses that we were too busy to watch television. Naturally, both Lenny and myself pleaded with our overbearing taskmaster, using a series of well-planned arguments and reasons why we should have access to apparently special privileges, such as being allowed out to play after the shop closed at 6.00pm or special dispensation to attend midweek and weekend school football matches, but the superpower was a surly old dictator who would deny and dismiss our basic child rights and privileges on a whim.

We were really annoyed by this, as the next day at school fellow pupils and friends would recount how much they enjoyed an inter-school football match, sports day, badminton or judo class. Instead, we had to trundle down to sombre Silvertown and stack Anchor butter, baked beans and soap powder on the voluminous shelves. We detested being underpaid and overworked, and we therefore used our own initiative to devise and organise our own unique brand of resistance.

On one level, our overall plan of action was to obey and comply with our father's unreasonable imprisonment after school; but on another level, we treated school as playtime, either by playing truant or misbehaving in class. More often than not, the teachers were only too glad that we were absent and would not go out of their way to report us.

I must confess – and I am sure some teachers will agree, such as the Deputy Head, Mr Talbot, or the resolute maths teacher, Mr McCarthy – I was an out and out terror. I rarely enjoyed classes as I was invariably up to mischief. But, when I did give a topic my undivided attention, it was usually in art, geography or woodwork classes. I suppose the lack of desire and enthusiasm for anything remotely academic meant that I was destined to be manual labour fodder for the diverse industrial factories that peppered the East London area.

As with the latter years at Star Lane Primary School, I was always getting myself into trouble with the teachers for talking in class, swearing, fighting or being out of school bounds at the local corner sweet shop. I lost count of how many times I received four or six of the best from Mr McCarthy's cane. Despite being an excellent maths teacher, Mr McCarthy was the school disciplinarian. He was very strict but remarkably fair and thus gained the respect of almost all the school.

As was Pretoria School's wont, I was placed in a more advanced set or class where classroom behaviour and discipline were more rigid and authoritarian. As a result, my ability to comprehend complex concepts and arguments began to suffer enormously. Put succinctly, on an intellectual and developmental level, I was way out of my academic depth. My education had been compromised by self-imposed discipline and control problems.

As an example, if and when there was an organised school outing or trip planned, I was invariably told, along with my ever-growing cohort of teenage subversives, that we were too disobedient or disorderly to be trusted and therefore we would not be considered for such treats. Gripped by Spartacus-like anger and indignation, we select few of little worth decided to organise and orchestrate our very own extra-curricular outings. No doubt our teacher-less adventures would turn out to be far more exciting and exhilarating than theirs anyway.

It must be said, we never played truant at the primary school, chiefly because we had the same teachers day in, day out, who were able to monitor their charges more strictly. But the secondary school collegiate system of changing both teacher and classroom after every lesson was open and vulnerable to abuse and, being master exploiters of the school system, we took full advantage of it.

On any given day, without any forethought or reason, our ragged band of deeply aggrieved pupil-cum-adventurers – Gee Ashman, Gerald Fisher, Boozy Freeman, Mickey Perrin, Kevin Lewis, myself and many more truant wannabes – would club together our dinner money and put it to a democratic vote which part of our marvellous metropolitan capital we would explore. Provided that we set off early and returned to the school site by the end of the school day so as not to raise suspicion among our parents, we would visit the Royal Parks, London Zoo, the Tower of London, Epping Forest, the local lido in the summer season or, our favourite venue, the Natural History and Science Museum at South Kensington. To conserve our meagre funds, we would bunk the train fares there and back, either artfully dodging the ticket collectors or brazenly bolting past them and hoping that they would not chase us. Believe it or not, we had visited the Natural History and Science Museum so many times we knew every part of its labyrinthine corridors by heart. We would spend hours upon glorious hours exploring the different and diverse sectors or themes of the museum.

One of our favourite pastimes was to gaze adoringly at the stuffed British birds and their complete set of eggs in the animal section. We were all avid bird egg collectors, each with our own set of birds' eggs at home, from the largest mute swan to the diminutive wren's egg; this was no trivial game to us, it was a serious business. We raided libraries for bird books, swapped eggs with each other and did all types of amazing and daring feats to acquire the best egg collection within our exclusive cadre.

For example, Gee Ashman was crowned king of the crow's nest climbers, as this particular species, the Carrion Crow, would build its usually visible large nest on the flimsiest of branches at the very top of lofty elm or oak trees. Obviously, being very competitive, I tried to emulate the supreme climbing skills and nous of Gee, but I must concede he was the guv'nor. We used to climb up to the nest in the trees and place the eggs in our mouths for safekeeping and climb back down again, sometimes doing many trips until the nest was empty. Paradoxically, we only wanted the eggshell as we blew the all-important life-giving yolk out of the egg via pinholes we'd pierced at either end.

To our delight, we found a specially adapted raised footpath which led from the banks of a lake at Regent's Park to the inaccessible island that bred and possessed some of the most beautiful British and tropical waterfowl in Great Britain. God knows how we found this path but its arcane secret was passed on to me and we would wade across the lake to the island and steal the rare and exotic birds' eggs under the watchful guardianship of the Royal Parks Police. On one hilarious occasion, Gerald Fisher was inching his way across to the island when he misjudged the direction of the secret path and slipped up to his neck in water. We all burst out laughing which brought unwanted attention to ourselves. Nonetheless, our dogged determination always guaranteed that we were successful.

Sometimes, if we had the money, we would hire a rowing boat and row under the protective chains to the main island and steal the birds' eggs to the great distress and anxiety of the combined duck, geese and swan population. The ensuing commotion and chaos would alert passers-by and onlookers, who would try to intervene by shouting at us, threatening to call the police because of our obviously selfish and destructive behaviour. Unperturbed, we were very experienced and resolute egg collectors, so we would ignore the joint clamour and din of the birds and protestors and make good our escape by rowing to the opposite side of the lake.

On another unofficial excursion, we decided to invade London Zoo at Regent's Park and try to steal penguins' eggs from the architecturally acclaimed penguin enclosure. We would jump over the wall and calmly walk down the slopes to the wooden nesting boxes and nick their eggs in full view of hordes of amazed onlookers. During another time we visited the massive Snowden Aviary at the Zoo. I climbed over the pedestrian footbridge, climbed up a metal pylon and nicked a white egret's egg right under the noses of onlookers who were now level in height with the egret's nest. I know that it was a liberty but we egg collectors were fanatics, as it meant everything to have the best egg collection.

During yet another paramilitary-type raid, we decided to steal some beautiful turquoise herons' eggs from a seemingly impregnable island at a secluded reservoir in Walthamstow, East London. At the time, these were very sought-after eggs for both their beauty and rarity. The only real problem we had was that the island had a lofty watchtower, as in a prisoner-of-war camp, from which both security personnel and bird watchers could look at and protect their charges. On one cold and windswept Sunday afternoon in February, about six of us waited until dusk, at which point Gee Ashman and I rowed across to the island in an inflatable dinghy. As we approached the island, the unexpected occurred. Unbeknown to us, the island had become a long-term roosting place for literally thousands and thousands of birds – sparrows, starlings, wood pigeons, crows and not forgetting the herons. Undeterred by the mass panic and hysteria of thousands of squawking and shrieking birds on the wing, we reached the island and climbed up the trees to the underside of the nests in pitch darkness. But because the nests were so large – the herons visited the same nesting site year after year – we could not circumnavigate the nest's wide circumference.

I had a novel idea, though. I said that we could punch our way through the underside of the nests to gather the prized eggs. This plan worked and we managed to grab up to 14 beautiful herons' eggs which we shared out equally with our friends. The very next day at school, Gee and I were accorded hero status as we had achieved the unachievable.

As I got older, my natural instinct and enthusiasm for bird-egg collecting began to wane. This was partly due to the social and cultural pressures of adolescent gatherings and adventures. It was also partly due to a very sad and poignant experience. I have always adored and respected swans, especially mute swans, for their stunning white plumage, repose and grace on the water. I find it hard to believe, as Geoffrey Chaucer proclaims in *The Canterbury Tales*, that the corpulent friar ate swan for his supper. Nonetheless, a fellow egg collector and inveterate rogue called Kevin Lewis came to me and said that he had found a swan's nest on the River Lea at the rear of a scrap metal yard in Canning Town. He claimed to have raided the nest two days running and retrieved a solitary egg on each occasion after a fight with the swans. This was not so far-fetched, as Kevin Lewis was renowned for his brute strength and sadistic willingness to use it upon vulnerable classmates and creatures. I went with him to the nest by the River Lea and, sure enough, the swan was there on the nest with her proud and dignified spouse beside her. As Lewis went up to the swan with a lump of 4x2 wood in his hand, the swans both put up a terrible fight. As he tried to hit them with the wood, the swans flapped their massive and powerful wings in defiance. It was a very disturbing scene to watch and I was feeling very uneasy. Then, during a respite in the proceedings, sensing imminent defeat, one swan waddled over to its nest, flapped its massive wings on purpose over the nest and smashed the sole egg. Amazingly, it then picked up the broken eggshell in its beak and waddled over to the river edge and deposited it in the water. It did this at least twice and I was absolutely gutted. To see this living creature sacrifice its own offspring in this extremely moving way was devastating. It was then that I sensed that birds, like all other sentient creatures, have strong emotions and feelings and I knew that my egg-collecting days were coming to an end.

Most decisively, the last bird-egg-collecting mission came about when ten of us decided to invade the National Trust Bird Sanctuary at Walton-on-Naze, Essex. This was the nesting site of migratory sand martins, little terns and ringed plovers. On one Sunday at the height of the summer season, we caught a train to Walton-on-Naze Station and walked several miles north along the coastline. Upon entering the restricted National Trust area, we noticed special bird-watching canopies in the distance. I'm ashamed to say, we plundered the nesting sites and we all secured numerous eggs while being dive-bombed by these elegant and rare sea birds. In the distance, we spotted a very irate figure flailing his arms about in the air as if his house was on fire. We quickly decamped and headed back to the safety of the tourist area and the train station.

By now, however, this person, who happened to be a National Trust employee, had summoned the assistance of the local police and was driving around the Walton seafront identifying and arresting us. An unmarked police car screeched to a halt near me and a fellow jumped out and blurted, 'That's one of them,' and gave chase. I ran on to the beach, followed by the policemen, and managed to jettison all my valuable eggs while hurdling sunbathers. Thankfully, the sun-worshippers did not report the contents of my booty. In the end, though, I forgot to offload the sand martins' eggs concealed inside a specially adapted tin in which we kept the smaller, more fragile booty.

I was arrested and taken to the local police station where I was reunited with nearly all of my fellow egging compatriots. After providing the police with our names and addresses, we were all released without charge or caution. Months later, we were prosecuted with a private summons taken out by the National Trust and we all had to appear at the Magistrates' Court at Walton-on-Naze charged with stealing little terns' eggs, a rare and protected species of bird under British law. Much to the chagrin of the National Trust representative, we were all fined £5 each.

To be frank, I did feel sorry for the person who brought the summons. Obviously, he adored the birds, just as we did in our own perverse way, but unlike us myopic and selfish simpletons, he did not plunder their nests for fragile trophies. Please accept my belated apologies and genuine remorse for such unacceptable and stupid behaviour.

During this particular period, I did wonder aloud to fellow egg collectors, some of whom were grown men, why we didn't just find the nest, take a photo of the nests and eggs, and display that as conclusive proof that we could have had the eggs in our collection. That way we wouldn't need to deprive the bird population of much-needed rare species of birds. Moreover, I have often wondered if there is a scientific correlation between bird-egg collectors and kleptomania, as I have observed, especially within our specific social group, the two tendencies appear to be linked to adolescent criminal behaviour.

One of the major difficulties for me as an avid bird-egg collector was that it was absolutely necessary to be out in the field, so to speak, in order to search for the nests and collect the eggs. The biggest obstacle for me was my dictatorial father, who required my presence at his prison-like grocery shop. God, I hated that shop, that remote and soulless monstrosity called Barnwood Court, Silvertown. Nonetheless, because he was bigger than me, I had to endure it.

In order to compensate for this brutal segregation from nature and freedom, I would meticulously read and study my stolen library bird books, my favourite being *The Observer's Guide to British Birds and British Bird Eggs*. I would sit for hours and hours reading about specific birds and their habitats, nesting preferences, styles of bird song and how many clutches of eggs the birds would lay each year. As a result, this was why I was very good at egging. I did my homework, to the extent that I drew birds and their colourful eggs in great detail.

My father, the sadistic superpower, knew of my intense love and affection for this topic and, although he took no interest in my chosen hobby, he knew that it was my weakness. By that, I mean, when I used to play truant, it was inevitable that occasionally I would be 'grassed up' by locals who would go into my father's shop and tell him, 'I saw your son today, in Hainault (or Epping or wherever) ... what was he doing all the way over there?' Little did these informers know that they were feeding the rage of a brutally sick man, for he would accost Lenny or me, depending on who'd been grassed up, and give us a good hiding with the broom handle. Not content with this, he would then seize our much-treasured and prized egg collection and smash them up in the dustbin. This crucified me and he knew it. For me, he wasn't a father; he was the living image of evil and hatred, someone to be despised for eternity.

As the childhood passion for egg collecting subsided, I adopted and embraced new interests and pastimes, like a desire for speed on my bicycle. I would scour all the old bombsites and debris in Newham for old bike frames, wheels, tyres, etc., and build my very own bike. Again, I threw myself into this hobby with great gusto and worked on building the best bicycle in the area. I would rub the frame down to bare metal, paint it or spray it red, then fit it with chrome handlebars, brake levers, a double-cogged crank and a five-speed racing rear wheel. In cockney terminology, 'It was the nuts.' I loved it, it was a work of art and all my school friends wanted to copy my ideas and style. Again though, I was grassed up for playing truant, and this time, knowing that the beloved bike was my latest cherished possession, the demented dictator took a claw hammer and smashed the bike to pieces. The strength and effort it must have taken to reduce this bicycle to a heap of twisted metal defies belief. Years later, I recounted this true story to a close friend, Billy Adams, while in prison, and he said, 'Your father must have been fucking sick in the head!' Yeah, he was.

I do not know if 'danger' is my middle name, but I certainly do have an unhealthy appetite for death-defying feats. For example, on returning from our unofficial outings from central London, we would have to face the awkward dilemma of either bolting past the ticket collector at West Ham Tube Station, or alternatively waiting until the train was out of sight and run across the live railway lines to a nearby fence where we would drop down into a nearby street, thus evading apprehension by the ticket collector. If I said, between the ages of ten and fourteen years, we performed this act of madness more than 50 times, it would be an understatement. We use to kid ourselves that, once the train was out of sight, the electric rails were not live. Thinking back, if one of us had fallen across those live rails we would have been fried alive. It makes me shudder.

At this time, between the ages of 12 and 14, the desire for excitement and adventure was stronger than ever. Anyone who knows the A13 trunk road that currently runs through the heart of East London will have seen the artificial ski slope at East Ham. Well, in 1972, when I was about 13 years old, the ski slope used to be a mountainous slag heap for the local Beckton Gas Works. Somehow, it always fascinated me to know what was up on top of this mountainous peak. So, along with my school friends, Tony Osborne, Clifford Donovan and Mark Watkins, we decided to visit this enigmatic landmark and conquer its mystery.

On reaching the summit, we were disappointed to see a moon-like, sun-scorched flaky surface. As I began to walk along the ridge, however, I began to sink, as though in quicksand, into a black, viscous-like substance or sludge. Once I had taken the first few steps, I couldn't turn around and head for safety. So I scrambled along on all fours and maintained momentum for dear life until I had reached the other side of this slaggy death trap. My friends, Tony and Clifford, were shocked at what they had just witnessed as I'd nearly died in front of them. Mark Watkins, however, who years later turned out to be a wrong 'un, was laughing hysterically at my fate. Annoyed at this scumbag's insensitivity, I rounded on him and tried unsuccessfully to push him into the danger zone but sensibly he ran off. Another lucky escape; will I ever learn?

On another one of my schoolboy adventures, I told to my best friend Tony Rawlings that I had seen hundreds of pushbikes outside a remote train station in Essex; did he fancy going down there and nicking one each, and pedalling back home to London? In any event, we bunked the train fare to Benfleet, Essex, nicked two of the best racing bikes there and pedalled back to London before school was over. The theory was, no one would be looking for stolen bicycles in Canning Town that had been nicked from a station 25 miles away.

When I was 13, there was a teenage craze for air pistols and, as always, I had to have the best. Most of my school pals had 'GAT' air pistols, which fired a 177-gauge pellet, and although potentially harmful to any living creature, it was not lethal. The air pistol that I wanted was a Webley .22-gauge, which had a spring-loaded barrel. Basically, it took all your strength to pull back the barrel to cock the spring. Once fired, however, it could blast through thick Perspex street lamps and explode the glowing filament inside. At school, a pal of mine, Mickey Perrin, equally audacious and my regular truancy partner, said that he had seen a sports shop in Barking town centre which had a Webley 22 displayed in the shop window. He asked me if I would like to go to Barking and commit a smash and grab on the property. It sounded interesting to me and I was indeed up for it.

As a result, we left for Barking one Wednesday evening. Once there, we cased the joint, selected our respective air pistols and smashed a massive brick through the shopfront plate-glass window. Almost immediately, the sports-shop burglar alarm was activated, while we dived inside the window, retrieved the two prized air pistols and sped off down a nearby alleyway. Unbeknown to us, two older schoolboys, obviously potential prefects, witnessed this daring raid and our subsequent escape, and gave chase, but they were unable to catch us.

When we got to the end of the alleyway, we loaded our weapons with the much more lethal air pistol darts and started pinging all the street lamps. During our gun-toting escapade, we got lost and walked along several roads until we had a major dispute about which way to go. I suggested one direction and Mickey suggested another. In any event, we followed Mickey's intuition and found ourselves about an hour later walking past Barking Police Station and, by sheer coincidence, who happened to be coming out of the police station as we walked past? The two schoolboys who'd witnessed the smash and grab. We ran off and split up. I got away and hid my Webley 22 air pistol in my bedroom.

The next day, I went to school – no Mickey! The following day, still no Mickey! Then, several days later, the familiar outlines of two burly cozzers approached our house in Grange Road, Plaistow. You've guessed it! The cozzers came about the Barking smash and grab as Mickey had lollied me. I went to my bedroom and retrieved the Webley air pistol and gave it to the detectives.

Later, on 10 April 1972, I appeared at Barking Juvenile Court and pleaded guilty to my first criminal offence and was sentenced to a 12-month supervision order. From the day I was arrested, Mickey Perrin, one of my closest and most reliable mates, was not to be trusted. Unfortunately, this turned out to be the story of his blighted life, as he went on and on to lolly many other people throughout his criminal career. For some inexplicable reason, Mickey just had to sing like a canary every time he found himself in a police cell.

In spite of this unprecedented encounter with the law, my sense of adventure and pushing personal limits was undiminished. Therefore, on one boring day during the summer school holidays of 1973, I had this overwhelming urge to visit my grandmother Dolly who lived 50 miles away in the Essex countryside. I had no money or food, but I had the all-important freedom of my cherished bicycle. Without staying anything to anyone, at 9.00am I set off from Canning Town and pedalled all the way to Romford, up the A12 to Hatfield Peverell, then through the sinuous and picturesque country lanes to Little Totham, Essex. To the complete surprise of my beloved grandmother, Uncle Derek and his wife, I cycled up their driveway. The journey took me three hours exactly, non-stop. If I had got a puncture, I would have been in big trouble.

As it was, I spent a superb week at my grandmother's country bungalow doing odd chores for her. One of the most enjoyable chores was to cut her overgrown grass with a large petrol lawnmower. While cutting the grass, I frequently went over pieces of bark, timber or stones, making loud, metallic grinding noises from the rotor blade. On one occasion, I checked to see what I had churned up, only to find out to my great distress that I had accidentally run over a pheasant sitting on its nest. With a great deal of concern, thanks to my natural love of birds and animals, we tried in vain to incubate the eggs artificially. This episode really hurt and haunted me; I blamed myself, as I had purposely pedalled down to the countryside for this to happen. Uncle Derek reassured me, though, that this frequently occurred at harvest time when mechanical combine harvesters cut the wheat in the fields, while pheasants and partridges simply refused to leave their nests, succumbing instead to a gruesome death. When it finally came for my trip back to London, the return bicycle journey took me two-and-three-quarter hours in the pouring rain.

A seminal moment occurred during my wayward adolescence of the 1970s when Pretoria School underwent a root and branch transformation, undergoing the enforced transition from a drab and lifeless Secondary School into a vibrant and dynamic mixed-sexed Comprehensive School. Built as a modern senior school in 1932, it was renamed Eastlea in 1973 after its geographical location east of the River Lea. Nonetheless, the seismic conflation of sexually inexperienced young virile boys with the over brimming oestrogen of young nubile girls was tantamount to releasing a fireball in a firework factory. Not surprisingly, the whole school went ballistic. Whatever chance I had of acquiring a worthwhile education before this volcanic mix of the sexes was minimal. As things stood now, I became a high-octane, super-charged social predator with one overriding aim in life – to splice together an inherent desire for adventure and excitement with the equally fascinating exploration of girls, sex and peer group acceptance.

Faced with this type of social and academic upheaval in 1973, albeit by design or fortune, the regular gathering of between 40 and 60 teenagers at the top of our road, Grange Road, Plaistow, evolved into a very visible and vocal adolescent gang. We were called the Manor Road Gang, due to the fact that many of the members came from the squalid and dilapidated tenement buildings in nearby Manor Road, West Ham. To be a qualified member of the gang, basically you had to come from the local areas of West Ham, Plaistow and, of course, Canning Town.

The gang itself was highly territorial, in that we defended and protected our patch against all invaders and infidels with extreme violence. Surprisingly, there was no set hierarchy amongst the gang, but obviously some members were accorded more status and prestige due to their superior age, contempt for authority and a natural ability to dish out blood-curdling violence.

Among the higher echelons of the gang were the likes of Steve Burns, Ray Church, Martin Davison, Steve Reynolds, Paul Hearn, Tallman and my brother Lenny. Lower down the ranks, but still die-hard members, were Terry and Gee Ashman, Mickey Perrin, Kenny Ryan, Willie Church, Martin Modeste, Paul Hearn, Keith Dawkins and myself. Naturally there were countless others, but these individuals formed the nucleus of the gang.

Generally speaking, the external threat of insufferable parents, uniformed authority and rival gangs meant that there was little internal competition. The Manor Road Gang was, in effect, bonded together through the adolescent cement of violence, crime and a compelling desire to be different. By that, I mean we all religiously supported our local football team of West Ham United, whereby we frequently went to away matches and tried, with great success, to infiltrate and take by brute force the main opponents' vocal end of the stadia. We always, along with the more dedicated football hooligans and strategists, managed to overrun or 'take' the North Bank at Arsenal, The Shed at Chelsea and The Shelf at Spurs. Despite my heart not being 100 per cent in the vagaries of senseless football violence, I did my penance by spitting at a policeman at Norwich City and getting frog-marched out of the ground before the match. Perhaps at the time, our biggest rivals were Millwall who had an equally dedicated and ferocious following.

Occasionally after home games at Upton Park, we would catch the tube train to the terminus at either King's Cross or Euston, and wait to ambush the departing away fans from other London matches. Manchester or Newcastle United fans were always good for a decent row and sometimes we use to pre-plan meets at these stations with Millwall fans and give it to the opposing northern fans with the weird accents.

The Manor Road Gang was not exclusively made up of male teenagers. A few young, female thrill-seekers – Jean Revel, Marilyn Kent, Christine Allard, Kim Ashman and Beverley Turner, for example – gravitated towards our gang and were treated with respect. Interestingly, though, some of us had girlfriends, which, to some extent, for some macho or inexplicable reason, was perceived as a weakness.

One of our favourite criminal exploits was to raid the local drinks distribution centre along the sewer bank near Bromley-by-Bow. Mid-week, we would get a pram and climb down the sewer bank and relieve the delivery lorries of countless cases of Campari, Cinzano, Mr Soft drinks and Newcastle Brown Ale. God, it tasted vile, but we would store and conceal the fully loaded pram until the weekend and organise a party at the best available house or venue. I recall, after one particular night of wild debauchery at a party, I passed out in the street only to wake up in a strange house on the settee with some elderly woman snoring loudly in a nearby bed. I must have been comatose through the alcohol, and had been carried into this person's house for safety. In the morning, I let myself out of the house before she woke up.

To some degree, this speaks volumes of the type of genuine people that inhabited the East End at that time. It was a generous gesture which was done in a traditional community spirit.

At one of our pre-arranged parties at our house in Grange Road, a fellow gang member said that he had nicked a motorbike and asked me whether I wanted to take it for a spin with him. I was at that impressionable age when I loved anything to do with the control and thrill of speed, especially motorbikes and cars. So, with this particular member as pillion, we raced around Canning Town when a police van spotted us and chased us through Rathbone Market. Knowing the area well, I let the police van follow us into the market and then darted through the pedestrian bollards. I took a right liberty and zoomed straight across the main Barking Road to get away. This frightened the pillion passenger and he jumped off and was arrested. I continued through some well-known alleyways and dumped the machine at the bottom of some flats and slipped home on foot. By the time I had reached my home 30 minutes later, the police were already waiting for me. This guy had talked and I was nicked.

As a consequence, on 14 February 1973, aged 14, I appeared at Newham Juvenile Court on charges of taking and driving away a motor vehicle (TDA) and was sentenced to 24 hours' Attendance Centre and conditionally discharged for 12 months.

In many respects, the Attendance Centre was the latest political 'quick-fix' to prevent the pervasive spread of football hooliganism and violence. Basically, those sentenced to the Attendance Centre had to attend a local school on Saturday afternoons between 3 and 5pm (kick-off time) and participate in a double session of strenuous physical exercise and making soft toys. This non-custodial sentencing policy was effective in that, to some degree, it reduced antisocial behaviour at football matches and it acted as a weekly reminder that one's sentence by the court was not over.

As a result of being firmly rooted in a predominantly working-class area with high unemployment, many of the Manor Road Gang's parents were themselves on the poverty line or caught in the poverty trap and dependent upon State benefits. There is little wonder then that many members of the gang turned to crime in order to counterbalance the social and economic results of poverty. Admittedly, because my parents owned two grocery shops, most outsiders thought that Lenny and I wanted for nothing. But this was not the case. The only time our parents saw fit to provide us with much-needed clothing was on special occasions, such as Christmas and birthdays. Other than that, we had done our best to provide for ourselves.

Many of the Manor Road Gang, but not all of them by any means, committed a wide range of crimes and, more specifically, burglaries on local warehouses, factories, retail outlets and selected homes in order to benefit from the social and cultural activities of the 'normal' hard-working population. We all knew that this was legally and morally wrong and that we ran a real risk of detection and imprisonment. But, without some form of financial income, we felt that we were unfairly excluded from society and therefore, in some way, different from everybody else.

One of our favourite social events was our weekly visit to the Keir Hardy school disco in Canning Town. Every Thursday evening, we would dress up in our best clobber, guzzle a bottle of cider and do our best to emulate socially sophisticated adults. Being quite bashful and shy when speaking to girls, the bottle of cider, together with the popular music of T Rex, Rod Stewart, Sweet and Slade, had the desired effect and induced a mild sense of euphoria. Unlike contemporary tastes and vices, there were no drugs around at this time. Quite a lot of the gang smoked cigarettes but, as a rule, drugs did not exist for us then.

On one particular occasion, however, I worked very hard at my father's shop at the weekend and, at the opportune time, I asked him in advance if it was all right if I went to the Keir Hardy disco the following Thursday. He gave me permission, but on the day of the disco itself the lying bastard reneged on the agreement without valid reason. This provoked a terrible sense of injustice in me, and I decamped to the think-tank of my bedroom. While pondering on the implications of reversing a 'done deal', one that had almost been etched in stone, I donned my crimson satin jacket (à la Rod Stewart) and bolted out of the top bedroom window over the cemetery and into the night. By committing this bold act of defiance, I knew that I could not return to the police state of the despotic superpower, for it would entail the pain and humiliation of another severe beating and subsequent penalties, so I decided to run away for the umpteenth time.

This would have been at the height of summer in 1973, when I was enjoying a sweet and loving relationship with a beautiful girl from Plaistow. She was a year older than me and we got on really well. Leslie was not only a very attractive girl with a stunning body, but she also really cared about me and it is no surprise that I lost – and rather enjoyed losing – my virginity at the fumbling age of 14. Our sweet and affectionate teenage romance was terminated, however, when I ran away from home and was imprisoned for a burglary on a school canteen with three black boys while in search of food.

Ostensibly, my burgeoning friendship with Selvin Brooks, Clayton Joseph and little Victor had evolved due to the fact that we were all being physically abused by our excessively violent fathers; so much so, that we often discussed, shared and compared each other's tales of beatings and accompanying humiliations. It was because of this common malevolent shadow in our lives that we decided to run away and live together. Amazingly, we all slept in a rat-infested railway arch under a brick-built viaduct at Manor Road, Canning Town. Initially, we survived on food given to us by close friends and cherries picked from trees at a nearby park.

This being inadequate, we decided to burgle a school canteen and ate some tinned Spam. The canteen itself was not far away from our makeshift home and the police raided the arches at 2.00am one morning and took us all into custody. We were all charged with burglary and all remanded into custody. The police, for whatever reason, must have had me down as the ringleader as I was taken to Ashford Remand Centre in Middlesex, while the others were placed in the care of the local social services.

Aged 14, I was the youngest prisoner in the institution. I'll always remember, even as unconvicted prisoners, we had to file in and march from the detached block to the main food hall like in the classic American films. It was quite a shock for me, as well as a useful learning point, as I'd always remember that I had squandered a valuable and irreplaceable week of my life on remand. I was determined not to waste any more time in prison ever again.

4

Seeking Approval

After a very long and introspective week in the doleful confines of Ashford Remand Centre in Middlesex, I reappeared at Newham Juvenile Court and was remanded into the care of the Local Authority. Little Heath Lodge Assessment Centre in Chadwell Heath was a semi-secure unit for male juvenile delinquents and run by the London Borough of Newham. The self-contained modern unit held about 20 to 30 boys of various age groups up to 16 years old. Essentially, the operational and functional role of the unit was to assess and evaluate seemingly unmanageable children and teenagers with social, behavioural and psychological problems. An observational report would then be compiled and either reviewed by a special review panel at the unit or submitted to the courts for sentencing.

Some weeks later, on 15 August 1973, I again appeared in court and, like my brother Lenny who was also incarcerated in the unit at this time, I was placed under a Care Order. Basically, this was due to the offence of burglary and the attendant issue of persistent physical abuse in the domestic home. Initially, my reaction to this sentence was one of relief, but gradually, as time progressed, I came to realise that all I had done was to exchange one problem for another – the regular parental beatings had been supplanted by the painful loss of childhood freedom and independence. It must be said, not many 14-year-olds would have been able to make sense of all this. Quite clearly, it was a sad indictment of my parents as it labelled them as abject failures. It transpired that they were so engrossed in a lemming-like pursuit of material prosperity that they were blind or ignorant to the deeper issues that mattered in life.

To exacerbate matters for me, while in Little Heath Lodge my parents applied for and secured permission to take my brother Lenny on a long-standing summer holiday to the Spanish island of Ibiza along with my sister Audrey. But, once again, I was left out of the equation. At the time it did not bother me; it was only later that the full impact of the callous act hit me. I was not alone, however, as these children's homes were full of unfortunate souls who had been abused, abandoned, alienated or parked up on the adolescent scrapheap. I often thought about escaping – the romantic notion of being a teenage fugitive appealed to me – but where was I going to escape to? Who wanted or needed me out there? Alas, the brutal answer was no one. No one cared, no one bothered. The sad, incontrovertible fact was that I was indeed better off imprisoned inside a secure unit. They fed me, clothed me and even took us to the local swimming baths, cinema and occasionally to a West Ham United football match. Most importantly of all, the arbitrary physical abuse had stopped. Little Heath Lodge had become my home.

I was making such good educational and behavioural progress at Little Heath Lodge that the staff offered me a Case Review. Everybody at the unit knew that, if you were offered a Case Review and your parents turned up and said all the right things, you were invariably discharged that very day. I was so excited about the prospect of the review that I had set my heart on going home and going back to normal school again. The Review Panel even offered to hold the review on a Wednesday afternoon to coincide with my father's half-day closure at the shop. But my mother was unable to attend the review because she did not have time to close her shop. The Review Panel, therefore, would not and, indeed, could not begin to consider the release of anyone back to 'normal society' without the expressed participation of their parents in the review process. Painfully for me, the Case Review was cancelled. Naturally, this was a huge emotional and psychological blow to me, a chilling act of cold indifference, rejection and betrayal that was gradually becoming a recurring theme throughout my life.

As a consequence, I was kept in Little Heath Lodge for five long months and I was making excellent progress in all areas. So much so, the staff themselves made a personal and impassionate plea to the Head of the Centre to do his best to get me back into 'normal society' but, without the genuine desire and support of my parents, I was doomed to be sent to a long-term Approved School until I was 16 years old.

Ardale Approved School – later renamed Ardale Community Home – was situated in the somnolent outskirts of Grays, Essex. But for its huge grey water tower and accompanying brick chimney, you would be able to drive past it on the new A13 bypass and not even know it was there. Unlike the semi-secure confines of Little Heath Lodge, Ardale was a long-term, open-plan institution run also by the London Borough of Newham. It consisted of four modern residential house blocks, an education centre, a decrepit gymnasium and a full-size football, rugby and cricket pitch.

On arrival, I was allocated to Shackleton House which was home to 20–30 boys per unit. My brother Lenny, who had arrived several months earlier, was allocated to the adjacent Nelson House with our friend Peter Bolger. Despite serving, in reality, a custodial sentence, the inhabitants were allowed weekend home visits in order to promote, maintain and sustain family ties. On each house block there were a housemaster and housemistress. These were normally a husband and wife team who generally policed and supervised the premises and kept things ship-shape.

The delegated guardians of Shackleton House were Mr and Mrs Stevens. Mr Stevens was a stout 6ft-plus, 16st mountain of a man who maintained a healthy balance of light-hearted buoyancy and discipline in the unit. Mrs Stevens, however, was a short, petite, mouse-like woman who, despite being preoccupied with the day-to-day running of the unit, always had time to listen to any general or personal problems of those in her care. In spite of bringing up their own very young family in living quarters adjoining the housing unit, they worked very well as a team and were, in return, respected by the boys.

In theory, Ardale was renowned for its newly built education block with a full complement of teachers. It encouraged most of its residents to partake in a series of basic educational courses and examinations but, in practice, this was rarely the case. Although strict order and discipline were essential in the house blocks, they did not necessarily filter through to the education centre, as in the time-worn adage, 'You can lead a horse to water, but you cannot make it drink!' This was part of the problem at Ardale; very few inhabitants took advantage of its educational facilities but lots took advantage of its sporting activities. Put simply, the stark options were, either you sat in a boring classroom with little or no discipline, or you went over to the gymnasium and played football, basketball, badminton or took part in weight training or gymnastics. I loved it. Every day, a score or more nascent athletes would pound away at the altar of exercise and savour the inner pleasure and self-esteem that it brings.

The PE teacher, Mr Doherty, an ex-professional football player, taught us everything that he knew about the game. If we were not playing friendly matches against local factory teams, we were playing competitive matches against the local schools in the Thurrock area. In fact, Ardale did the league and cup double while I was there, winning all our matches in the school league and beating St Mary's School 2–1 in the School Cup Final. Mr Doherty was so impressed with our footballing development and prowess that he even wrote to nearby Southend United Football Club in order to secure Geoff Hewitt and myself a trial. If the Youth Training Scheme (YTS) had been up and running then, the likes of Geoff Hewitt and I may have reached professional status. Southend United did, indeed, offer us a trial in the South Eastern Counties League, but we did not have the money for the fare to travel to Southend.

Similarly in the sphere of basketball, Ardale trounced all-comers and went on to win the local schools league. Not surprisingly, the team gave me the nickname of 'Five Fouls Smith' – with basketball being a non-contact sport, I was invariably in the sin-bin enduring the mandatory time-out penalty period.

The Shackleton housemaster, Mr Stevens, who himself was an accomplished football, rugby and cricket player, would frequently join in the games against adult opposition. I recall he use to belittle our opponents with cynical banter or steam into them if they manhandled or misjudged a tackle against one of his boys. He was a sterling sportsman, someone you could depend on when the going got tough. Later, four or five of us were recruited to play football for Aveley Town FC's junior team and we were invited to train with the former Millwall icon Harry Cripps once a week. We used to knock the ball to him in training and he used to flick it up perfectly every time for us to head it into the goal. The Aveley first-team players, knowing that we came from a school of dubious character, made us very welcome in the clubhouse. Playing serious competitive football and guzzling copious pints of lager appeared to be part and parcel of growing up in boomtown Essex, and we were not complaining.

Although the competitive sporting activities of football, rugby and basketball were successfully channelling my unquenchable thirst for excitement, I also needed to satisfy my irrepressible desire for adventure. This was partly resolved by the availability of outward-bound courses, such as a week-long camping trek up and over Snowdonia or, more significantly, a sailing course with fully fledged mariners.

The London Sailing Project was the brainchild of some Lord or other who thought that the youth of London were getting soft and needed the rigours of the sailing world to toughen them up. To be frank, he was not wrong.

Despite needing to be 16 to qualify, I volunteered at 15 for this week-long sailing adventure on the south coast of England. On arrival at Gosport, Hampshire, I was allocated to one of three tall sailing ships called *The Rona*. This was a proper hands-on 60ft sailing vessel where everything was done through brute strength and bare, salty hands. All the rigging, the anchor and even the bilge pump had to be operated manually. Initially, we sailed out into the calm waters of the Solent to get used to our roles on board, and then we were going to sail to the port of Cherbourg, France, the Channel island of Guernsey and then back to Blighty.

I recall having a full and hearty meal while on the Solent and then sailing past The Needles off the Isle of Wight. It was then that the nightmare trauma of violent seasickness hit me. I felt like I was going to die. *The Rona*, with the wind in her sails, was forced over on to her side at such an angle that the water practically swamped half the upper deck. Rather stupidly, and without telling anyone, I unclipped my safety harness, thinking the vessel was going to capsize and sink. If a freak wave had hit us, I would have been washed overboard. The combination of wave after wave for hours on end crashing into the bow and the attendant disorientation of seasickness was horrendous. Lord So and So was 100 per cent right – in the sphere of the sea, spume and salt water, I was a grade 'A' wanker, and I was not afraid to admit it.

We sailed for countless hours through the night, crashing into the unseen waves until we reached Cherbourg harbour, and then I was placed on first watch in case any large container ships decided to sail near to us. This was an unbelievable nightmare, and I had volunteered for it.

On the return trip to England from Guernsey, it was obvious that I was not cut out for sailing. To try to take my mind off the downside of seasickness, the captain placed me at the helm, but it was not for me. Believe it or not, when things got really rough, I began to thrive on it. Towards the end of our journey, we were in sight of land, caught up in a force eight gale and the waves were mountainous. The omnipotent power of the sea in all its dramatic rage was awesome. It was like all the best rides at the fairground in one; it was adventure at its apex. Even a Royal Navy Minesweeper came alongside us to ensure that we were not having difficulties.

During this exciting storm, not only had all fear and loathing of the sea dissipated, but also the wretched seasickness. I was buzzing. Now *this* was what I'd come for ... God, it was exciting! Alas, back at the sedate tidal vacillations of Gosport harbour, the captain called the crew one by one to the front of the vessel to give us our progress report. He told me that I had failed the sailing course and, to be honest, despite being a very competitive person, for once in my life I accepted the stigma of failure with open arms. The motion of the ocean definitely did not get my devotion.

Uncharacteristically, the next adventure was of a musical variety as I learnt to play the French horn in the developing Ardale brass band. Basically, this was the brainchild of the deputy housemaster. He taught about 15 of us to read music and play various woodwind and brass instruments, such as the tuba, euphonium, horn, clarinet and cornet. I really loved playing the French horn as it had a very distinctive, mellifluous tone, which invariably monopolised the solo scores. The band itself later joined the Air Training Corps (ATC), but despite flying Chipmunks over Cambridgeshire and playing rugby for the RAF, the brass band never had its public debut. This was a big regret as we practised and practised and had become worthy of a public performance.

As with Little Heath Lodge Assessment Centre, Ardale also had Case Reviews but rarely, if at all, were residents discharged at the conclusion of a review. In 1974, aged 15, I had a Case Review and, once again, my parents were invited. Once again, only my father turned up, but it did not bother me ... or so I thought. Also present at the Case Review were Mr Stevens, the housemaster, a female psychologist, a representative from the education centre and a designated social worker.

Rightly or wrongly, I felt that I had developed into a tough young man, playing football and rugby against adult opposition; generally, I felt I could handle myself. I really thought that I was physically and emotionally strong. But, for whatever reason, this was not the case. I was given the opportunity to express my personal views about any progress and development that I had made ... at which point I just couldn't hold it together. I broke down, sobbing uncontrollably, accusing my parents of not caring for or about me, and especially my mother who was always making derogatory or cynical remarks about me when I was allowed home at weekends.

I was not looking for sympathy. I did not intend for this embarrassing event to occur, it was a genuine emotional breakdown. Quite simply, I could not help it. Years and years of pent-up emotion and frustration came tumbling out and cascaded down my face in a pool of sorrow on to the floor. It was decided, due to my emotional state, that I should go home there and then with my father for an extended weekend.

We drove home to Plaistow in total silence. Then, would you believe, as soon as my mother saw me walk through the front door of our house with my father, she blurted out, 'What the fuck are you doing home? You're not due home until Friday!'

The white light of truth had finally pierced my father's consciousness. He had just witnessed his son sobbing uncontrollably, and now he knew what I'd said was true. Nothing had changed. I remained at Ardale until my sixteenth birthday and was legally released to fend for myself in the congested labour market of East London.

5

Borstal Boy

After nearly two years of various types of custody or confinement, I was, at long last, let loose on the street. The future was not exactly rosy, but I had hope. One of the golden rules of the Smith clan was, in order to remain at the Grange Road dwelling, you had to have a legitimate job and work. According to the work ethic of the Smiths, work equates with income and income equates with respectability. If you did not have a job, you were perceived as a good-for-nothing layabout who lived off the backs of others. Therefore, it was imperative that I sought some form of employment, even if it was to appease and satisfy the work ethic of the tyrant.

My first ever source of employment was at a fruit and vegetable distribution factory in Silvertown. This was a low-paid, boring job, requiring me to stack tomatoes or aubergines into cellophane cartons, loading them on to pallets and then on to lorries for delivery around the country. The work itself was about as exciting as waiting to see a doctor at a busy surgery. The pay was £25 per week; out of that I had to pay £5 emergency tax and £5 'keep' money to my mother for board and lodgings. By the time I took a pound a day for bus fares and dinner money, I had the best part of £10 to lavish upon myself.

Quite clearly, then, this was a dead-end job and I was going nowhere.

To aggravate matters, I used to come home from work on Fridays with my meagre wage packet and see my brother Lenny with wads of cash from the proceeds of crime. In order to circumvent the pervasive work ethic of 'no job, no board', Lenny quite cunningly used to buy his own formal wage packets from the stationer's and insert a wad of cash inside the packet, staple it down and open it every Friday teatime in front of my gullible mother as if he had been working all week. It worked a treat, as all my parents were concerned about was the cash and not its provenance.

Not surprisingly, the promotional prospects of an enhanced fruit packer did not appeal to me. The combination of robotic menial tasks along with a Third World pay structure was enough to transform me into a Marxist revolutionary. I lost the job and became another statistic for the Minister of Employment. At the Grange Road citadel, unemployment was synonymous with leprosy and, within a week, I was evicted with all the grace and finesse of a ham-fisted bouncer ejecting a persistent drunk.

To his credit, my half-brother Stephen came to my rescue. Being a reluctant recipient of countless evictions himself over the past decade or so, he sympathised with my plight and let me live with him at his ground-floor flat in Clarence Road, Canning Town. In return for this superlative generosity and kindness, I used to help him with his milk round.

We would rise at 4.00am and be finished by 1.00pm, providing a lingerie-wearing, sex-starved woman did not accost him over some inconsequential query at the street door.

Moreover, Stephen was a proficient car mechanic and spent a great deal of his time under the bonnets of motor vehicles. He used to teach me the basics and, although I found this immensely stimulating and intellectually rewarding, it did not pay the bills or put food in my belly. Therefore, in the scorching summer heat of 1975, I stupidly returned to crime and it was not long before I was arrested for two burglaries and being driven in a stolen vehicle. I appeared at Snaresbrook Crown Court on 29 July 1975, and was sentenced to six months' Detention Centre.

Due to the popular political concerns and anxieties of rising crime in the mid-1970s, the Government of the day decided to adopt and embrace the punitive policy of the 'short, sharp shock'! These were secure Detention Centres that espoused a quasi-military regime of strict discipline, vigorous physical training and menial work. I was sent to the notoriously austere Detention Centre at Send in Surrey.

As soon as you stepped off the prison van, you were frog-marched into the reception area and given a crash course in abject degradation and humiliation. But as luck would have it, I knew the reception orderly, a fellow 'Towner' with the same name as mine, Terry Smith, who asked the reception screws to drop me out of the Gestapo treatment.

In any Detention Centre, the first week is the worst week, as everyone has to endure the dreaded week-long induction period of 'medicine balls and benches' in the gymnasium. For a solid hour every day, we had to run around the gym holding a medicine ball in front of you, above your head or to the side of your body or any combination of these strength-sapping positions. Then three or four of us would have to hold a long bench above our heads and run around the gym, backwards and forwards, or lower the bench from side to side until our arms were numb. In any event, the more we did it, the fitter and stronger we became.

After the physical horror and pain of the first week, we progressed to circuit training. In many respects, Detention Centre transformed boys into fit young men. It took boys at the optimal time of physical growth and development, during which period the before-and-after philosophy of character and muscle building was discernible on release.

Despite having the desired effect on discipline, respect, hygiene and so on, the downside for the Government was it made fitter, faster and more determined young criminals who could, more often than not, outrun the police.

The intense physical exercise was combined with hard menial work, like cleaning the toilets, scrubbing the appropriately named M1 corridor with a toothbrush or working in the kitchen. I was allocated the job of washing-up in the kitchen, but after several weeks

I got the sack for pointing out the detrimental aspects of slave labour.

One disturbing feature of Send Detention Centre was the 50/50 ethnic balance and its attendant bullying. It was common knowledge amongst all the screws and detainees that the vulnerable white prisoners were being bullied or 'taxed' by the stronger West Indian cliques. I and a handful of other white prisoners had several fights with some of the West Indian detainees and, once they realised that we were up for a fight, they left us alone. Other much weaker white prisoners went through hell.

While at Send, I had to appear at Newham Magistrates' Court for an outstanding charge and was dispatched in a taxi with one portly screw and driver. After appearing in court, on the journey back to Surrey, the screw said that he had to make a phone call. By pure coincidence, the taxi driver stopped at a phone box on Barking Road, Canning Town. Once he left the vehicle, I could have easily jumped out of the taxi and got lost among the mosaic of alleyways and subways of Canning Town. But once again, I wondered where the hell I would go. Who would look after and support me? Would I be more of a burden than a benefit? It was the perfect opportunity to flee, but I never seized it. This still rankles with my conscience now as human instinct dictates that all captive prisoners should have a bone-deep duty to escape from imprisonment or anything that causes them pain or suffering.

Nonetheless, in Send they had a progressive system of enhanced privileges by wearing either blue, green or brown ties. The blue ties represented the induction regime; the green tie, intermediate privileges; and the brown tie, the enhanced regime. After six torturous weeks of physical and psychological sweat and toil, I was awarded the most prestigious job in the institution. I became the gym orderly. Unfortunately, I only had this job for one week as I was carted off to court to face the outstanding court case.

One of my lasting memories of Send Detention Centre was that I was in a state of perpetual hunger. It seemed as if there were never enough calories to counterbalance the intense physical training. On Sundays, however, Send held a five-mile cross-country run around an enclosed sports field. As an incentive to do well, the first five detainees to finish in the weekly run were given extra food at Sunday lunch. Seizing this opportunity, I finished fourth and was given extra grub for my grumbling stomach.

With regard to screw–prisoner intimidation and humiliation, it went on all the time. In fact, it was all part of the natural ethos of Send to keep its captives on their toes. One of the screws' favourite pastimes was to pinch our nipples and painfully twist them, pull our sideburns violently, slap us round the back of the head or punish the prisoners collectively by marching everyone out into the courtyard at 7.00am in only our underpants and forcing us to do star-jumps. The more reluctant dissenters were taken to a remote holding cell and given a beating. This never occurred to me, but I was aware of it. All in all, the punitive and disciplinary benefits of Send Detention Centre were all in vain for me as, on 12 September 1975, I appeared at Woodford Crown Court for an outstanding burglary charge and was sentenced to a period of Borstal Training for six months to two years.

On a psychological level, this was a serious blow, as to be halfway through a six-month Detention Centre sentence and then be sentenced to Borstal Training was a rarity. From Woodford Crown Court I was transported to Wormwood Scrubs Prison where I was processed and kitted out in an antiquated reception area. I distinctly recall having to walk from the reception to 'B' Wing – the Borstal Boys wing – on a cold and windswept September evening. Looking up at the grotesque Victorian architecture of the massive wings filled me with underlying trepidation and awe. It was as though I had been transported back in time to the sinister workhouses of the Industrial Revolution of the mid-nineteenth century.

As we entered the echoing, eerie interior of the wing, the future looked bleak. In any event, I was placed into a two-up cell on the threes landing and, as the screw opened the cell door, it reminded me of a Third World dungeon. The cell was filthy dirty and freezing cold, with all its small windows broken and, remarkably, it had an insect-ridden straw mattress on the wrought-iron bed. This was more reminiscent of a condemned jail of centuries past than a seemingly well-resourced prison in the mid-1970s.

While learning to adapt and conform to the new austere surroundings and conditions, I was informed that all Borstal boys had to endure a three-week assessment period at Wormwood Scrubs before being allocated to a specific Borstal institution. Basically, prison officials took into account previous convictions, a written aptitude test and a cursory wing report in order to determine whether or not a prisoner would be suitable to go to an open or closed Borstal. For example, those convicted of offences involving violence or robbery would be sent to Dover or Rochester Borstals, and those convicted of less serious offences, such as burglary or stealing vehicles, would be allocated to Hollesley Bay, Huntercombe or Gains Hall Open Borstals. At the end of my assessment period, I was sent to Hollesley Bay Borstal near Woodbridge, Suffolk.

On 1 October 1975, about 12 Borstal boys, including me, were loaded on to a green prison coach and driven up the A12 from London to Suffolk. Once at Hollesley Bay, we had to spend two weeks on an induction wing, where further tests and analysis were conducted to see which house block and employment best suited us.

It was not long, however, before I was involved in a serious assault on another Borstal boy. I recall mopping a corridor when the big fellow came up to me and tried to bully me by snatching the mop and bucket. Sensing immediate danger, and noticing that this fellow was wearing his very own Dr Marten's high-leg boots, a palpable symbol of violent thuggery, I thought it was time to stand up and be counted, so I delivered a peach of a right hook flush on the geezer's chin and he was carted off to the nearby medical centre with a broken jaw. No one saw the incident, but news travelled fast and I was soon down the block facing a Governor's report. Such serious offences against 'the good order and discipline of the institution' invariably meant being 'shipped out' back to Wormwood Scrubs for reallocation to the more forbidding venues of the closed Borstals. Quite remarkably, on the Governor's adjudication, I was sentenced to two weeks' loss of association (with other prisoners) and also two weeks' loss of prison earnings.

As part of the training regimen of Borstal, everyone had to learn a trade of sorts. At Hollesley Bay, they provided an intense four-month

Trade Training Course in either bricklaying, plastering, carpentry or painting and decorating. Seeing as it was now mid-October and winter was not far off, the *al fresco* trade of bricklaying did not appeal to me, neither did the sloppy wetness of plastering. Hence it was either carpentry or painting and decorating in the warmth and comfort of a workshop. I opted for carpentry, as I have always had an affinity with trees and the versatility of timber. It seemed like a building trade which had a dynamic future as carpenters were always in demand, especially in the construction industry.

The course itself was excellent. Initially, I learnt to plane and square off a basic piece of timber, then cut and fit lap joints, cut mortise and tenons, and then moved on to the more advanced fixture and fittings of making and hanging doors, sash windows and even the construction of a mock timber roof. In the final examination, I had to fit out a complete room with joists, floorboards, skirting, a dado rail, architrave, doors and windows, and at the end of it I was awarded a laudable B2 pass.

After the induction period at Hollesley Bay, I was allocated to one of four modern residential units called Hoxon House, where I was reunited with fellow Towners Jimmy Tarrant and Gee Ashman. Despite Jimmy being several years my senior, we got on really well as he had a natural sense of style and vigour about him. Jimmy was heavily into contemporary fashion, particularly men's clothes and music, and invariably he had the wherewithal to look the part. Jimmy was a trendsetter in Canning Town where many of his contemporaries tried to imitate and emulate his undeniable style and class.

It was not long before I was selected to play football alongside Jimmy in the Hollesley Bay Colony team. In many respects, the team itself was like Canning Town revisited as we had Gee Ashman in goal, Paul Hearn and Ray Church in defence, and Jimmy and I dishing out the stick in the midfield. There was not a game that went by during which Jimmy and I did not sandwich a Suffolk bumpkin in a bone-crunching tackle. Hollesley Bay Colony was not the most skilful team in the world, but every Saturday afternoon, somewhere in Suffolk, us Towners would leave our mark.

Throughout the incarceration at Send Detention Centre and

Wormwood Scrubs, I did not have any visits. I was writing to family and friends, but no visits materialised until I reached Hollesley Bay. This was partly due to the fact that my brother Lenny was in the nearby Detention Centre and we used to be allowed joint visits with our family. More interestingly, I was writing to two former school friends, Donna and Christine. Unbeknown to them, they were directly responsible for keeping my spirits up while I was in Borstal. Under the artful guidance of a fellow Borstal boy and very good friend, Egan Blackford, I was taught the persuasive art of writing love letters and the subsequent effect they had on the fairer sex. Thus I embarked upon a very sensual and enjoyable correspondence with Christine, which later developed into a truly affectionate relationship. We did not share any visits, but she was there for me and that spoke volumes.

After the completion of the carpentry course, I was allocated to work on 'Site Five', the construction of a new and secure Young Prisoners institution built exclusively by screws and Borstal boys. I was detailed to a team helping to build a concrete roof over the Segregation Unit. If I had had a little foresight or had been a little wiser, I should have refused this assignment on the basis that it would become a temple of isolation, segregation, subjugation and suffering. But I was only 16 at the time, and ignorant of the moral dilemma involved in aiding and abetting the construction of a prison block.

After about seven or eight months at Hollesley Bay Borstal, a review board stated that I was to be released on 9 June 1976. When the glorious day came, I bade farewell to the 'college of crime' and was escorted to Ipswich Station and placed on the London-bound train to Liverpool Street. In Borstal-boy folklore, once at Liverpool Street Station it is traditional to skip across the road, have a pint of beer in 'Dirty Dick's Bar' and stick your discharge travel warrant on the wall for luck. This we all did and then went our separate ways into the on-rushing and formidable future.

6

The Sniper

When you are a teenager, there is something supremely sacrosanct about Fridays. For if Saturday is a day of intense retail therapy and Sunday is a day of God, then Friday was seemingly tailor-made for teenagers and excitement. For teenagers, Fridays tend to symbolise the be-all and end-all of everything. To miss a Friday night out with your friends is like missing the very last train to the sun-blessed isle of euphoria and hedonism. Put in plain and simple terms, Fridays mean fun, freedom and escapism from the mundane monotony of the modern world.

It was with no surprise then that, when I was released from Borstal on a Friday, that meant a long-awaited reunion with a tumult of Towners at the Windsor Castle public house in Canning Town. For some time, this had been a regular social and cultural meeting point for us, where we would all become progressively inebriated and lay siege to the Norseman nightclub on the Barking Road, Canning Town. We used to harass and terrify the owner with our late-night brawling to such an extent, both inside and outside the club, that he decided to employ a minder, someone who we would not only respect, but who could also keep the nightclub in order. He chose a well-known face called Nicky Gerard, who had become a very dangerous and violent villain.

In many respects, this called a brief halt to our adolescent antics and forced us to dip our tentacles into other late-night venues throughout East London and Essex, such as The Dug-Out in Silvertown, The Lotus in Forest Gate, The Room at the Top in Ilford and Cherries on Hackney Marshes. It was not that we went out purposely to cause trouble, but it was inevitable that the lethal cocktail of adrenalin and testosterone, combined with gallons of lager, would express itself in an impulsive explosion of violence and mayhem by the end of the evening. There came a time when it was impossible for all of us to go to the same venue as each other, as at least one or two of our crew were barred from one club or another for brawling or violent behaviour.

When I say brawling, I should say violent fights and affrays that blossomed into the vicious gang culture of slashing your rival's face with a Stanley blade or an equally sharp knife. The halcyon days of a good old straight-up fight or giving your opponent a traditional kicking were over. The overriding notion of that time was to stripe your opponent down the face and see the skin of his face flap open with lashings of blood. The knife culture of cutting your rivals was seemingly justified and legitimised by witnessing adult gangsters and villains do the selfsame thing in pubs and clubs like the Norseman in Canning Town. To cut someone was the ultimate in leaving your mark and this occasionally precipitated a cycle of revenge. But, all in all, it was a fad, a rage, good guys and scumbags got cut for literally anything. Our slogan at the time was 'Cut or be cut ...' Get in first!

Once again, back at the Grange Road sanatorium it was essential to seek out employment. The all-important work ethic of the Smith clan still applied. Hence my brother-in-law Steve Perryman securing me a job at Graham Wood Steel Stockholders on the Isle of Dogs, East London. I was commonly known as a 'slinger'. By that, I mean it was my role to sling a hook and chain around massive steel girders and let the crane driver above lift and load them on to 20-tonne lorries for delivery around the country. This may sound like a boring and thankless job, but in fact it required more than a smidgen of skill to judge the balance of the load correctly, and also an element of fitness and athleticism as the job entailed jumping on and off lorries all day. I was working with a mixed workforce, with me being the youngest at 17, and the oldest being grumpy Joe who was nearing his pension.

Generally, they were a good team to work with, as there needed to be an element of trust between the crane operator and the slingers on the ground – one slight mistake and you were dead. There were no second chances when five tonnes of the best British steel was being lifted above your head. It was very dangerous work, to the extent that a representative from a life insurance company used to visit the firm every three months without fail. I was so concerned about the risks associated with the job that I only used to go into work about three times a week, just enough to get me out clubbing at the weekend and to keep the fascist dictator happy back at Grange Road; and, more interestingly, to give me time to work on my embryonic career as a semi-professional burglar.

Without wishing to lecture or make moral judgements about burglars generally, I never burgled private homes as our property at Grange Road had been broken into at least three times and we all knew the heartache and despair that it caused. To my way of thinking, burgling someone's house made it personal. Alternatively, however, burgling a large, juicy retail outlet, factory or warehouse was impersonal and therefore a valid economic target.

Prior to getting organised, we used to jump on to a bus or train to our intended target, case the property and then return at about 9.00pm the same night and raid the premises. Then, with our booty stuffed into black bin liners, we would catch the last bus or train home. To a great degree, this was very dangerous, even suicidal, as we were sitting ducks for the police patrol cars and I suggested that we all club together and purchase a small van to upgrade our *modus operandi*.

After our next successful mission, therefore, we bought a small Vauxhall Viva van and I would generally drive the team to the venue to be raided. Then, using scissor jacks – burglar alarms were a luxury in 1976 – we would jack open the thick metal bars on the window at the back of the large clothing or electrical outlets and load up the van. If it was very late, we would park up the van for the night and drive the stolen goods to our buyer or 'fence' first thing in the morning. My favourite target was a well-known men's clothing store for, despite us all coming from poverty-ridden backgrounds and having very little cash in our pockets, we were without doubt the best-dressed gang of burglars in East London. I even recall taking two natty suits up to Chelmsford Crown Court for my best friend's father, old Tommy Hole, who was on trial with George Davis *et al* at the time for stealing a lorryload of whisky.

For once, life at the Grange Road asylum seemed to be going well. During the day I was working as a 'slinger' and during the evening working as a burglar. That is until I caught a so-called girlfriend canoodling with a mini-cab driver in his car. If I had not been on the razzle that night I might have swallowed it, but I ended up attacking him with a broken bottle and getting nicked for malicious wounding and assault on the police. The girl herself could not have been that concerned about me as she even came to Plaistow Police Station and without my knowledge cunningly identified me as the attacker.

Therefore, on the brink of Christmas 1976, I received a bland court summons to appear at Snaresbrook Crown Court the next day for trial. Knowing that I was going to plead guilty, this would have meant a definite Christmas inside one of Her Majesty's piss-holes, so I slipped up to the local hospital and acquired a doctor's certificate stating that I was unable to attend court due to a serious back injury. The next day, two burly policemen visited our house but, being alone, I did not open the front door.

Then on the night of Christmas Eve I was in bed at about 3.00am when I heard loud banging on our heavy brass doorknocker. It was a definite Old Bill knock if ever there was one, as no one knocked on the tyrant's door at three in the morning like that. Bemused and confused, I quickly jumped out of bed, slung on some clobber and tried to get out of our top bedroom window, but, seeing as the tyrant had nailed it shut to deter burglars, I smashed the entire window out and bolted across the nearby cemetery as fast as a whippet. One of our neighbours who'd heard the commotion screamed out of their window, 'I see him, I see the burglar!' as I left a trial of dust in my wake.

The next day, Lenny and my father found me at a friend's house. It wasn't the police at all, it was an alcohol-sodden Lenny coming home who had forgotten his front door key. Fancy knocking on the front door like a policeman in the dead of night, the dope!

In spite of the damage, the commotion and confusion of the comical event, I had an enjoyable Christmas and New Year. Then on 6 January 1977, I was again summoned to Chingford Crown Court to face the malicious wounding and assault on a police officer charge. I pleaded guilty and was sentenced to a Borstal Recall. This basically meant that I had to return to the gloomy world of HMP Wormwood Scrubs and then on to Hollesley Bay Borstal for four months. Unlike the original 'fresh whack' Borstal sentence, however, I did not have to suffer and endure the training aspect all over again.

At Hollesley Bay, I was allocated to the much more liberal and relaxed pre-release unit called Saint David's House, where we slept in large dormitories and could watch TV until the Queen came on at the end of the transmission. It was not long before I was appointed House Captain and given my own private room. Being the kit orderly as well, I had access to all the kit for the house block. Evidently, the traditional blue-striped prison shirts had become a fashion statement and were in great demand outside. I soon solved the problem by leaving a box of new prison shirts down the lane for my pals to collect after their next visit. The four-month sojourn at St David's soon evaporated and it wasn't long before I was released in early May 1977. Just in time for the summer.

On release from Borstal Recall, it was straight back to the vibrant and dynamic life of Canning Town, and I loved it. Such was the magnetism of the gang culture in the area, three distinct sub-groups of colourful villains emerged. These were called 'The Mini-Snipers', 'The Snipers' and 'The Piranhas'. The origin of the names of these sub-groups most probably derived from a very witty and humorous Piranha member who classified the diverse gang members. The Mini-Snipers were gang members aged between 13 and 16 who earned their money and kudos through creeping private premises and pilfering credit cards or wallets, committing random burglaries and minor robberies such as till snatches; The Snipers' ages ranged from 16 to 21, and they were slightly more organised and bought their vehicles to commit their crimes, such as 'joey-ing', which meant driving vans into factories and warehouses and loading up with goods and driving away. They were responsible for committing professional and well-organised burglaries in London and the provinces, and serious robbery, normally with a hammer or squeezy bottle filled with ammonia. The robberies usually targeted till snatches, night safes and the occasional small firm wages snatch.

As for The Piranhas, these were very well organised and ravenous armed robbers who did not snipe about like the Mini-Snipers or Snipers, but voraciously seized their prize with boundless relish and aplomb.

Essentially, my brother Lenny and I were subsumed into The Snipers' group along with the likes of Ray Church, Jed Freeman, Gee Ashman, Tony Pitters and Dennis Lancaster. Some members of the gang were born and bred workers and did not participate in the villainy, such as Gary Ishmael, Stephen Reynolds, Dermot Mullins, Andy Roland and Tony Croft, but nonetheless they were an integral part of the gang.

At this time in 1977, The Piranhas were very active and usually targeted night-safe drops, betting offices, building societies, post offices, banks and security vans. In fact, Steve Kelt and Eddie Chamberlain each received a ten-year prison sentence for robbing a security guard outside the local branch of the National Westminster Bank in Canning Town. By far the most proficient armed robber in E16 was the legendary Rooky Lee, whose natural flair and audacity ranks him as one of the most prolific armed robbers to come out of Canning Town. Rooky subsequently drew a seven-year sentence in the mid-1970s for a string of armed raids throughout the London area.

What was very interesting about these clearly defined sub-groups was that there were invariably examples of overlapping or cross-group collusion and organisation between the different gang members. For example, a Sniper would hear about the extraordinary gameness of a particular Mini-Sniper and invite him to join them on a particular criminal venture. Similarly, I might be recruited by a member of The Piranhas for a specific robbery or whatever; and invariably, over the course of time, the best joey-ers, creepers, fraudsters, burglars and robbers would gravitate towards each other to create a quasi-league system of criminal efficiency and effectiveness.

This is perhaps how I came to meet my best friend, young Tommy Hole. I had heard about him being the criminal driving force among a group of Mini-Snipers who were robbing tills, betting offices and petrol stations, and we decided to join forces as we shared and exhibited many similar characteristics, such as audacity, ambition and expertise. When all was said and done, we got on so well that after only a short time we became inseparable. Whenever we saw each other, we both experienced a frisson of excitement and adventure, which invariably resulted in us having an excellent time together.

At about this time, young Tom introduced me to his Mini-Sniper friends Jimmy Murphy and Tony Martin. We all had our own unique character and personality and enjoyed each other's company immensely. Not only were we united by the gang culture, poverty and crime, but we all shared a burgeoning distrust and hatred of the police as each of us had a vivid tale to tell of being beaten up by a cozzer or two, especially in the Special Patrol Group transit vans that patrolled E16 at the weekends and randomly selected gang members, dragging them into the van under the pretext of being drunk and disorderly and given them a beating. I recall once, Jimmy Murphy was dragged to the police van and he made out that he was unconscious to avoid further trouble, so the police sprayed him with a fire extinguisher to wake him.

On one memorable occasion, we were all walking past a nightclub in Essex when we noticed a uniformed policeman wilfully harassing courting couples outside the nightspot. This so incensed us that, without dwelling on the subject in detail or planning it, we all walked over and surrounded the cozzer and, without further ado, someone flopped him from the side and he went down and he got a good kicking. In the mêlée, no one noticed the unmarked police vehicle until it screeched up alongside, and we all dispersed into the crowd except Tony Martin, who was enjoying himself so much leathering the cozzer he was arrested and sent to Borstal for it.

At about this time, I was the proud owner of a 15cwt Ford Thames van that I'd bought off the local scrap-metal dealer Dennis Ferrier for £20. Of all the luxury vehicles I have had over the years, this old, reliable beast of a van gave me the most enjoyment of all. We all nicknamed her 'The Sniper-mobile' as it was a dual-purpose machine, acting both as essential transport to social events and playing a valuable role in the burglary business. Despite having neither driving licence nor insurance, I had three overriding rules – no drinking and driving; no driving at night, as the vehicle was liable to be stopped by the police; and third, all passengers were welcome to contribute to the petrol fund. Therefore, it became The Snipers' own battlewagon. We even painted it dark blue to blend in with our naughty nocturnal activities. She was a beautiful beast with a three-speed column gear change and was as reliable as a Volkswagen. Despite her, sweet-sounding 1500cc engine and cute persona, the police used to pull us over at least once or twice a day on the manor and give me 'producers', which we would plaster on the panels inside the van. If there was one major disadvantage about the Sniper-mobile, unlike Tony Croft's Mark 1 Cortina with his two-tone paintwork and fluffy dice, she was not a bird-puller ... more like a bird-doer by the time I'd faced all the police producers at the Magistrate's Court!

During the daytime, seeing as most of the Mini-Snipers, Snipers and Piranhas were either unemployed or unemployable, we use to congregate at Squire's or Bianchi's Café in the Barking Road, Canning Town. Then we would either set off on some criminal adventure or play football, 20–30 strong in the local car park. The best player by far was David Bailey, who, with his grammar school education and silky ball skills and control, could have gone on to be the Johann Cruyff of E16.

Throughout the highs and lows of adolescence, and the seemingly endless cycle of imprisonment, release, imprisonment and release, I had several female admirers and companions, but none with whom I could say I spawned a deep and loving relationship. To be frank, I was not into the soppy, sentimental world of late-night lovers' trysts. That is, not until I spotted a young, very attractive starlet called Tracey Etherden. Tracey was a year younger than me, smaller than me, but with a very beautiful face and a sensual figure.

Late one night after enjoying ourselves in the Norseman club, I offered to escort Tracey home. On reaching her home, she invited me in for a cup of coffee. Within minutes, her panicking mother came trundling downstairs to verify that Tracey was all right and then left us alone for five minutes. But then the demented pet dog called Skinny knocked piping hot coffee over my nether regions and bolted out of the front door. Ah, the joys of romance and seduction. Any chance I had of exploring Tracey's inviting curves had long evaporated and I departed feeling deflated. Nevertheless, unlike other girlfriends that I had been attracted to, there was something that made her seem vulnerable, something that required the endearing strength and protection of my loving arms. I resolved to see Tracey again the following week.

By coincidence, as time progressed, I was to learn that my best friend, young Tom, was, in fact, Tracey's cousin, and therefore I had the good fortune of meeting two wonderful people who felt the same way about me as I felt about them. Whereas young Tom was funny, humorous and exciting to be with, Tracey was loving, affectionate and equally exquisite company. The three of us got on tremendously, drinking at the font of youthful exuberance and carefree laughter. That was until I was hospitalised with excruciating appendicitis and had to have an emergency operation to have it removed. It was then that I realised how much this girl loved me and wanted me as much as I wanted her.

We had our stark differences, though, as Tracey had been brought up in the healthy confines of a loving family home, whereas I had been dragged up in either a dysfunctional family asylum or state institution. Nonetheless, in her sweet and loving way, Tracey taught me the irreplaceable value of human warmth and togetherness. She was to become an extended part of me, someone who was with me even when we were not physically together. It's difficult to know whether we were officially 'in love' but, whatever it was that we had, it felt like I had been pushed headlong off the top diving board into a swimming pool and, once the initial surprise of falling into the water had passed, I wanted to do it again and again.

7

How Do You Plead?

By the onset of 1978, things started to go drastically wrong for me. In many respects, 1978 came to symbolise my very own *annus horribilis* as I was forever getting into trouble and getting arrested. By this time, I had already had two outstanding cases at Snaresbrook Crown Court for taking and driving away a motor vehicle (TDA) and actual body harm (ABH). Then one cold February morning, young Tom, Gee Ashman and I set off on one of our criminal excursions. The mission – which we had accomplished countless times before – was to venture out and nick a car for a robbery later that same day.

We all caught the train to Upminister Underground Station and slipped into the station car park where we nicked a green Ford Capri. But, unbeknown to us, we were spotted taking the car and the police were called. As we pulled out of the station car park, a police panda car spun around and followed us. It was joined by a police Rover V8 area car at the top of the road. We were in big trouble and a high-speed chase ensued. I drove along the High Street and did a sharp left into St Mary's Lane and, as we drove past Upminister Police Station, several uniformed policemen were outside and threw their truncheons at our windscreen which shattered. Undeterred, young Tom and I punched the glass out – *à la* the Sweeney films – and kept driving full pelt.

I recall jinking in-and-out of a tight gap and, much to their annoyance, the police area car smashed into a parked Ford transit van. I kept driving with the accelerator flat to the boards, when I approached a mini-roundabout at about 90mph and a mini van pulled out in front of me. We crashed into the rear of it and sent the mini van spinning into oblivion. They subsequently found one of its rear windows 200 yards up the road. The driver's door of the Capri was so mangled in the collision that we had to climb out through the front windscreen. We all got out of the Capri and found that we were surrounded by miles and miles of loamy fields. We skipped through a hedgerow and started running across the fields.

By now, the police were on the scene and could clearly see us running over the fields. We managed to get to about the third field and it became reminiscent of General Custer's last stand. The cozzers were coming from all directions. On foot, on horseback and a helicopter in the air. As we stood forlorn and dejected in the middle of the field, I said, 'Look, lads, before the police get here, I am not owning up to driving the Capri!' They all said OK.

Puffing and panting, the first cozzer arrived and arrested us. We were all carted off to Upminister Police Station, where some flustered police sergeant took over the case. Evidently, a policewoman had been injured in the police Rover and he was desperate to know who the driver of the Capri was. They had us for two days and none of us would own up to driving. The police sergeant was pulling his hair out! Years and years of experience with the police and court procedures told me that this was a 'refused bail' case, particularly as I still had the two outstanding cases at Snaresbrook Crown Court.

On the third day, the flustered cozzer came into my cell and I was just about to own up to the driving, when he declared, 'We know who the driver is ... it is your blond-haired friend Ashman!' Despite being in the back seat of the Capri, the police had it in their notebooks that Gee was the driver. On the other hand, Gee thought that he had a good chance of bail and decided to put his hands up to driving the vehicle. Some time later, we all had new clothes for court handed in to the custody officer. These were very smart suits and ties, the proceeds from one of our recent successful burglaries.

When the flustered cozzer came on duty and saw how his three inner-city scallywags had transformed into very smart and presentable young men, he nearly burst a blood vessel. He ordered us to take off the suits, but you can imagine our reply! He was really aggrieved that we scrubbed up so well.

Not surprisingly, we were all remanded in custody to Ashford Remand Centre in Middlesex. The prison regime at Ashford in the late 1970s was notorious for its 23-hour-a-day bang-up. In spite of countless suicide attempts by clinically depressed young prisoners – unfortunately, some of which were successful – the austere regime always remained the same: bang-up, bang-up and more bang-up. We remained there for four months until we appeared before His Honour Justice Greenwood, a stern sentencer at Chelmsford Crown Court.

Due to the bizarre juvenile sentencing policy or statute at the time, the judge could either sentence us to any period of time up to six months or any prison sentence over 18 months, but nothing in between. Alas, Gee Ashman was sentenced to 18 months' imprisonment, young Tom was returned to Borstal and I received six months' imprisonment. I only had to serve about another two weeks and I was home. The excitable cozzer nearly had another seizure.

During the time on remand, my girlfriend Tracey had been visiting me and writing letters and our relationship appeared to grow stronger and stronger through absence and adversity. On release from the Young Prisoners wing at Wormwood Scrubs, I was only out for ten days when I was nicked for aggravated burglary and remanded in custody back at the Ashford asylum.

My friend Jimmy Murphy and I had had to collect his mother Rita from a party in Hermit Road, Canning Town, and escort her home through a particularly dark subway that was notorious for muggers. When we knocked on the front door, a drunken partygoer accused us of being gatecrashers. A fight ensued and the belligerent partygoer attacked me with a hatchet, cutting my hand as I defended myself. The police were called and we were arrested and later released from the police station without charge. Several days later, at around midnight, five masked men kicked down the front door and steamed into the property. The owner, armed with a machete, fought his attackers and they ran off. I was arrested, placed on identification parade along with Jimmy Murphy, and remanded in custody.

In the interim, on 21 August 1978, I appeared at Snaresbrook Crown Court for another TDA offence of joy-riding and was sentenced to 18 months' imprisonment. If that wasn't bad enough, I appeared at the same court the very next day for ABH on two geezer birds. The incident occurred at The Lotus nightclub in Forest Gate where I had been enjoying myself on the dance floor when my half-brother's geezer bird and her friend were taking the piss out of me. Annoyed, I swore at her and she threw the contents of her drink over me. I shoved her out of the way and she fell to the ground and suffered minor cuts to her buttocks due to the glass still in her hand. I am very respectful of women generally, but if a woman wants to act like a man, then I feel obliged to treat them as I would a man.

Once outside the club, her mate ran the full length of the road screaming at me and attacked me, so I punched her. Apparently, they went to the police that night and, upon hearing the facts, the police did not want to pursue the matter. The geezer birds subsequently took out a private summons and the CPS took up their case.

At this time, I was caught up in a courtroom culture of pleading guilty just to clean the slate, so to speak. I should have fought the ABH travesty and, despite being slightly culpable for the incident inside the club, the second incident outside the club was undeniably self-defence. As I was already serving a prison sentence, I appeared in front of a female judge and pleaded guilty to both counts and was sentenced to a total of 12 months' imprisonment to run consecutively with the earlier 18-month sentence that I received the day before, making a total of two-and-a-half years in all.

At the time, this seemed like a long sentence for relatively minor crimes and I felt particularly saddened for Tracey, as we had only been together for about a year and, in that time, I had only been home for a few months. Not ones to grumble or complain, though, we both knuckled down and looked to the future. I was placed in HMP Wormwood Scrubs in atrocious, overcrowded and unhygienic conditions. We were packed three to a cell designed for one person, with one chamber pot to piss and shit in during the long days and nights behind the cell door. At first, I was on 'A' Wing, and was then transferred over to the more dynamic 'C' Wing, where the likes of Mickey Ishmael and George Davis had just been sentenced to 15 years' imprisonment for the Bank of Ireland armed robbery in Central London. From a teenager's viewpoint, it was a fascinating insight into human behaviour to see how these veteran bank robbers conducted themselves. They were not flash, arrogant or unapproachable, but thorough gentlemen worthy of respect, particularly from a young, impressionable teenager like myself.

Due to the draconian and claustrophobic conditions of Wormwood Scrubs at this time, it was inevitable that there would be inter-prisoner disputes and disagreements which would invariably blossom into fully fledged fights and assaults. At the time, I was banged up in a cell with two amiable geezers, Terry Frazier and Paul Gray from Bermondsey. Then, on New Year's Day 1979, we had a row with another prisoner in the prison library and I gave him a dig. Later on the landing, after collecting the best prison meal of the year, ham and chips with a succulent slice of pineapple on the top, this fellow ran at Paul Gray and me, smashed a bottle on the railings and attacked us. To combat the danger, I smashed him over the head with the metal tray on which we fetch our meals, and the alarm bell went off and I was frog-marched down to the punishment block to be charged by the Board of Visitors (BoV) with assaulting another prisoner. This quasi-judicial body had the power to take up to six months' remission from prisoners if they were found guilty of any serious infringement of the prison rules and regulations. It was imperative then that we all got out of this assault charge, as it meant a lengthy extension to our respective sentences.

Before we faced the BoV, though, I had to stand trial with Jimmy Murphy at the Central Criminal Court (Old Bailey) to face the aggravated burglary palaver. With significant encouragement from the police, the owners of the house came to court and gave their evidence. A mistrial was ordered, due a particularly prejudicial comment, and the owners had to give their evidence all over again.

Once all the facts came out during the trial, that we were not aggressive party gatecrashers but, in fact, victims of a vicious assault while carrying out a good deed, we were both cleared. Many years later, my co-defendant Jimmy Murphy had the privilege of meeting the female instigator of this escapade on a public bus. A violent row developed and Jimmy was once again arrested for assault and had to appear at Snaresbrook Crown Court. He was acquitted once again.

Meanwhile, back at the Scrubs I still had to face the BoV hearing. Prior to going into the hearing, a decent screw poked his head inside the cell door and said, 'Ask me any questions you want and I will agree with you!' During the hearing, I pleaded not guilty and, after the screw had given his evidence that Paul Gray and I were not the aggressors, the BoV found us not guilty. All in all, it wasn't a bad week – two 'not guilties' in seven short days!

What is astonishing, despite nearly a year of cramped cells, courtrooms and prison blocks, is that I still had one significant Crown Court case to face. The facts were, it was alleged, that a single policeman had been keeping static observation on a stolen MGB sports car in a dark alley near a nightclub in Custom House. It was alleged that young Tom and his girlfriend, along with Tracey and I, came out of the club and went to the sports car, sat in it, got out of it and went to a nearby cab office. After losing eye contact with us, the policeman identified us in the cab office and arrested us.

At the trial, young Tom and I denied ever going to the vehicle. We called both girls to give evidence on our behalf and things were going well until the prosecution called evidence to rebut Tracey's account of events. They alleged that Tracey had verbally confessed to going over to the car with 'Terry and Kevin'. Obviously, this was a disputed confession, as despite young Tom's real name being Kevin, no one ever called him that, more especially as Tracey was young Tom's cousin. As the prosecutor was putting words in Tracey's mouth, tears of utter disbelief and frustration were tumbling down her sweet face. We all knew that it was all lies, but the jury didn't and they found us guilty.

It is worth noting that, up until this seminal time in Tracey's life, she had always abided by the noble concepts of truth and justice. Tracey thought the police were doing an essential public service to the community and viewed them with high regard and respect. After this devastating experience, her favourable perception of the police as the guardians of law and order was fundamentally obliterated. Henceforth, Tracey would always view the police through a prism of deep distrust and cynicism. Her sweet, all-embracing innocence had been violated in a most brutal way. The judge was not impressed; he sentenced young Tom to 18 months' imprisonment and me to two years to run concurrently with the two-and-a-half years that I was already serving, which basically meant that I had to serve an additional nine months in prison.

When I returned to Wormwood Scrubs that night, I clumsily rolled my very first joint of ganja. I had no tobacco and no cellmate, so I rolled it neat and smoked it all to myself. Then I realised to my amazement that I could not get off the top bunk bed to turn the light off. I was immobile, but still slept very soundly, dreaming of running barefoot across fields and fields of pert, nubile nipples.

At long last, all the wretched Crown Court cases had been dealt with and the allocation prison officer at the Scrubs was only too pleased to be able to pass me on to another penal dustbin. As a Category 'B' prisoner, I could only be sent to a prison with secure conditions. There were several options available – Coldingley Prison in nearby Surrey, Blundestone Prison in Suffolk or the invidious sin-bin of Camphill Prison on the Isle of Wight. Need I say more ... I was off to the Isle of Wight.

From a prisoner's point of view, there are three types of penal institutions – progressive, static and regressive jails. Basically, being transferred to a progressive jail means that you have had a result and you are taking a giant step towards eventual release. On the other hand, static jails signify that you are treading water and are going nowhere. Lastly, regressive jails denote that you can slag the screws off as much as you want because you are in the worst possible piss-hole available.

HM Prison Camphill comes under the latter category as, not only was it the South-East Region's short-to-medium-term sin-bin, but it also, geographically speaking, put extra pressure upon your visitors as they had to travel to Portsmouth and then hop on the ferry to the island. What could easily start out as a pleasurable jaunt to the seaside for visitors invariably became a long, tiresome and expensive ordeal, where only the most determined and dedicated friends or loved ones would see the sentence through to the bitter end.

In 1979, there were approximately six wings at HMP Camphill. There were two newly built pre-release wings at the top end of the jail and four older Victorian-type wings at the bottom. Initially, I was placed on St Patrick's Wing, a relatively small wing of about 30–40 short-term prisoners with little or no atmosphere. Apart from one or two sensible fellows on the wing, I did not like it at all. As soon as I entered the wing and saw the highly polished floors, fresh paint and military-like orderliness, I thought I wouldn't be there long. The wing did not have that lived-in feel about it, that quaint amalgamation of strident music, scuffed lino and endearing chaos. In short, it resembled a morgue.

After a while, the screws offered me a job serving food on the hotplate at mealtimes. Although in some jails this is construed as a semi-prestigious job, as it allows you access to more freedom on the wing, extra food and Visiting Orders, it far from appeased my doubts about the wing and its clientele. For example, on my very first day behind the servery, we had finished serving the food and I sensed a lingering tension between another hotplate worker and myself. Primarily, this was an inter-prisoner territorial dispute – he thought he owned the hotplate, its food and its workers.

At the conclusion of serving the food, it is customary to share the remaining titbits in a civilised manner. I distinctly recall that there were three fried eggs and three of us. I proceeded to take one of the fried eggs and some fish cakes, when the geezer stated bluntly that the fried eggs were all his. Simple mathematics dictates that three divided by three equals one, therefore we were to have one fried egg each. Clearly, he was not having it and, in my view, this flew in the face of common decency and fairness, so I nutted him and decked him. Not being an experienced headbutter, blood started to pour down my face and I looked like I'd been in a motorway car crash. I was then taken to the prison hospital to have stitches inserted in my head and then swagged down to the punishment block to await another BoV hearing, where several weeks later I pleaded guilty and was sentenced to two weeks' loss of remission. What a palaver, all over a fried egg. I wonder what would have occurred if it had been over a piece of roast chicken.

There was one consolation from this episode, however, as the screws moved me to St Michael's Wing, a much larger wing with a vibrant atmosphere of laughter, pumping music and attendant skulduggery. More specifically, I was reunited with Paulie Gray and another Bermondsey pal called Billy Iverson. Also on another nearby wing was fellow Towner Frank Smith, and Mickey Reilly. Altogether, we made a colourful bunch of characters with a never-a-dull-moment attitude.

I remember one occasion when a particular South London State-paid police informer came to the jail and it was a matter of pride and honour that the Bermondsey lads served him up. He was only on the exercise yard a matter of minutes when he was slashed with a vast array of sharp implements. The alarm bell went and we were all swagged down to the punishment block to face an external police investigation. We were kept in solitary confinement until Hampshire Police had conducted their inquiry and decided to drop the case due to lack of evidence.

As a direct result of our sporadic violent and anti-authoritarian exploits, the screws at Camphill nicknamed us 'The Quality Street Gang'. Whether this was a compliment or an insult is debatable. But, whatever it was, we were potential London villains in the making.

It was at Camphill that I first met John Kendall. John was finishing a four-year sentence for burglary and was allocated to a wing in the top half of the jail. My attention was first brought to John when I was a teenager as there was intense rivalry and animosity between The Snipers and the Stratford mob. Over the years, the Towners used to clash with our Stratford and Custom House adversaries, normally on their turf at disco pubs and clubs. Kendall was known for being very ruthless with knives and ammonia and had acquired a notorious reputation. At Camphill, however, we got on really well and shared a mutual respect for each other.

In fact, I recall asking John, who worked in the administration block at Camphill, to secure me a special A4 size book so that I could write up notes on a painting and decorating Trade Training Course that I had enrolled on. It is my philosophy that, when you are in jail, there is no value in dossing about dwelling on the profundity of incarceration, and it's better to do something worthwhile and constructive – a bit like this book I'm writing at Belmarsh Prison – in order to take your mind off the psychological torture and anguish of captivity. The painting and decorating course provided the perfect foil for this, much like the earlier carpentry course which I'd completed in Borstal. It was a thorough four-month programme, taking us through the fundamentals of painting and decorating, from how to treat wall fungi to the gleaming finished product of a fully decorated room.

Despite throwing myself into this with great gusto, it did not pass without incident. The team of bin emptiers who visited our workshop once a week complained about the presence of wet and soggy wallpaper being thrown into the dustbins. It was not the complaint itself that was the problem, it was the tone and general demeanour of the central protagonist. In any event, a fight ensued and I whacked the fellow with a broom handle and broke his arm. Once again, back to the punishment block, a BoV hearing, and this time I was found not guilty.

Throughout this year-long period of incarceration at Camphill, at least once a month my girlfriend Tracey would make the long journey to the island where we would sit opposite each other at a visiting table and plan for the future together. We both knew that things had to change, as after months and months of long overdue introspection we both knew that I had to break this senseless cycle of petty criminality. Therefore, I made a concrete resolution never to return to prison again, not unless it was for something worthwhile, like earning chunks and chunks of money.

8

A Willing Pupil

On 15 April 1980, I was finally released from Camphill Prison on the Isle of Wight. I was picked up at the prison gate by my half-brother and was driven straight to my girlfriend's house in Canning Town. There I was given a real home-coming reception by Tracey's wonderful parents who made me feel like their own son.

Sadly, Pat and Iris Etherden, Tracey's parents, had lost a much-cherished son when he was only 13. Kevin, whom I never had a chance to meet, died tragically on a school outing when a coach rolled backwards and crushed him. This was obviously a very painful loss to the Etherden family and, although I could never replace Kevin, the entire Etherden family treated me as if I was their own son.

I did travel to see my parents, who had by now moved to Dagenham, and they offered me shelter at their palatial bungalow, but it was not for me. The tyrant, however, who had mellowed somewhat over the years, offered to secure a job for me at his workplace as a warehouseman. This I eagerly accepted as I wanted to show Tracey and her lovely family that I was making a sincere effort to reform my ways.

While I was waiting for the vacancy to come up at my father's workplace, I put my painting and decorating skills to good use and took on some decorating requests within the family. It was not long, however, before I was back out with my good friends young Tom, Jimmy Murphy and Tony Martins. I recall that I went on some comical burglary adventure in the wilds of Essex and, as we were loading up our truck with electrical goods from the store, we were tumbled by the police. Without further ado, we all dispersed into the local streets and countryside. I was unable to make it to the back-up vehicle and ended up sleeping with a horse in a stable. Then in the early daylight hours, I stole a vehicle and made my own way back to London. When I walked into the Etherden household at about 8.00am, I was cross-examined as to where I had been all night long. Thankfully, due to the overwhelming farmyard stench on my clothes, I was duly acquitted of any impropriety and reinstated within the Etherden fold, much to my relief!

After a couple of weeks, there was still no news regarding the job as a warehouseman, so I started to rob again. During one incident, young Tom's car was seen leaving the scene of a night-safe robbery. I went back with Tom to collect the car the following day with a mate of ours called Terry, and an unmarked police vehicle followed us to Canning Town. When the police confronted us, young Tom and I both bolted and escaped. Our friend Terry was captured. Young Tom phoned the previous owner of the vehicle – who was also an inveterate villain – and marked his card that the police might pay him a visit, and that he should say that he bought the vehicle from some travellers. As a result, the previous owner of the vehicle was pulled in and questioned at Hornchurch Police Station and, while he was in a custody cell, he was overheard shouting out, 'It is all Smithy's and Hole's fault that we are here. They committed the robbery!' Not surprisingly, the police then raided our parents', girlfriends' and other close relations' premises and we became fully fledged fugitives.

At this time, young Tom's father, old Tommy Hole, had been released on parole after serving a seven-year prison sentence for attempted murder, where it was alleged that he and another person had tried to run someone over with a car. There was one overriding proviso to old Tom's release, though; it was that he had to live outside the London area, so he was parked up in a pre-release hostile in Winchester, Hampshire.

Upon hearing about our perilous position as fugitives, old Tom proclaimed to his son, whether rightly or wrongly, 'You are a million to get nicked for a robbery sooner or later and go away for a long time. If you are going to rob and I cannot stop you, I may as well teach you properly.'

Therefore, old Tom, who had been an exceptional and well-organised armed robber in his time, began to teach young Tom and myself the noble art of armed robbery. Obviously, being a professional armed robber, old Tom was a little apprehensive and concerned about me, as he only knew me through my friendship and association with his son. But, once young Tom reassured him that I was a good gravy guy, we were all ears and willing pupils in this dangerous and fascinating trade.

Over the course of several weeks, old Tom taught us that being an armed robber was not a game to be taken lightly, it was a 24-hour occupation. He added that it is not just about robbing a bank or security van and spending the money, it is about how you behave before as well as after a robbery.

We were told that most of the best robberies were professional, trouble-free robberies where there were no shots fired, no possible facial identifications and no surplus evidence left behind. We were told that most of the top-grade professional robbers stole their own vehicles and put false matching number plates on them to avoid detection prior to a robbery. Moreover, most suppliers of stolen vehicles could not be trusted, especially if there was a particularly savage robbery in which a policeman or a security guard had been shot and it was given extensive media coverage. We learnt to steal our own motor vehicles; that way, no third party associates could do us any harm.

Additionally, old Tom added that 'pieces of work' or robberies evolved or materialised in two ways. This was either through inside information or through getting out there and finding your own work yourself. The safest and most reliable work is always found by the person committing the robbery, as it cuts out the ever-present risk or threat of an informant. Nonetheless, over the years, some of the best and most rewarding robberies have all derived from inside information and, although good information should not be dismissed, it should be treated with the utmost care and circumspection. As things stand then, these were the basic tenets of the noble art of robbery as expounded by a very experienced and supremely cunning professional armed robber.

Not surprisingly, we did not have long to wait to put this advice into practice. There was 'a bit of work' that several old-school East End robbers had been looking at and had even tried to get moving on, but with little or no joy. Old Tom invited his willing pupils to view it and, because we wanted to get established as successful robbers, we said that we liked it and that we would have it the following week. The only problem old Tom had – unlike the old school – was the heated dispute between his pupils as to who was going to get the prize first. The work itself was tricky, as the security guards only had a short walk from the armoured vehicle to the bank and the timing and judgement of one's approach and method of seizure was imperative.

On the day, of course, I got it spot on and caught the security guard between the bank and the security van. I relieved the guard of a juicy canvas sack full of money and made my way with young Tom to a waiting vehicle with old Tom at the wheel. We drove a short distance and changed into another vehicle and then reached our 'flop', or safe house, to cut up our well-earned spoils. All in all, by the time we paid out the expenses for the flop, cars, guns and miscellaneous bits and pieces, I had £8,500 for my whack. In the early 1980s, this was a small fortune to me and, when I slept that night and woke up the next morning, I felt decidedly strange. By that, I mean I had all these bricks of £10 notes surrounding me on my bed.

More specifically, despite the widespread media coverage about the robbery, it was, according to the gospel of old Tommy Hole, an overriding success. There were no facial identifications, no forensic evidence left at the scene and, most significantly, no one had been hurt. The only thing the police had was the customary reward money that was put up by the security company and a team of eager detectives running around looking for elusive leads and clues.

That first bit of work put the three of us bang on our feet, as, in effect, all three of us had recently been released from prison and we were skint. We all treated ourselves to new cars, clothes and jewellery. Perhaps the most sacred of old Tom's tenets was that we told absolutely no one about our business. For as they say, 'Loose lips sinks ships!' As a powerful incentive to compel us to adhere to the robber's culture of total secrecy and silence, old Tom pointed out wisely the painful shortcomings of previous villains and robbers, such as Bertie Smalls and Charlie Lowe, who had turned supergrass and given evidence against their former partners in crime.

In many respects, it was due to the supergrass era of the 1970s that family-orientated gangs of robbers like ours developed and evolved. No longer were individual robbers prepared to work freelance. They all knew the life-shattering pitfalls of supergrasses and therefore preferred to work in small, tight-knit family groups of robbers such as ours. Put bluntly, there were too many good but brazen robbers sitting in Albany and Parkhurst Prisons serving decades and decades of imprisonment due to the contagious criminal disease of supergrasses. Fortunately for us novices, with the wisdom and experience of old Tom we could, indeed, learn from their costly blunders and mistakes.

Now that I had my first ever serious armed robbery under my belt, and I was seemingly financially well off, a veritable calamity occurred. My father said that I had now been granted the job as a warehouseman and I was to start work the following Monday. Without wishing to declare the source of my new-found wealth, I pointed out to him that I was unable to start work as there was a warrant out for my arrest and that the police were actively looking for me over the night-safe robbery. I pleaded that the police were bound to check the income tax records to see if I was working. My heartfelt plea went over his head as he righteously proclaimed that he had put himself out to acquire me the job and, now that it was available, I did not want it.

Being a steadfast man of my word, and against my better judgement, I went to work as a poorly paid, slack-jawed warehouseman, lifting countless boxes of pet food on to countless pallets all day long which were then loaded on to lorries by forklifts for the deliveries the following day. To exacerbate matters, young Tom and a carful of our friends would drive around to my workplace during the dinner breaks and wind me up. It was copper-bottomed torment and torture.

At night, I used to creep out with young Tom to a local pub or club and return home at about 1.00am and have to drag myself up again at 6.00am to go to work. I was forever tired, as the work was not only strenuous and boring, but it also appeared never ending. Soon I became very depressed, as not only was I missing out on the youthful vibrancy of socialising with my friends, but, because I was living back at my parents' address in Dagenham, I was also badly missing my long-term girlfriend Tracey. Awkward circumstances dictated that I was unable to visit her house, as the police had raided it while looking for me after the night-safe robbery.

Then one morning, rather than getting a lift to work with my father as I usually did, I drove to work in my BMW car. As I drove past the gate lodge at the warehouse, I looked down towards the shed where I worked and I saw a police dog-handler's van parked there. Initially, I took no notice as the premises had been burgled several times in the past and I thought that it might have happened again. But, as I walked into the workers' canteen, a fellow worker said, 'The police are waiting around the main shed for you!'

Apparently, the police had not expected me to come to work in a BMW and missed me driving through the main gate. I left the car there and slipped through a side fence and caught a train to where young Tom was staying. We then drove around to my half-brother's flat and the police were there, too. It did not take the Brain of Britain to work out that someone close to us was an informant. The grass knew that I had stayed at my half-brother's place while I was working as a warehouseman, but what the rat did not know was that I had moved back to live with my parents in Dagenham. It had to be someone very close to us and we managed to narrow it down to one particular slag. Admittedly, in spite of not telling a soul about our secret professional trade, the BMWs, the Cecil Gee clobber, the pukka jewellery and attendant generosity caused or engendered widespread jealousy and resentment among some – but by no means all – of our friends.

It was hard not to notice an ever-increasing socio-economic gulf emerging between young Tom and I and our erstwhile friends. Obviously, we still wanted to associate and socialise with our lifelong friends, but things had changed. We were different, we acted and behaved differently, as if someone had waved a magic wand over us and we had abandoned the benighted social mores of Canning Town and evolved into a higher species of sophisticated criminality. As old Tom astutely proclaimed, 'The Metropolitan Police (in 1980) employ 21,000 cozzers in London alone, and every one of them wants to jump on the back of a bank robber!' He was 100 per cent right; successful armed robbers had to be on their guard at all times.

Due to the overriding success of the first robbery, old Tom introduced us to his long-standing friend and excellent robber Lenny Carter. Lenny was primarily one of the old school of East End robbers who rubbed shoulders with the Kray twins in their heyday and had a very good reputation and name. I took to him immediately for, if old Tom was our inspirational college tutor in the art of robbery, then Lenny Carter was our university mentor. I would not say that Lenny was more cunning than old Tom, but he possessed and exhibited a far deeper understanding of what made a supremely successful armed robber.

The golden rule according to the doctrine of Lenny Carter was: *never underestimate the police*. They have all the money, cars, computers, experts, resources and manpower to nick professional armed robbers, as we are perceived as 'very special and dangerous people'! Lenny would claim, 'Anyone can be an armed robber, but not anyone can get away with it every time.' It takes a special person indeed to become proficient and efficient at nicking large chunks of cash from the state and security companies. One of Lenny's tricks was always to plead poverty in the pubs and clubs around the East End, even to the extent where he would borrow money off other drinking friends and pay them back later. Also, he advised us never to buy a flash and expensive car when an old Honda Civic would do. And always use public transport to look at a bit of work, as this enables you to give your eyes a chance to see if you are under police surveillance.

Another one of Lenny's tricks was to remove the lead shot from a shotgun cartridge and put long grain rice inside it instead. That way, if he had to shoot anyone, the target experienced all the traumatic effects of being shot but, in fact, they'd only been hit with rice. Over the course of several months, I became very close to Lenny and we used to sit in his council flat and plan and discuss future bits of work. Sometimes, he used to say to me, 'I've had a good think,' which invariably meant that he had thought up some classic idea with which to orchestrate our next blag.

On a social level, particularly if we were out guzzling in one of our remote back-street pubs in the East End, we would spend the best part of the day and night in each other's company. If old Tom was humorous, charismatic and somewhat restrained in getting the drinks in, Lenny was hilariously charming and endearing company. As well as being warm-hearted, he was exceedingly generous to the extent that, if you said you liked his tie, shirt or jacket, he would take them off there and then in the bar and give them to you. He was also very down to earth. Whereas most people liked old Tom, everybody, without exception, loved Lenny. They made a terrific duo.

If there was one apparent weakness in old Tom and Lenny Carter's approach to robbery, it was that they were, to some degree, still caught up in the 1960s notion of robbing security vans with four or five robbers. This appeared totally archaic to our point of view. Why take four robbers on a bit of work when two robbers were more practical and efficient? Strength in numbers may be required at times and it may also engender confidence, but invariably it was surplus to requirements, resulting in the necessity and supply of extra get-away vehicles and this always meant more evidence for the police and their forensic experts.

It was not long before we cracked the ice with Lenny and, on the basis of some useful information, we attacked a security van in the Midlands. It was not the most profitable robbery in the world but, in terms of knowledge and experience in finding an escape route and clever change-over points and the avoidance of motorways, it provided a steep learning curve. According to Lenny, the overriding problem with robbing security vehicles outside the inner-city areas was that robbers could be up to ten miles away from the scene of the crime and still be in a very dangerous and arrestable position. On the other hand, being a couple of streets away after a major robbery in a densely populated area is worth up to ten or fifteen miles away in the countryside. Moreover, the manpower resources of police forces in the metropolitan areas are invariably overstretched, and if the robbery is not particularly dramatic or sensational in its execution, or it does not yield any overt evidential features or leads, after a month or two, the inquiry will start to gather dust on the top shelf somewhere.

Alternatively, out in the sticks where a stolen macaw makes the headlines, a serious, well-planned robbery will mean a full-strength squad of terrier-like detectives will be put on the case who will pester and hound their metropolitan neighbours for possible, probable and potential candidates for the robbery at hand. Therefore, as Lenny would proclaim, provincial robberies were not only hard work in selecting successful escape routes, but there was a real threat that the investigating squad would let the inquiry run on and on. British prisons are waiting for robbers who venture out into the fertile pastures of the countryside. The risks are too great in comparison with those committed within the inner-city areas. It follows, then, that perhaps the most sacred rule of robbing – after keeping *schtum* – is that, if the escape route is not viable or available, do not go ahead with it. Lenny would add, why take an unnecessary chance, when an inconvenient river, railway line or forest cuts the escape route down by 50 or 75 per cent. It does not matter how good the prize is, or how scrumptious the work looks; do not take unnecessary chances as the money is of little value if it ends up as a mere exhibit in a forthcoming trial.

As a result of a possible informant on the fringes of our company and the subsequent spins at my workplace and my half-brother's flat, I decided to move in with some distant relatives in Essex. I was living there for about nine months and they made me feel very welcome. In fact, living in Essex became a real revelation as it compelled me to assess and analyse the potent magnetism of Canning Town and its unavoidable pitfalls. Living in Essex was a bit like living outside a goldfish bowl; my vantage point enabled me to look in at E16 and see how short-sighted some of the local villains were. It was essential, therefore, that if an ambitious villain wanted to progress up the pyramid of crime and success, it was indeed imperative that one had to move out of the Town and into the leafy lanes and avenues of Essex.

After the second robbery, young Tom and I were getting more and more confident. More specifically, when we put the idea that we had been working on of robbing a particular security van to old Tom and Lenny, they were slightly indifferent about the work as they were content to savour the success that we had had so far. As for us young bloods, however, we were just warming up and we went against their advice and judgement and committed our next robbery without them. They realised that we were not prepared to wait about for the old school, as we knew what we wanted and we wanted it now. Despite being slightly aggrieved at our dissent, we appeased them by cutting up our £25,000 prize equally with them. Not only did this benevolent gesture put a smile on their faces, it also came to symbolise our appreciation and loyalty towards our ageing mentors.

As the months passed, we would, as a rule, commit about one robbery per month. At this time, we were content to just take the bags of cash off security guards, but we were getting, bit by exciting bit, more and more ambitious and confident. The exercise of running up to a security guard, putting a gun under his nose and nicking the prize was exciting and fun, but we wanted to entertain more challenging tasks. I recall one occasion when I had a security guard up against a security van and young Tom blurted out, 'Stand and deliver!' At the time, these formed part of the lyrics of a popular Adam and the Ants song. Young Tom and I knew what we were doing was very dangerous and the consequences of being caught were very high, but we wanted – needed, in fact – to have a little fun as well.

Perhaps one of the most dangerous situations an armed robber can face is that of a 'ready-eye'. By that, I mean, when the police are aware that a robbery is going to take place and armed police are lying in wait, either at the scene or back at the flop. To set up a ready-eye is a very difficult process for the police, as they want to get as many armed police officers near to the scene of the robbery as possible. This means that they will invariably disguise themselves as milkmen, dustmen, postmen, telephone engineers, cab drivers, window cleaners or even double-glazing operatives. Throughout my lifetime as an armed robber, I have walked into three known ready-eyes and I have tumbled them each time. Twice I was only there to look at the work and once I was actually there to have the work. Most robbers would have been nicked at these ready-eyes, but if you are professional about your work and you do your homework like visiting the scene of the robbery several days beforehand to get the natural feel of the plot, and even visit the scene of the robbery early on the morning to make a mental note of the surroundings, social settings and pedestrians in the area, this will help to highlight anything odd about the location when the time comes for action.

For example, if a bus stop has been moved several yards closer to the target and a nondescript woman is standing at the bus stop desperately trying to look inconspicuous, abandon the work. Or if the road sweeper is not the normal guy you have seen there for weeks on end, drop the work out. In fact, if things are that bad, it is probably bang on you, so go and find a legitimate job.

In the meantime, the police were still looking for us and were also going mad looking for two other East End villains called Jamieson and Hutchinson, who were wanted for the murder of an elderly couple in New Barn Street, Plaistow. Concerned that we would get caught up in the hunt for them, we decided to leave the capital until they were captured, which they were a very short time later. Eventually, they were both convicted and sentenced to life imprisonment for the senseless crime.

By pure coincidence, on another occasion, young Tom, Jimmy Murphy and me were out clubbing and I suggested that they come and stay with me at my Essex bolthole as my relatives were away on holiday. Fortunately, they accepted my advice as, later that night, the police blocked off the street and raided young Tom's girlfriend's flat looking for him. Obviously, the informant was still active.

A couple of weeks later, young Tom moved into his mother's flat and they were pestering me to decorate their front room. I was very reluctant as I didn't need the money, but I could hardly refuse as I respected young Tom's mother as much as my own loved ones. So I agreed to decorate the front room, providing they bought me all the painting and decorating tools that I required and that in itself would act as the payment. Everyone was in agreement and young Tom and I drove to Ilford to acquire the appropriate painting and decorating paraphernalia. But I did not take into account one thing; young Tom was an inveterate kleptomaniac, and even if he had £1,000 in his pocket he would still feel the urge to nick things. Young Tom possessed a natural compunction to steal. In fact, he was so good at it he could have easily made a criminal career out of it. Anyway, we both raced up to the local DIY store in our respective BMWs and pilfered every single item that I required, save a large, heavy-duty black plastic bucket that I needed for wallpaper paste. Our pockets were absolutely bulging with miscellaneous brushes, scissors, scrapers, plumb lines, etc. We had everything.

As we left the store and crossed Ilford High Road into a nearby street where we had parked our vehicles, I thought that I had better look round in case some eagle-eyed store detective had been following us. As I turned round, I saw two big, burly geezers about to pounce on us, so I pushed young Tom out of their reach with one hand and whacked the geezers with the bucket in the other. As we sprinted off down the side street, a phalanx of plain-clothes detectives appeared out of gardens and doorways with handguns pointed at us as they tried to stop us. But, in the chaos and confusion, we ignored them and I hurdled several garden fences until I was finally cornered. I was then dragged into an unmarked police vehicle, laid face down on the back seat, handcuffed and then sat on by the two burly cozzers whom I had just mugged off earlier with the bucket. I could hardly breathe and I thought that I was going to suffocate and die. I was then taken to Ilford Police Station and chucked into a cell.

Young Tom had run down the same side street as me and shoulder-barged a cozzer, who later claimed that he had broken his ribs. He was also taken to Ilford Police Station. While in the police cells, I was listening at the crack in the door jamb – as you do – when I heard someone say that we were being transferred by Hampshire Police to Portsmouth Central Police Station.

Apparently, some months earlier, a Securicor security van had been attacked and a security guard had been robbed by gunmen of £25,000 outside a bank on an industrial estate in Portsmouth. As part of their extensive enquiries, the police at Hampshire wanted to quiz us about the robbery and put us on identification parades.

Once in the police cells at Portsmouth, on the advice of my solicitor I refused to answer any questions about anything, but stated that I was prepared to go on an ID parade. Throughout the five days that I was held in police custody prior to the ID parade, I wore a distinctive short, black leather jacket. I never took it off once, not for the police interviews, solicitor's visits, meals or anything. The jacket looked like it was superglued to me.

Shortly before attending the ID parade, I viewed the volunteers who were to be on the parade with me. After studying their appearance, I agreed that they were all of similar appearance to me as they had all come from the local Royal Navy training barracks. As the police inspector conducting the parade called the first witness to the robbery and the runner went to fetch him or her, I quickly changed positions in the line-up and also swapped the black leather jacket with a squaddie and put on his Parka coat. Throughout the whole exercise, I continued to change positions each time the runner went out of the hall to fetch the next witness. You may not be surprised to note that I never got picked out once, but my poor black leather coat was picked out seven out of twelve times. It might be that black leather clothing is symbolically associated with crime and criminals. It might be that all the volunteers wearing the black leather coat resembled the robber's appearance, or there might be a more sinister reason for this coincidence. Who knows ... but the charges were dropped against both of us.

We were then transported separately back to Romford Police Station in Essex to face the night-safe robbery allegation. On the advice of my solicitor, I made a written defence statement; in it, I admitted going to the car used in the robbery, but not actually getting into the car or committing the robbery. The Crown Prosecution Service (CPS) eventually dropped this charge as well.

Lastly, the police charged young Tom with GBH for shoulder-charging the cozzer at the time of our initial arrest, and I was also charged with ABH for hitting the overzealous cozzer with the bucket. At a preliminary court hearing, young Tom elected to go for trial and the CPS dropped my ABH to common assault on a policeman and asked me to plead guilty at the Magistrates' Court. Refusing to accept the advice of the solicitor defending me, I fought the case and made the overzealous cozzer come to court to justify his actions. He was livid.

In essence, my defence was that young Tom had been receiving threats from a well-known villain which was, in fact, true and, when I saw these men about to pounce on us without warning, not realising that they were, in fact, policemen, I hit one with the bucket in self-defence. Due to the fact that the charge had been dropped to common assault, the case could not be tried in front of a jury. Not surprisingly, at the Magistrates' Court, the bench found me guilty and I was fined £200 with time to pay. Unfortunately for young Tom, he had broken his parole licence and was remanded in custody. Later, he appeared at Snaresbrook Crown Court for the GBH charge and was unanimously acquitted.

While young Tom was serving the remainder of the parole licence, we all decided to adopt a low profile for a while and hang up our weapons, until one day I received a phone call from an old Piranha pal who was eager to start working with me. This particular Piranha had an excellent pedigree as a robber as he had been working with a tasty little firm out of South London. He had become increasingly disillusioned with them, because, although they were very game and efficient robbers, they were cowboyish after the event and all he could see was plenty of grief in the distance. So he wanted to work with me and I introduced him to the old school.

Prior to the introduction, however, I had cracked the ice with the Piranha by having several bits of work with him two-handed. In many respects, we were so much alike – game, ambitious, audacious yet also cautious. We were both increasingly aware of the sophisticated surveillance techniques that the police were using and we treated even a simple meet with great care and caution.

It was this person, the Piranha, who introduced me to the essential advantages of owning and riding a motorbike. I started off with a Honda 250cc Super Dream and gradually progressed into riding much larger, more powerful bikes. I used to set off at 7.30am and travel all over London in search of potential work. The only place that was out of bounds was central London, because the IRA was very active at this time and the police were stopping anything that moved in the Square Mile of the British banking system. I had heard of countless stories of robbers driving to commit robberies elsewhere in London who'd been caught up in an improvised roadblock in search of terrorists. We were not about to make that mistake.

Now that I was no longer a wanted man by the police, I could return to the exquisite family environment of the Etherden household. By now, Tracey was pregnant with our first child and we managed to acquire our very first home together in East Ham outside the goldfish bowl of E16. Then on 10 April 1981, Tracey gave birth to our first son, Terence Eugene Smith. Because Tel-boy, as he was known, was born prematurely at six months weighing 6lb 12oz, he was placed in an incubator on the special care ward. Then, one day after his birth, I was driving to Barking Maternity Hospital to visit both mother and child when I noticed that the police had stopped all the traffic at a junction on the A13 and an ambulance with a police escort drove past. I thought, God, someone's in trouble. When I reached the hospital, Tracey informed me that, due to Tel-boy's poorly condition, he was being transferred from Barking to a special intensive care ward at the University College Hospital in Paddington, central London.

I am not one to show outward emotion, but on this occasion I could not contain myself. Tracey and I sobbed like children in each other's arms. We really thought that Tel-boy was in big trouble. Tracey was still too poorly to be with Tel-boy at the inner-city hospital, so I used to travel up to Paddington on my motorbike. I would slip into the hospital at any time and sit with him while he was cocooned in his incubator with tubes all over his tiny body. I used to put my finger inside and let him grip it with his hand. I used to sit there for hours and pray to God or Allah or whoever that he would pull through this testing and delicate period. Looking at the other premature children nearby, however, some no bigger than a 2lb-bag of sugar, inwardly I knew that Tel-boy would be a survivor. It certainly put things into perspective for me. Here I was gallivanting around London, attacking security vans for selfish, materialistic reasons, while many ultra-fragile babies were tenuously hanging on to their lives by the slimmest of threads. It definitely made me think! After several weeks in University College Hospital, Tel-boy was allowed home with Tracey where he ate and ate and ate and now he is a mountain of a man, thank God.

If the problem of stealing large chunks of cash is not hard enough, the headache of where to store the money throws up even more problems. Some robbers invest it, some bank it, some acquire safety deposit boxes, some spend it lavishly and some depend upon friends and family to look after it. Once I had no reason to reside at my distant relatives' abode in Essex, I decided to leave some money there. Not a lot, but enough to be locked in a briefcase. Occasionally, I would visit them either to make a small deposit or a withdrawal.

One day, I noticed that some of the money was missing. In order to be 100 per cent sure, I left a little trap in the briefcase and, sure enough, the next time I opened the case I was another £1,500 down. All in all, I had lost £4,000. Naturally, I confronted the relatives and they jointly denied it, with the added caveat that it was such a serious accusation that they should call the police. That day, for the paltry sum of £4,000, I lost relatives who had helped me while I was in trouble. I loved and respected them and it really hurt me when I had conclusive proof that they had been picking the lock of the briefcase and pilfering its contents. It was then that I learnt that access to large sums of money changed some people. If they had been clever, they could have had a moody burglary and said the lot was stolen. I put the problem to the old school who wanted to punish the culprits, but I decided not to as, deep down, I loved them and their sweet children, and they had helped me when I was in trouble with the law. Nonetheless, to this day, some 20 years later, they have suffered the traditional wrath of Smith obstinacy as my family and I have never spoken to them since. They were good people and now they are nobodies.

This would not be the last time that relatives would dip into the prosperous pot of stigma and shame. Evidently, this type of marrow-deep betrayal occurs more frequently than villains like to admit. Many well-known and successful robbers have walked through the prison gates at the end of their sentences only to find that their hard-robbed and blagged dosh has been raided by so-called close family and friends. Losing the filthy lucre is secondary; it is the loss of bone-deep, irreplaceable loved ones that is the hardest to swallow.

In May 1981, my brother Lenny was in Wandsworth Prison serving a seven-year sentence for possession of a shotgun. Seeing as he did not have any dependable visitors, such as a steady girlfriend or reliable pals, I used to visit him at least once a month and look after his convivial and economic needs. Although I detest visiting prisons, I do derive great satisfaction from visiting close relatives and friends and letting them know that I am there for them. On this occasion in 1981, Lenny met an old friend of his called Steve Pearson, a very game and active armed robber who was also serving a seven stretch. He told Lenny that he was going to attempt an escape off the prison coach on the way to court. But, if he was successful, he wanted somewhere to go and stay. Without my knowledge, Lenny furnished him with my phone number.

In any event, the escape was successful and four of the prisoners overpowered the screws, escaped from the prison bus and ran off down nearby streets. Out of the blue, he phoned me up and I went to meet him at West Ham Underground Station. To be honest, I did not really want to have a red-hot escaped prisoner hanging around me, so I took a couple of grand with me in the hope that he only wanted financial assistance. As things transpired, Steve had money and it was the safety and warmth of an anonymous abode that he really wanted. Not one to refuse a fugitive in need, particularly one whose mugshot was splashed all over the local TV news and tabloids,

I decided to let him stay with me. As things turned out, he was an excellent fellow who wanted to work with me, but I was ultra-loyal to our own team of robbers and, sadly, I had to park him up.

Steve was recaptured after being grassed up by an erstwhile girlfriend who let the police wait in her flat for him to walk into a swinging truncheon as he entered the living room. Nice gal, eh! Nevertheless, I continued to visit Steve throughout his sentence and picked him up outside Maidstone Prison on his release. A couple of years later, in 1983, Steve was involved in a fatal traffic accident while on his beloved motorbike. Apparently, it started as an innocuous traffic accident in which Steve was laughing on the ground, only for a lorry to roll over him. As fate would have it, his new bubbly girlfriend was heavily pregnant at the time of the accident. It is bizarre how many young fathers die shortly before the momentous birth of their child. Steve was a fabulous guy who had reached his full potential as a wonderful human being. He is sorely missed.

It was not long before young Tom completed the remainder of his sentence for breaking the conditions of his parole and he was home. I had been relatively active with the Piranha while young Tom had been away and young Tom wanted to get back to work. At this time, we had been working on a major bit of work in which we had to storm a secure area and seize money being loaded on to security vans. It was rather a complex robbery that required military-like planning and split-second timing, using up to six vehicles in the process.

Actually stealing the vehicles for the robberies was a cinch for me. I loved the idea of stealing cars for robberies as it invariably meant that we were going to work soon. We always approached the task of stealing vehicles with the same degree of professionalism as the robbery itself. We would wear suits, shirts and ties and travel out of the East London area to nick cars. Our favourite hunting ground was South London, as we liked the notion that the Rotherhithe and Bermondsey blaggers would get the blame for our robberies. Similarly, many years later, I learnt that the South London robbers would plunder East London for their vehicles and return the focus of the Robbery Squad upon us. I bet we gave them a few headaches.

Eventually, we stormed the compound and caught the guards

loading their security vans, before stealing in excess of £100,000. The only problem was the noise. The security company had installed these monstrous sirens and it sounded like the blitz. Consequently, we alluded to this particular bit of work as 'The Raid on Entebbe' after the way armed troops stormed a hijacked aircraft at an airport in Africa. It was a real buzz and, in the end, I don't know whether I was addicted to the thrill and excitement of a successful robbery or the money. All I know is that, after each and every successful robbery, it was another feather in my cap and I loved it.

It goes without saying but it has always been traditional or customary for decent villains to look after each other's loved ones and families while the main man is in prison. To the best of my abiliity, I have always done this and made sure that, if I had to visit someone's wife or girlfriend while their partner was away, I would either take my girlfriend or a close friend with me as a moral safeguard against malicious innuendo or accusations.

In early 1982, old Tom was visiting his friend, the respected and feared villain Nicky Gerard. Apparently, old Tom had become friends with Nicky while they were in Albany Prison together in the late 1970s. But, in my view, old Tom made one overriding mistake, as he used to drive Nicky's wife and children down to the island to visit him. Even if nothing was going on, which I believed there wasn't, it looked really bad and old Tom should have known better. Both the Piranha and I strongly disagreed with this visiting set-up, as we both knew there was always an ulterior motive behind any of old Tom's altruistic acts or gestures. It was not long before Nicky came home and old Tom and him were the best of buddies. The rest of us knew that they were up to some form of illegitimate business together and we were not party to it.

To compound the underlying malaise in the camp, some of my stolen cars were mysteriously going missing and they were being used on other robberies throughout East London. Old Tom was renowned for his laziness at stealing cars and would use the same vehicle again and again if it had not been spotted, or he would use one of my stolen cars. I used to let this go but it was annoying us, and particularly when I read about one of my stolen cars that had been used on a bit of work, when we all thought the police had probably found it and towed it away.

To aggravate matters even further, the Piranha and I had lined up three brilliant pieces of work – we thought so, anyway – and we kept urging the rest of the team to have them. But we kept getting put off, stalled or delayed with some excuse or other, while the rest of the team were obviously slipping off and robbing with someone else. This is very dangerous, as an outside robber or robbers may contaminate an otherwise sterile team. It has got clever robbers arrested in the past and it will no doubt happen again in the future. Things came to the crunch when I stole a powerful motorbike and parked it up in a safe place late one night, only to find it was gone when I returned very early the next morning. We all knew that old Tom wanted a motorbike for some reason and mine had disappeared.

So the Piranha and I went and had a lengthy heart-to-heart with old Tom and pointed out that we were disillusioned with the way things were going. We cited the lack of enthusiasm on his part, our stolen vehicles going missing and being used for other work, and the tacit knowledge that he and the other members of our team were freelancing with other firms. In true Machiavellian style, old Tom denied all the above and added that he had invested £50,000 in a long firm with Nicky Gerard.

Whatever the situation, enough was enough, we were implacable and decided to pull away from them and work on our own. It was an amicable split and it obviously suited old Tom, as he did not try to persuade us to remain in the fold. If there was one fatal flaw in old Tom's disposition, it was his greed. He was the greediest robber I have ever known, in that he wanted his finger in every pie and was always reluctant to put his hand in his pocket to pay for expenses. He was so mean. I recall one night we had to put a small fleet of stolen vehicles into position for a major bit of work and one of the stolen vehicles had been sitting there for so long the car battery was flat. Seeing as it was old Tom's particular duty to move the car, he said later at a briefing, 'We have got a problem ... the battery is flat on my stolen car ... we will have to go out and nick a car battery.' For a minute we were all taken in by this seemingly serious setback, until someone wisely said, 'Why don't you go and buy a car battery?' as it would save the danger of committing another crime and the possibility of getting caught. Reluctantly, old Tom agreed, but then he promptly asked for a £5 whipround to contribute to the purchase of the car battery. Amazingly, here was a man going out on a robbery the next day that could net tens of thousands of pounds, and he was having a £5 whipround for a car battery. For all old Tom's supreme expertise and cunning at robbing heavilyladen security vans, this made him appear ridiculous.

Over the next few months, the Piranha and I had the three special bits of work that we asked the others to take part in, and we cracked it. These particular robberies usually required three or four robbers, but we were dedicated and determined and slightly pissed off at the way that we had been treated and we really cracked it. Bang ... bang ... bang ... they were carried out and we were absolutely in the money and all the others knew it.

While all this was happening, Tracey gave birth to our second son, Bradley Javier Smith, on 18 February 1982, weighing 6lb 10oz. As a precaution, because he was prematurely born at six-and-a-half months, Bradley also had to be placed in an incubator in the special care unit at Barking Maternity Hospital. Unlike the situation caused by the serious complications that Tel-boy endured when he was born, I was allowed into the delivery suite to watch the phenomenal experience of Bradley being born. I distinctly recall watching him come into this world and take his first breath; it was brilliant.

In the summer of 1982, we bought a caravan on King's caravan site on Canvey Island, Essex, and savoured the intrinsic joys of family life. The Piranha and young Tom both bought Staffordshire terrier pups and urged me to follow suit, but the macho image of the robber and his tough-looking dog was not for me. One day, as I was driving through the picturesque expanse of Essex, I came across a sign outside a farm proclaiming 'ducklings for sale'. So I stopped and bought a little fluffy duckling and took it back to the caravan. I put the duckling in a paddling pool with boy-Tel and Brad. We called him Quackers and they loved him. Quackers the duckling quickly developed into a Muscovy duck and we had him as a family pet for many years, much longer than the Piranha and young Tom had their furniture-chewing dogs.

One Friday in July 1982, I drove to London to visit relatives and, on my way back to Canvey Island, I bumped into Ray Church at the Hermit Road traffic lights in Canning Town. He shouted to me, 'Are you coming to that Rolling Stones concert that I told you about? It's today and we are setting off in a minute!' Not one to miss the Stones in concert, I did a U-turn and we picked up Keith Dawkins, Eddie MacMarne and another bloke. We all piled into my vehicle after buying some puff – well, how could you go to a Stones concert without puff? – and drove to Wembley Stadium for a marvellous concert fronted by a super-fit Mick Jagger. At the gig, I recall seeing my uncle Tony in the crowd, but I did not say hello to him as I was stoned and I did not want to mug myself off.

After the concert, we drove back to Canning Town where I dropped them off before and motoring back to Canvey Island, as I knew Tracey and the children would be scared in the caravan alone. On reaching the caravan, none of them were there, so I went to a phone box and phoned her mother's house and Tracey's sister answered the phone. She said, 'Have you heard the news? Nicky Gerard has been shot dead outside The Eagle pub in Stratford.'

I was gobsmacked. It meant the beginning of the end. To some degree, the police will reluctantly tolerate armed robberies, providing there are no fatalities involved, but, when armed and extremely dangerous villains start blowing people's heads off, it is obvious that they are going to come down hard, extremely hard.

On a personal note, I felt for Nicky, his family and children, as, of all the dirty, rotten, no-good, police-informing slags in the East End, someone had to shoot and kill a good guy. Admittedly, it is well documented that Nicky had reputedly committed his fair share of villainy, cuttings, shootings and, some say, murders in his time, but this left a bad taste in my mouth. Inwardly, I was very relieved that we had pulled away from the others when we did, as I don't mind stealing large chunks of cash from security vans but, on a moral level, there is no value in topping people as it all, one way or another, comes back on you in the end.

Almost immediately, over 30 very experienced Murder Squad detectives were out and about in the East End pubs and clubs, pumping for information. They even had secret informers pumping for them in the boozers as well. I always recall that everyone I'd spoken to who had been pulled in or quizzed about the murder by the police had been asked, 'Who do you think is capable of committing this murder?' It was not long before the focus of their attention was being directed at our fragmented criminal group. Apparently, the murder of Nicky Gerard had all the hallmarks of professional robbers, as the assassins had jumped out of a nearby stolen van wearing masks and later drove to a change-over vehicle. Not surprisingly, old Tom, young Tom, Lenny Carter, the Piranha and I me all become suspects and we were all placed under close police surveillance.

What made things worse, evidently the murderers had chased Nicky Gerard and clubbed him with the butt of a shotgun which fell off, leaving behind the vital clue of the shotgun's serial number. The serial number of the gun was traced to the previous owner, allegedly a small-time crook in the Midlands. He apparently passed the shotgun on to Patsy Feeley's brother-in-law in Southend in Essex. The brother-in-law said that he gave the shotgun to Patsy Feeley. At the time of the murder inquiry, Patsy was serving an eight-year prison sentence in Wandsworth Prison and had received numerous police visits and was offered immediate early release on parole if he would name the person or people he gave the shotgun to but, being a very staunch man of pride and principle, he refused to assist the police.

It transpired that Patsy Feeley's brother-in-law had seen all the others and me at a Christmas party in 1981 and therefore stuck my name up as a possible or probable recipient of the shotgun. I therefore became one of five main suspects for the murder allegedly committed by two assassins. Not only was my telephone tapped, but I was also being followed everywhere by police surveillance vehicles, including a black taxi, motorbikes, several small saloon cars and even nondescript vans. I used to drive to the West End of London to visit nightclubs and note the vehicles following me. When I left the venues at between 4.00 – 6.00am, the same surveillance vehicles were very easy to spot on the ultra-quiet roads leading to the London suburbs. I had nothing to fear, however, as I knew that I was innocent. The main problem for the Piranha and me was that we could not continue our fertile careers as robbers as things were too hot.

Then, on Friday, 19 November 1982, Tracey and me were driving away from our flat in East Ham when our path was blocked by unmarked police vehicles. We were both arrested and taken back to East Ham Police Station. There I was interrogated by Detective Inspector Craig of the Walthamstow Robbery Squad. DI Craig was a very proficient and effective senior detective who had put more than his fair share of armed robbers inside British prisons. I was aware of his ruthless reputation for attaining convictions, but it became patently clear to me that he was not aware of my reputation and expertise. I say that because he quizzed me about a wide variety of armed robberies with varying degrees of seriousness, skill and expertise. These included robberies at a jewellery shop, supermarket, post office, bank and a cash-in-transit blag. Surprisingly, he obviously did not have a clue as to what type of robberies I was responsible for and it became more of a hit-or-miss exercise than one predicated upon precise police knowledge and intelligence.

I recall DI Craig alluding to me in a police interview as 'a dangerous and precarious robber'. At the time, this suited me, as he did not have a clue as to how professional and organised I had become.

On the following Sunday morning, 21 November 1982, I was taken to an interview room and quizzed by the Murder Squad detectives dealing with the Nicky Gerard case. They brought with them stacks and stacks of witness statements that they had accumulated over the months since the incident. Up until this point, I had been saying, 'On the advice of my solicitor, I wish to say nothing,' to all the police questions. This time, however, I decided to open up a little bit and tell the truth, as I could distinctly recall where I was that day. I remember telling the police, 'I will tell you once and once only. On the day of the murder of Nicky Gerard, I was at the Rolling Stones concert at Wembley with Ray Church, Keith Dawkins and Eddie MacMarne.' I was aware that they knew all this information as they had interviewed Ray Church at length about the murder, as he was himself an earlier suspect. In fact, Nicky Gerard had attacked Ray some years earlier and, although Ray refused to press charges, the police knew about the source of his grievous injuries. Therefore, by establishing the veracity of Ray's alibi for the murder, they had indirectly gained evidence of my whereabouts on that all-important day.

I remember the murder squad detectives sifting through copious witness statements and cross-referencing my account with that of those who were at the Rolling Stones concert with me. As the cozzer looked through these witness statements, he looked up numerous times and reluctantly nodded his head in agreement to his colleague next to him. They really thought that I was somehow involved in or responsible for this heinous crime.

In the light of the overwhelming alibi evidence, the Murder Squad still wanted to put me on a formal identification parade along with old Tommy Hole, who had also been arrested at this time. It was only at the very last minute that they withdrew me from the identification parade for the murder.

Then police officers from Essex Police wanted to interview me about two serious armed robberies in their area. At this time, I felt like a tin can at a fairground firing range. It was open season and I was a reluctant target in real fear of receiving a stray bullet. Perhaps DI Craig summed up the situation in a barbed aside, when he predicted, 'Don't assume that you'll be playing football at the weekend!' Alas, he was right, as I still had to face the worst situation of all – a cozzer who would bend, break and batter the rules in order to secure his holy grail, a conviction.

9

Take Him Down

After being passed about like a condemned man from squad to squad, I was finally passed over to Essex Police who wanted to interview me about serious robberies in their picturesque county. The first was a very violent robbery in Clacton, Essex, in the summer of 1982, in which Security Express security guards were delivering cash to Barclay's Bank in the town centre. Apparently, armed raiders, who included a busty blonde female accomplice, shot a security guard and a member of the public and escaped with £25,000.

The second robbery was at Corringham, Essex, in May 1982, in which two armed robbers wearing dark wigs and moustaches attacked a Brinks Mat security guard and stole £20,000 in cash while was being delivered to Lloyds Bank in the town centre. Despite different *modus operandi* being employed during both robberies by the robbers, such as handguns, disguises and stolen vehicles, Essex Police were inwardly confident that it was the work of the same team in that the robbers in both crimes had used change-over vehicles at conveniently situated railway lines.

Seeing as I was under no obligation by law to answer any questions being put to me, I chose to say to all the questions, 'On the advice of my solicitor, I wish to say nothing.' The enthusiastic Essex Police officers, however, were paying particular interest to Tracey, my long-standing girlfriend, who had blonde hair, and were accusing her of being involved in the Clacton robbery. This was absurd, of course, and, when I was told of the actual date of the robbery, I recalled that at the very time that the robbery was in progress, at 9.50am, I was appearing at Bow Street Magistrates' Court some 70 miles away in central London for a drink and driving offence.

The evening before the Clacton robbery, I drove up to the West End of London to go clubbing with a car full of revellers. During the journey, my BMW clipped a central reservation in Shaftesbury Avenue and, as a result, I got a puncture, so I parked it the wrong way in a one-way street. Stupidly, I reversed the car back out on to Shaftesbury Avenue and had to find a new parking place. As I drove back down Shaftesbury Avenue, two uniformed police asked me to stop as I was driving with a puncture, but I just floored the accelerator and jumped a red traffic light. A black taxi coming along Trafalgar Square T-boned the BMW at about 40mph. The vehicle spun around and I jumped out of the severely smashed BMW and legged it down Charing Cross Road, through some remote alleyways and on to the Embankment. The uniformed cozzers could not keep up with me and radioed for assistance and then the Old Bill appeared from everywhere.

They eventually caught me, put me in a police van and restrained me severely. I taunted them by saying, 'You can't hurt me, you wankers!' At that, one overzealous cozzer was so wound up the others had to drag him off me. I was then taken to Bow Street Police Station – the birthplace of the London Bobby in 1870 – processed and charged, before they released me at 7.30am to reappear at the nearby Magistrate's Court the same morning of the actual robbery. I appeared in court at 10am and the case was adjourned to another date. In order to save Tracey the unnecessary hassle of remaining in police custody, I related this account to Essex Police. Naturally, given the innate cynicism and negativity that is characteristic of most policemen, they refused to believe this alibi evidence.

Due to the fact that I was the focus of three separate criminal inquiries by three separate specialist police squads, I was transferred from East Ham to West Ham Police Station for identification parades. When we pulled into the courtyard at the rear of West Ham Police Station, the uniformed policemen walked me some 30 yards across the courtyard to the rear entrance of the police station. Unbeknown to me, all the witnesses to the various alleged crimes were housed in the police canteen on the top floor of the police station, which had windows that overlooked the courtyard. This was to become a very controversial and significant issue at a later trial. Did some of the witnesses, through hours of enforced boredom on a Sunday afternoon, look out of the windows and see me enter the police station?

After consulting with the solicitor, I elected to go on all the ID parades that the police required of me. In total, I had to face about 30 potential witnesses to various major robberies. I was not identified at all for any of the London robberies, but remarkably identified as being a robber at the Corringham robbery in Essex that had occurred some six months earlier. Evidently, a middle-aged woman, who'd been out shopping with her close friend at the time of the offence, identified me.

It was not until a bail application later that the police said that I had been picked out twice. It transpires that the cozzer in charge of the case, a man with a mission, had personally selected these two witnesses out of a possible ten to fifteen witnesses to the Corringham robbery and collected them from their homes in Essex on a Sunday afternoon and drove them to West Ham Police Station. In all fairness, the first woman picked me out, but, when the second woman came into the parade, she stood next to the police inspector conducting the parade and carefully looked along the line-up and said quite clearly that she was unable to recognise anybody. She then left the parade and it is alleged that, during the journey back to Essex in the police car, she broke down and cried claiming that she did recognise the robber; he was the one with the shiny buckle on his shoes.

Believe it or not, this stood up as a valid and legitimate identification at a later trial. In my opinion this makes a nonsense of the law and police codes of practice. How can a potential witness to a serious crime be allowed to participate in an identification process and, after failing the purpose of the test, later claim he or she did recognize the suspect but was too frightened to identify him?

Admittedly, however, there was other significant evidence against me to the Corringham robbery. Namely, a pair of prescription glasses that were allegedly found outside the driver's door of the change-over vehicle several miles away from the scene of the robbery where the robbers switched to a red motorbike and sped off across the countryside. Despite the glasses being of a low prescriptive strength, they were very similar to the glasses taken from me for comparison purposes at the police station.

If this evidence wasn't damaging enough, the Opel vehicle used on the robbery by the robbers was stolen from a car dealership some time before with some other car keys. These keys were later found in a lock-up Chelmsford garage in Leigh-on-Sea along with another stolen vehicle. This significant discovery of evidence by the police was because the person who rented the garage had failed to pay the council rates the on property and the perplexed owner called the police to investigate the contents of the garage when he received the bill. The police forced open the garage and found the stolen car and, realising the significance of the car keys, set up static observation on the premises.

It is alleged that I came along with another person to the garage in a Jaguar XJ6; we then discovered the police observation and, after a short car chase, we made good our escape. Subsequently, the police found the Jaguar abandoned several miles away and, lo and behold, they found my fingerprints all over it.

To summarise, the evidence against me was one definite identification of me as one of the robbers, and one disputed identification; a pair of prescription glasses that were very similar to mine; a police officer who said that he identified me as going to the lock-up garage in Leigh-on-Sea; and, lastly, my dabs all over the abandoned Jaguar car. Taken individually, a barrister should have ensured that the ID was thrown out of the trial, and he should have sought to discredit or undermine the remaining evidence. But taken all together, it constituted a very difficult and precarious case for me.

To compound matters even more, I was in the judicial catchment area of Chelmsford Crown Court, a green-belt area renowned for guilty verdicts on the flimsiest of evidence.

As a result of this evidence, and particularly the identification evidence, I was charged and remanded in custody to Brixton Prison in South London. A dirty, overcrowded Victorian monstrosity, where, once again, prisoners were confined three to a cell and expected to urinate and defecate in a single slop bucket. A week later, I was taken to Grays Police Station in Essex, where I faced several other witnesses on an ID parade for the Essex robberies. No other independent witness picked me out, save a police officer on night duty at Grays Police Station a week earlier, who claimed he recognised me as the man at the lock-up garage in Leigh-on-Sea several months earlier.

Back at Brixton Prison, I bumped into old Tommy Hole who had been picked out on ID by one independent witness to the Nicky Gerard murder. He was looking rather slack-jawed and was proclaiming his innocence at every opportunity. As a result of one of his alibi witnesses being extremely ill, his trial was brought forward. At the trial, the judge dismissed the eyewitness evidence as unsafe and he was discharged.

Shortly after our arrests, young Tommy Hole and his pal Bobby Butler were arrested after a bungled robbery in central London. It is alleged that they attacked a Security Express security van making a delivery to a bank in Farringdon Road, Holborn. It is claimed that this bit of work was particularly tricky, because the security guards were very suspicious of any pedestrians in the vicinity and would not transfer the bulky canvas sacks of cash from the security vehicle to the bank unless the pavement was completely clear of pedestrians. Evidently, young Tom came up with the novel idea of struggling along the walkway carrying a 56lb-sack of potatoes. The security guards fell for the ruse and young Tom pounced on the security guards as they conveyed the £25,000 cash bag across the pavement. After seizing the prize, young Tom sprinted to a nearby alleyway and escaped on a motorbike being driven by his accomplice Butler. They sped away, but only for a short distance, when young Tom's crash helmet, which was strapped to the side of the motorbike, collided with a concrete pillar as they squeezed through a small gap. This sent them both flying from the motorbike.

By pure coincidence, walking down the alleyway towards them were some policemen. They began to chase the robbers, who fired their pistols above the policemen's heads as a warning not to approach them. Sensibly, the police officers kept their distance. In a panic, because the motorbike refused to restart, both young Tom and Bobby hijacked an *Evening Standard* newspaper delivery van, which they also crashed after a short distance. As they abandoned the hijacked van, young Tom fell out of the vehicle more or less into the waiting arms of the Chief Inspector of a provincial police force who was in London to visit a computer exhibition being held at the nearby Barbican. Butler ran off and tried to hijack another vehicle in the busy London traffic but was overpowered and arrested. At the trial later, Butler pleaded guilty and was sentenced to nine years, while young Tom chose to fight the case and was, amazingly, acquitted, claiming that he was in the area collecting a genuine debt for his father.

To a great degree, it was imperative that young Tom was acquitted, as while on remand he had been involved in a mini-riot in the top-security Category 'A' unit at Brixton Prison. As a result, young Tom was transferred to the notorious Kafka-esque punishment block at Wandsworth Prison where the screws were eager to 'give it to' young Tom.

At that particular time in 1983, Wandsworth Prison was infamous for its brutality and cruelty towards prisoners. On one occasion, a friend of mine was being persecuted so much in the punishment block that he knew that the only way to stop the problem was to make the problem worse. He did this in order to get the Board of Visitors involved in the hope of securing a transfer to another prison. He saved up the contents of his piss bucket for days on end and chucked it over the screw who'd been picking on him. The screws used the mop that had soaked up all the human waste and pushed it into his mouth. What a way to get a transfer!

As for me, I was reluctantly transferred to Pentonville Prison in

North London as the jail came under the catchment area of Chelmsford Crown Court. Once there, I met up with John Kendall and his other co-defendants, Tony Smith and Tony Trinder. They had been arrested and charged with a string of paramilitary-burglaries in London and the Home Counties. I learnt that they were a very well-organised outfit of burglars who targeted large tobacco warehouses. They would crash through the wall using a lorry and then pull up a large box van and rapidly load up with boxes and boxes of cigarettes. As a fail safe, they would have spotters strategically placed several miles away to tell them when the police were coming once the alarm on the premises had been set off. It was not long, however, before the South-East Regional Crime Squad based at Barkingside were on to them and they were all arrested after lengthy police surveillance and intelligence reports.

Later, on 16 June 1983, Kendall and his team, which included a guy called Danny Shankshaft, were handed out long custodial sentences with Kendall copping a sentence of ten years' imprisonment. Throughout this sentence, other prisoners would frequently hear Kendall crow, 'Ten years for what? I am only a burglar!' While at Pentonville Prison, Kendall and I became close friends, particularly as we were invariably lodged down the punishment block together for minor infringements against infantile prison rules and regulations. In order to keep Prisoners in isolation for longer, excessive periods, the prison Governor would activate a widely abused prison regulation – Rule 43(a) – for the 'good order and discipline' of the jail. In short, it was a bit like being remanded in custody in the punishment block without a fair trial or explanation. It was like being held captive in a prison within a prison.

The Prison Governor, with the Board of Visitor's monthly consent, could keep you in these dehumanised and demoralising conditions indefinitely. It was the epitome of a totalitarian State, in which the Prison Governor could, in theory, behave like an unrestrained Third World dictator. Who would guess that, in a tiny speck of cosmopolitan London, there could be a Stalinesque regime of isolation and sensory deprivation ... and it still exists today in prisons all over the country.

The only highlight for me at this time – the Easter Bank Holiday weekend of 1983 – was that the Security Express depot in nearby Curtain Road, Shoreditch, was being robbed of over £7m in cash. Not only had I a cast-iron alibi for this supreme bit of work, but also the vivid media account of it in the tabloids and broadsheets gave me countless hours of pleasurable reading.

Potentially more significant for me, however, in early June 1983, was that I had to appear at Chelmsford Crown Court to face the trial for the Corringham robbery. It was to be staged at the Number One Court in front of His Honourable Justice Greenwood. In my corner, I had the very eloquent and charismatic Ron Thwaites, who appeared on the brink of taking silk and lacked the all-important élan of old, as I'd seen when he'd represented my co-defendant in 1979 for the aggravated burglary case. The prosecutor was a seemingly efficient and effective barrister, who'd obviously seen better days. It must be said he did not appear to be anything special, particularly when compared with the sterling oratorical prowess of Mr Thwaites. I distinctly recall the prosecutor, in his opening speech, harping on about the significant circumstantial evidence in the case, urging the jury not to allow such evidence to 'degenerate' or deteriorate in its overall value or worth.

Alas, as soon as the jury were sworn in, I could tell that I was a gonna. The men on the jury were all wearing blue or green shirts and ties as if to signify a pro-police resonance. From the outset, then, this was undoubtedly a 'lions versus Christians' foregone conclusion.

As Caesar sat high up on the bench and cast his stare upon the proceedings in this modern-day Colosseum, it was only a matter of time before he tilted his all-important thumb towards Hades. Things were really that bad. I was really up against it. As a taster of things to come, during the very first day of evidence, three Brinks Mat security guards gave their testimony and, despite all of them picking out the same person on the identification parade, a bloke who was not me, I felt that, if the jury could have retired there and then to consider their verdicts, they would have found me guilty.

The next witnesses to take the stand were the all-important two women bystanders who said that they saw two armed men run across a car park and get inside a vehicle and drive out of the car park. There was some evidence to suggest that the robbers may have been wearing wigs and, in any event, the conditions of the identification were momentary. In order to compensate for the tenuous nature of the identification, one woman witness claimed that, as the robbers' get-away vehicle drove out of the car park, it suddenly stopped and the driver said to the passenger, 'Look, those women have seen us ...' or something to that effect, and then the robbers carried on and drove away.

I recall that there were some persuasive arguments as to the admissibility of evidence regarding the female witness who did not pick me out on the ID parade but, like an elephant stamping on an ant, the judge overruled the defence argument and allowed the jury to hear it as *bona fide* evidence.

Then we argued, quite compellingly, that the witnesses could have seen me come through the police courtyard on the day of the ID parade. As we put this to the first woman witness, she was not ready for this line of questioning, but when the second witness took the stand she was well primed and said that she could not get to the windows that overlooked the courtyard as someone had arranged a line of chairs there to stop anyone from looking out of the windows. Whatever the case, the determined judge was having none of it. It was like trying to shoot down a B52 bomber with a flintlock.

What is more amazing, while I was in the dock listening to the melodramatic performance of the women witnesses, two young men in their early twenties, of similar age to me, sidled into the court room to kill some time. Apparently, they had submitted some stock at the local Chelmsford auction rooms and were killing some time before they went to the auction to collect their takings. After they'd heard the evidence of one of the women witnesses, as she walked out of the courtroom after her evidence, one of the young men whispered, 'You fucking grass!' The police immediately arrested them and charged them with contempt of court. The judge then remanded them both in custody to Brixton Prison until the end of my trial.

To exacerbate matters, they also came from the Rainham area of

Essex, which was close to Dagenham, where my parents lived. This was also the address that I gave to the police when I was originally arrested. No doubt, because these two people were of a similar age to me and also came from the same area, the police and judge mistook them as close friends of mine, which was not the case. Alas, at the conclusion of the trial, the judge sentenced them both to six months' imprisonment. The sad fact is that I did not know either of them, the poor sods.

The prosecution produced the evidence regarding the prescription glasses allegedly found outside the driver's door of the get-away vehicle and claimed that the prescription of the lenses was very similar, but not identical to those taken from me. The prosecution could not prove that these were my glasses but it was compelling circumstantial evidence nonetheless.

Like a consummate idiot, I chose not to give evidence and relied upon my alibi evidence and witnesses to get me home. This was a fatal mistake, as all juries want to hear what the defendant has to say and I should have gone into the witness box. A close friend of mine, whom I was later to meet in a dispersal prison, boasted to me that he had endured the psychological anguish and anxiety of seven trials for various offences. During six of them he had given evidence and was duly acquitted. During the seventh trial, he refused to go into the witness box and was found guilty. He spent many years in British prisons fighting for an appeal against his 12-year sentence. Once the appeal was granted, the Court of Appeal ordered a retrial. At the retrial, he gave evidence from the stand and the jury acquitted him after two hours' deliberation. Admittedly, all juries and trials are unique, and it is wrong to generalise over these issues, but if I could turn the clock back and give some explanation to the jury about how I ended up being accused of this offence, I am sure the outcome would have been different.

Once the prosecutor, defence counsel and the judge concluded their closing speeches, the jury retired. The jury came back into court and asked a pertinent question about the identification evidence, but any rebellion in the jury room in my favour was short-lived and I was found guilty. The recommended sentence for a robbery of this magnitude and seriousness was 12 to 14 years, but the judge pronounced solemnly, 'Stand up. Terence George Michael Smith, you have been convicted by a jury of robbery. This was carefully planned. Arms, firearms of some sort or another, were used. This was a bank robbery involving a vast sum of money – £20,000 was taken. You have played for high stakes, now comes the punishment. You will go to prison for 15 years. Take him down please.'

On hearing this, the jury recoiled and gasped in shock at the severity of the sentence. They must have thought that I was only going to receive five to seven years. To this, I blurted out, rather poignantly, 'I hope it rests on your conscience all your life!' And I sincerely hope that it does, sending a young, bold, daring and debonair armed robber away for at least a decade was an out-and-out liberty!

My poor girlfriend Tracey was devastated. She broke down sobbing as she witnessed the love of her life being dragged away down to the cells. As for me, I was electric and all hyped up. The adrenalin was gushing through all the gateways and gulleys of my tensed body, leaving me feeling like I was preparing for some major calamity ... and indeed it was. It was then, at that moment, that I made a self-fulfilling resolution that I was not going to serve a decade of soul-sapping servitude in British prisons which were notorious for draining the spirit and life-blood out of young career criminals like myself. For the very first time in my life, I had someone out there who loved and wanted me and the State, with all its omnipotent authorities, wanted to grind me into the ground, overwhelm and oppress me and incarcerate me yet again. I was going to escape! I knew that I would only have the one chance and, when it came, I would seize it voraciously with both hands. I was going home ... I wanted to be with my beautiful family Tracey – Tel-boy and Bradley. They wanted me, they loved me and I worshipped them. Never, but never, underestimate the power of love. For, if you are fortunate to have it in your life, you are capable of anything.

I knew that I was clever enough to escape but, at that time, I was devoid of a viable plan. The main thing was that I already possessed all the core ingredients and characteristics of a successful escapee – determination, dedication, organisational skills, the ability to keep *schtum* and the overarching love of a good woman and family. Some people believe that your biggest enemy is your own mind, as it limits and restricts your achievements by planting seeds of doubt and uncertainty. On the contrary, the seeds of escape were already germinating within my mind.

Over the next 18 months, with diligent and careful cultivation, the escape plan would blossom into a viable and achievable proposition. No way was I going to serve the outrageous sentence of 15 years' imprisonment while in the prime of my life. To succumb, surrender and submit to this sentence would be synonymous with saying that I am a grade 'A' wanker and that I don't love and cherish my family, otherwise I would use all the physical and intellectual tools that I have to help me mastermind a successful escape.

It would have been very easy for me to have sat back and rolled the umpteenth joint of giggle weed and let my long-standing girlfriend and family trundle all over the country, visiting distant and doleful jails, providing me with goodies while I puffed and puffed away my existence in a cloud of inertia. No way, the only word in my vocabulary with real substance was 'ESCAPE'!

Bollocks to jumping through sycophantic hoops of good behaviour and attendant humiliation; bollocks to the elusive carrot of early release on parole; bollocks to the Court of Appeal, which had clearly stated that it was not a court of clemency or mercy. I was going home thanks to one of mankind's most primal instincts – a biological, physiological and psychological desire to escape from my captors.

10

Fight or Flight?

Down in the cells at Chelmsford Crown Court, I had the customary post-sentence visit through a glass partition. In spite of the grave disappointment of being convicted and sentenced to such a swingeing term of imprisonment, I was in control of events. As all my direct family looked on, I basically said, 'Don't worry about me, I can serve this sentence, just don't leave me in prison to rot and waste away.'

Saddened by the tragic outcome, every one of them swore allegiance to the cause and said that they would continue to support and visit me throughout the long incarceration. I suppose that this heartfelt appeal was the product of lingering doubt and insecurity on my part, as a 15-year sentence is no short, sharp sprint but a long and monotonous marathon that requires the stamina and endurance of a truly devoted and loyal family. Only the prevailing wind of time would tell whether they would be standing there at the end, or be blown away by the grinding attrition of absence and despair.

As I was transferred from the court to the formidable confines of Wormwood Scrubs Prison, a million thoughts and feelings went through my mind. The most significant of all was the new route the prison coach was taking back to London. Was this a standard precaution or were the screws already aware of a possible escape attempt or plan? Either way, as I wistfully looked out of the prison bus window on a sultry summer's evening and witnessed hundreds of people going about their normal lives, it gave added emphasis to the totality of the tragedy. It was as though a massive wedge had been driven between my loving family and myself. It was a truly painful experience, but I had to discard all feelings of sadness and self-pity and become just as hard-hearted and ruthless as the judiciary and penal system. In spite of being a sentient being, capable of human warmth and emotion, the authorities regarded me as a dangerous bank robber who had to serve a very long sentence with a three-fold purpose to punish the offender, to deter others from committing similar crimes and to protect society from serious career criminals like me.

On a personal level, however, the sentence had other repercussions, as I would not only be prevented from adding to my family, but its unstated aim was to severely debilitate or crush my spirit before eventual re-entry into society. On an entirely different level, though, I viewed the sentence as a major challenge in the rich tapestry of life, a challenge like a genetically acquired physical handicap that could only be overcome by the exercise of sheer determination and will-power to escape.

At the Scrubs, I was allocated to 'C' Wing, a long-term wing for miscellaneous miscreants and mutineers who had recently arrived from Albany Prison on the Isle of Wight due to a well-publicised riot that had occurred in May 1983. Unlike the unconvicted regime of Pentonville Prison, where I was invariably placed in the prison block, the Scrubs was a vibrant and exciting human aviary with the buzz of promise and expectancy.

Almost immediately, I met up with two close pals, Kevin Brown and Perry Terroni, who had both recently been sentenced to seven years' imprisonment for conspiracy to rob. Kevin broke me off a sizeable chunk of cannabis and gave it to me and this left me in a much-needed herbal stupor for a week or two. Then I was introduced to an endearing character called Johnny Massey, who wisely gave me a crash-course in the ways to approach, manage and conquer a long prison sentence. At this time, John himself was a cogent authority on long-term imprisonment as he was already a decade or more into a life sentence with a recommendation to serve a minimum of 20 years for murder. It is alleged that John was in the company of a friend who lost an eye in a fight with a bouncer in the mid-1970s. John is reputed to have gone back to the scene of the fight on the same night and shot and fatally wounded the culprit.

As I got to know John, I could see there wasn't a day of his sentence that passed without him regretting this crime. Although John was not one to publicise his problems, I could tell that he was genuinely remorseful and deserved another chance one day back in society. Also with John was another very charismatic character called Tommy Green, who was serving 15 years for robbery and who loved to wind up the screws.

In many respects, the presence of the Albany mutineers was a godsend to me at this difficult time. Not only did they boost my spirits, but also one prisoner in particular had recently attempted to escape from Maidstone Prison in Kent and, without wishing to broadcast the reason of my interest, I wanted to know everything about it. Evidently, the escapee had managed to get out of the prison by climbing an ingenious escape rope to scale the prison wall using a pendulum to counterbalance his body weight. He scaled the prison wall and was running away from it when the prison alarm was raised. This alerted all the squaddies in the nearby Army barracks who captured him a short while afterwards. If only he had had some outside help, he would have got clean away.

As all this information was being stored in my memory, I asked the fellow to expand on how the pendulum – escape rope – principle worked. Apparently, he said, if you attach a PP9 battery to the end of a broomstick and the other end of the broomstick to a rope strong enough to carry your weight, then throw or place the broomstick on the other side of the prison wall, this would act as a type of hook on the wall which would allow the escapee to pull himself up to the top of the prison wall. Then the escapee would have to reverse the process to lower himself down the other side. This is ideal for medium- or low-security prisons, such as Maidstone or Camphill, but the pendulum principle would not work at high-security jails which all have the geoscopic dome on the external wall. Nonetheless, it was a start for me as it was my ambition eventually to get allocated to a jail like Maidstone and attempt to escape. Already, thanks to the upheaval of the Albany Prison riot, a plan had evolved due to this unfortunate escapee. Was the convergence of our paths due to luck or fate? Who knows, but meeting this chap was a veritable oasis in a desert and I was desperate to drink at the font of knowledge in the art of escaping.

While at the Scrubs, my friend John Kendall arrived with his co-defendants who had been sentenced for their part in the paramilitary-style burglaries. It was good to have John around as he possessed a very upbeat sense of humour, although invariably it was at someone else's expense, which often got him involved in violent rows and confrontations. At this time, however, the brunt of his infectious humour was directed at himself as he had made a determined effort to stay away from committing armed robberies in order to avoid the pitfalls of a long prison sentence, but now John was serving ten years for burglary and everybody knew it.

As the reluctant recipient of a long sentence myself, I felt that it was only right that I faced up to the problem of the long-standing loving relationship Tracey and I shared. I perceived it as wholly unfair and unreasonable to expect Tracey to wait for me and therefore I wrote to her and asked her to 'drop me out' and find someone else. Tracey was a very attractive young lady and I did not want her to miss out on the youthful joys of life because of our enforced separation. As a consequence of the prison sentence, Tracey suffered a breakdown due to an attack of Crohn's Disease and was hospitalised. Deep down, I knew that I could not put this beautiful and fragile butterfly through more unbearable heartache and pain. We arranged a visit at the Scrubs and we discussed the situation at length and, in an amazing demonstration of love, devotion and undying loyalty, Tracey declared that she did not want us to separate but, instead, wanted to wait for me because she loved me. Not for one moment did I doubt her unyielding love for me, nor my love for her, but it was the ominous prospect of years and years of separation that concerned me. For example, would our love be strong and resilient enough to withstand the endless attrition of time and change?

We came to a mutual agreement that we would remain together as one and work hard at maintaining and sustaining our relationship. If, after two years, however, we were still with each other and still in love with each other, we would reinforce and consolidate our togetherness with marriage in prison. This, in turn, would provide Tracey with the strong sense of security and assurance that is often lacking in long-term prisoner–girlfriend relationships. It was not the perfect answer to the problem of separation but, somehow, we had devised and constructed this relationship-saving mechanism in order to cope with the catastrophe of enforced division and detachment. It was a testament to our love for each other that we were able to confront and overcome this mountainous problem. Tracey was more than a beautiful girlfriend who had given birth to our children; she had evolved into a remarkable woman of substance, principle and fidelity. A very rare gem indeed!

After several weeks at Wormwood Scrubs, the screws became uneasy at the strong sense of camaraderie amongst the prisoners on 'C' Wing and decided to transfer some of us to various jails around the country. As a result of this mini-exodus, Kevin Brown, Perry Terroni, John Kendall and me were called to the allocation office and informed that we were to be shipped out to Parkhurst Prison on the Isle of Wight. Under normal allocation circumstances, we were a dead cert to go to Albany Prison but, due to the riot and the lack of space at the jail, an alternative was found. In short, Parkhurst was a notorious jail known as the end of the line for long-term prisoners, where the screws were older and wiser and were more willing to adopt and embrace a relaxed regime, one that allowed long-standing subversive prisoners to body-swerve the petty rules and regulations of the more militaristic regimes in the prison system. In fact, Parkhurst Prison was a dumping ground, a penal dustbin of the dispersal system where a mixture of old lags and rebellious agitators were left to get on with their time in relative peace and quiet.

One of the drawbacks of being a Parkhurst prisoner, however, was that the concept of parole or early release was non-existent. Hardly anyone ever received parole at the jail. But it did not bother me, as I was going to initiate and develop my very own parole in the form of unauthorised and unstoppable leave.

On the day that we were to be transferred, the four of us, all renowned for varying degrees of audacity and gameness, decided to have a pop and try and overpower the screws escorting us and escape off the prison bus while we were in transit between the jails. To be perfectly honest, I only wanted to attempt this if there was a very good chance of the escape being successful, as I did not want to squander the one and only chance I would get on a half-hearted or half-baked attempt with no back-up. As the old adage proclaims, 'If you fail to plan, you plan to fail!'

We all knew that a short while before our imminent transfer, a determined group of prisoners had overpowered the screws on the same route and managed to escape. Again, due to the lack of preparation or back-up, some were captured not far from the escape and only one or two made it home. Any potential notion of escape was shattered, however, when we entered the prison bus, as we were all shackled American-style to the floor of the vehicle by handcuffs and chains. More depressingly, as we linked up with the A3 trunk road at Putney, we noticed that we had a police escort all the way to the Isle of Wight. It transpired that the earlier, semi-successful escape from the prison bus had led to a revision of security of prisoners being transferred to the island and our only destination that day was Parkhurst Prison.

According to British penal history, in 1834 an All-Party Select Committee was appointed to find an alternative to the rotting prison ships or hulks which contained prisoners that were sentenced to transportation to the Australian colonies. These included children as young as six years old. Initially, Albany Barracks was the recommended site for the new prison, but this was rejected in favour of the old military hospital at Parkhurst. As a result, Queen Victoria signed a Bill to build the prison in 1838. Evidence of the Black Hole dungeons, where the children were incarcerated under 'C' Wing, are still in existence today. In 1950, Parkhurst became a Preventive Detention Centre where repeat offenders had their sentences extended as a deterrent to others. In 1963, the focus on security changed and a Special Security Block (SSB) was built to contain some of the most infamous prisoners of the Sixties, such as the Great Train Robbers and the Kray twins. More recently, in October 1969 and again in 1979, Parkhurst endured two well-publicised riots which nearly destroyed some of the wings. As a consequence of this colourful history, Parkhurst acquired a reputation as a powder-keg jail where anything could happen and often did.

It is not surprising, then, as we drove through the ominous prison gates of the jail in the hot summer of 1983, that I was possessed by an underlying feeling of awe, dread and excitement. Parkhurst Prison was like a living legend, with its huge rectangular Victorian wings steeped in human misery and torment; I wondered what it had in store for me. Initially, we were all allocated to 'B' Wing, which was reminiscent of the aviary atmosphere of Wormwood Scrubs, a long, echoey wing with five landings of cubbyholes where people were reduced to prison numbers and forced to endure a dehumanised existence.

After a week of induction courses, by choice we all moved over to 'C' Wing, which was basically a continuation of 'B' Wing. Despite 'C' Wing being smaller than 'B' Wing, with a prison roll of about 120 prisoners, it contained a good group of guys from all over the London area. Among those who were there at that time were John Laveve, John Massey, John Dunlop, John Wickes, Dave Bailey, Peter Flynn, Clive Cumberbatch, Pat Dobson and Pat and Joe Lee. Among the more mature prisoners were Reggie Kray, Bob Maynard, Freddie Sewell, Jimmy Simpson, Joe Beveridge and some staunch IRA prisoners such as little Ronnie McCarthy and Billy Armstrong, who bombed the Old Bailey in the 1980s. In spite of all these very distinct and diverse characters, we all got on together with very little trouble or animosity. If there was any inter-prisoner violence or discontent, it was usually the result of a unique mental state called 'the Parkhurst Ps', which described a general state of prison paranoia in which prisoners embraced an intense fear or suspicion of persecution. This normally entailed the misconceived fear or notion that someone was plotting to harm you.

This veiled unease or insecurity was compounded by the nearby location of the prison hospital, or 'Wendy House' as it was called, which acted as a halfway house between the prison system and those deemed criminally and who were sent to secure mental hospitals, such as Broadmoor, Rampton or Ashworth. The senior psychiatric consultant at the hospital-cum-mental mansion was the infamous Dr Cooper who invariably strived to reintegrate some mental patients on to 'normal' wings within the prison. This would, to a significant extent, justify and reinforce the 'Parkhurst Ps' as no one wanted to die in prison, particularly at the hands of a mentally deranged or demented psychopath who would, unbeknown to you, view you as the enemy and possibly slip up to you and stab you for no apparent reason.

This may sound far-fetched, but these things did happen, as in the case of our good friend Rocky Harty who was fatally injured in the prison kitchen by an oddball who'd taken offence at something he'd said. There were many occasions where one of Cooper's Troopers were behaving oddly and the prisoners would refuse to go behind their cell doors until the unstable crackpot had been removed from the wing. At first glance, this may appear a radical and unfair response, but many of us had families and we all wanted, one day, to be reunited with them no matter how long we were serving.

More or less as soon as I arrived in Parkhurst in July 1983, Leon Brittan, the Home Secretary, scrapped early release on parole for all serious offenders. Although this did not affect me as I was not eligible for parole at that time, it did impinge upon many long-termers at Parkhurst who were due to be considered for early release. I recall the Prison Governor at Parkhurst who was in favour of the parole system allowing a TV news crew into the jail to assess and evaluate the response of the prisoners. Anyone with a modicum of common sense could see that it was a cheap scam by the reviled Conservative Party to portray themselves as the pre-eminent anti-crime political party. All the prisoners knew that we were political pawns in a much wider game. I recall being interviewed by the TV crew, pointing out that I had just been sentenced a month earlier to 15 years' imprisonment by a judge who obviously had parole in mind and now it had been scrapped. I concluded the interview with the pithy soundbite: 'No Parole, No Control!' Whatever the case, parole did not feature in my plans; the only early release I was planning was to go over the wall at the earliest opportunity.

Although I had only been at Parkhurst for a short while, with careful guidance and tuition from my friend John Massey I rapidly realised that the successful cornerstone to serving a long prison sentence revolved around three basic principles: maintain strong ties with your family; use the gymnasium and education departments regularly; and enjoy the occasional cell party in order to relieve any built-up stress, tension and aggression.

Sport was extremely popular at Parkhurst, with its plentiful sports facilities on the exercise compound, such as football, badminton, tennis and basketball in the large plastic dome gymnasium or pounding the miles around the figure-of-eight running track. There was also a small weights gymnasium in the main body of the jail that was always in use and a spacious punchbag room at the back of 'C' Wing where we used to enjoy stress-relieving boxing circuits with Reggie Kray, John Massey, Kevin Brown and others. In many respects, competitive sport and intense physical training was the mainstay of good health and sanity. Ironically, we all trained like lunatics to keep the possible threat of lunacy at bay and, as a product of this, we all developed into competent sportsmen and athletes.

For many prisoners, the highlight of the week was the 'big match' on Sunday mornings on Parkhurst's infamous sloping football pitch, where, at its low point, the touchline was a mere 12in away from a 2ft drop to the walkway. I have seen many a flighty winger run pell-mell along the touchline and get barged off the pitch, only to rapidly negotiate the perilous 2ft drop. Naturally, there were injuries, such as severe cuts and grazes and the infrequent broken bone, but to complain about this ever-present pitfall would be a sign of weakness and everybody used to consider it worth the risk to enjoy a decent game of football.

I used to organise 'theme' matches, such as South London versus

East London, or Terry's Tigers versus (Paul) Edmonds's Heroes. These matches were invariably played in good spirit, although the competition was always intense. No one liked to lose face in a tackle when half the jail was watching from the sidelines. We even had our own referee, an elderly Parkhurst lag called Holbie O'Brien, who oversaw the game in full referee regalia and who would not hesitate to dip into his top pocket and pull out a yellow or red card no matter who the player was. It was hilarious stuff, as a yellow card had no punitive value at all, save the melodramatic act of a stern-faced Holbie reprimanding the offender in front of a hysterical and vociferous crowd. God forbid if the red card was issued as, if the player ordered off refused to leave the pitch, Holbie would pick up the football and simply refuse to let the match continue until he had his way. The referee's make-believe behaviour became almost surreal when, in a supreme display of brinkmanship, he would lecture and chastise hardened villains as if they were back at school in front of the headmaster. Even with passions running high, the doughty referee always managed to get his own way, which resulted in hysterical laughter and strident comments from the spectators on the sidelines. Holbie O'Brien was a character and a half, and appeared to be an intrinsic part of the Parkhurst fabric and fittings.

Once a year, generally in August, the prison held its half-marathon and 'Superman Competition'. For some prisoners, including me, this was a time to compare and contrast all the training we had done against each other. Many prisoners refused to enter these prison competitions for a wide range of reasons, but I enjoyed them, as there was no point in pushing your body to extreme levels of peak fitness if you could not compete against others. The Superman Competition was a two-day event, covering about ten disciplines, including the 100 and 1,500 metres, shot-putt, discus, press-ups, squat thrusts, long and high jump and how many basketball baskets one could complete in one minute. In the true spirit of the competition, I recall that I was leading the field right up to the last two disciplines, when a supreme athlete nicknamed 'Bobby's Ball' came through to pip me at the post.

The half-marathon was a different story as the prison invited in outside competitors from a local running club. I fancied myself to win this, as there was no one in the jail who could beat my times, except an IRA prisoner called Tony Clarke. We called him the 'Red Flash' due to his distinctive trainers. Boy, could this fellow run! Generally, IRA prisoners refuse to participate in sporting events organised by the prison authorities, as this could be perceived as their tacit acceptance as common criminals over and above their perceived status as political prisoners. I recall speaking to Tony about this matter on the morning of the half-marathon and I could see that he really wanted to run in the race but the dilemma of his position was bugging him. I like to think that I helped Tony overcome this dilemma when I said that he was a born runner, he loved running and that he should ignore the politics for this one day and get out there and win the race for us. As a result, Tony won the race, completing the distance in slightly over an hour, and I came a proud second in 1 hour and 27 minutes. For me, it was a substantial achievement, which only leaves me in awe of those who complete the full marathon of 26 miles, 376 yards.

It would be facile of me to claim that drugs did not exist in prison and I would lay myself open to ridicule if I tried to deny their existence. Of course, drugs exist and are taken in large amounts in jails up and down the country. In Parkhurst, however, the majority of the long-term prisoners enjoyed the relaxing and soothing effects of cannabis. Some would puff first thing in the morning, some last thing at night and some not at all. Like most long-termers, I became embroiled in the culture of drug-taking. To some degree, those prisoners who sought their daily dose of legalised medication, such as Largactyl, were perceived as hobbits, as it was seen as a weakness of character to become dependent upon such powerful, zombifying drugs and everyone knew it. On the other hand, smoking cannabis was seen as socially and culturally acceptable, as it helped to dissolve or overcome tension and frustration and could transform the most aggressive of agitators into seemingly model prisoners. The screws knew that we all puffed and they would not go out of their way to confiscate it, providing that it was not rubbed in their faces.

Purely on a personal level, to maintain an element of discipline and direction, I used to puff for six months and then have six months off. I did this for several reasons. First, I found that the long-term daily use of cannabis was affecting my short-term memory. It also made me paranoid and, after a while, for some strange, inexplicable reason, I could not talk to someone face to face when I spoke to them as it felt terribly uncomfortable. Oddly, I had to focus on another object when I spoke to others. This disturbed me and, although I did not openly discuss this with anybody else, I did recognise the same behavioural traits in many other prisoners. Second, and most significant, there came a time when I was looking forward to a visit to secure the puff more than enjoying the company of my visitors, who had travelled over 100 miles to see me. It was then that I knew that something was wrong. How could I put the puff before close friends and family? It was then that I stopped puffing altogether. It was not right for cannabis to replace my loving family as the focus of my attention.

Of course, there are long-term cannabis users who do not experience these unfortunate side-effects and who would put them down to a biochemical or psychological weakness on my part. I am not specifically pointing to the harmful effects of cannabis-smoking as a propaganda exercise. I am merely saying that, when taken in moderation, I found smoking cannabis a wonderful and thought-provoking experience, but puffing day in, day out, did not suit my personality.

I was also introduced to acid the hallucinogen, at Parkhurst, and the phenomenal experience remains one of the most remarkable days of my life, save that of the birth of my children. As part of a pre-planned exercise, 16 of us decided to avoid or cancel our visits on a specific Sunday in the height of summertime. As we were unlocked on the morning in question, we all went for our breakfast, but that day's sustenance was not the pallid porridge, but a 'Superman' trip of acid. As the drug began to take hold, by dinnertime we all were experiencing potent waves or rushes of the drug and we were 'right out of our nuts' making humorous remarks about each other and giggling like mischievous children. I distinctly recall that I could focus on someone's facial features and I could tell if they were happy or sad, healthy or poorly, wracked with worry or carefree in spirit. Over the dinnertime bang-up in our single cells, we all blasted our music and enjoyed the most amazing experiences and hallucinations. I looked in a small prison-issue mirror and saw myself as a Roman gladiator, complete with strong facial features and attendant carefully honed muscles. When the cell door finally opened after what appeared like aeons, we all piled out on to the exercise compound to play the maddest game of five-a-side football in my life. There were nine of us playing who were flying, and one player from another wing who'd not taken anything. I'll never forget it. I was a real blood-and-guts gladiator and I ran around and around so much when the game was finished the soles of my trainers were flapping on the tarmac pitch. The straight player who did not know that we were all tripping could not make out the sheer madness of the game. We were all running about like it was the World Cup and as if our release dates depended on the outcome. I recall having a bone-crunching tackle with Perry Terroni, who crashed to the floor in severe pain and lay there motionless like he was dead. I ran over to him thinking that he was mortally wounded and saw that his face was covered in a mixture of sweat and grime from the tarmac and, in all earnestness, I asked, 'Are you all right, Pel, are you all right?' to which he replied, 'Did you get the number of that bus?'

The gladiatorial football match came to a halt, however, when the naturally gifted Dave Bailey took a simple free kick and booted the ball what seemed like miles and miles into the firmament and beyond the prison wall. We all walked up to Dave in amazement and said, 'Dave, what have you done, why have you booted our ball over the prison wall?' He replied, 'I don't know why ... I just felt like doing it!' End of the game, but not end of the fun.

Then someone came up with the idea of swinging across the crossbar on the goalpost from end to end like a monkey. All ten of us decided to do it for a laugh. We all lined up at one end of the goalpost and swung across the goal like monkeys to the amazement and disbelief of the screw in a nearby sentry box who was scribbling down frantically the names of those taking part in this extremely odd behaviour.

I know that it sounds incredibly irresponsible for a 25-year-old father to be taking powerful mind-altering drugs, but you must remember we all had very little to look forward to save years and years of bang-up behind the cell door and this, especially for me, helped me to clear the cluttered-up office desk of my mind. The very next day, it felt like I was starting my prison sentence afresh.

The 'Superman' tripping experience had been such a success that we planned another one about a month later. This time, by coincidence, a local theatre group came into the prison to stage a dramatic production about a cricket pavilion caper or something, so we duly took the acid and sat back to enjoy the show. I remember sitting through the production absolutely spellbound by the authenticity of the actors. The only downer for us was that one of our exclusive group had been unexpectedly called out for a visit. This was a real nightmare and, to compound matters, this well-respected individual was religiously protesting his innocence – in fact, as I write, the Criminal Cases Review Committee have just referred his case back to the Court of Appeal for reconsideration – and Dowager So-and-So had come to Parkhurst to discuss his case. When he returned from the visit, we all asked him how it went. He replied, 'I couldn't lie to them, so I told them the truth that I was tripping!'

While all this mind-expanding experimentation was going on, I was still determined to escape and I noticed that every year at Parkhurst they sent five or six prisoners to Maidstone Prison to take part in a six-topic O-level education course which lasted for one academic year. Without telling anyone, and I emphasise *anyone*, I enrolled on several education classes in order to learn basic maths and English at the jail. Initially, I said that this was to assist in my letter-writing, but I was also willing to take a couple of elementary exams to prove to the teachers that I was indeed a genuine and diligent pupil. To be perfectly frank, although I was conning the education department, I did, in fact, like the teachers and enjoyed the idea and practice of acquiring a belated academic education. I would not say that I am overly superstitious but, as I get older, I believe certain coincidences occur because of something more than pure chance. For example, the prison service in the early 1980s produced an artistic bookmark that showed a pile of books stacked up against a prison wall with the caption 'Escape with Books' upon it. This was, indeed, what I intended to do, escape metaphorically by reading and studying the books, and also literally by securing a transfer to Maidstone Prison to break out.

While I was at Parkhurst, Tracey and our two young sons used to travel to the Isle of Wight for visits as often as they could. Due to the long journey from London and the added aggravation of coming to the island by ferry, the prison had an exceptionally liberal policy of issuing Visiting Orders. For example, visitors could come to the island and stay at special prison accommodation for anything between two and seven days at a time. So it meant young families such as ours were able to savour and enjoy some real quality time together. Invariably, the wives of prisoners would meet with other wives who were faced with the same hardship of visiting prisons up and down the country and forge long-standing friendships. They used to travel and stay together at the prison accommodation for security, support and companionship.

It was during one of these extended visits that Tracey intimated that our family would be complete if we could have a baby daughter to complement our two lovely sons. Naturally, I agreed, but there was no way that we could manage such a delicate act on a visit. By now, obviously, Tracey was aware that I did not intend to serve my sentence and that I was going to escape. In fact, when we used to write letters to each other, at the bottom of the page I used to draw a matchstick man, woman, two small boys and a pram with a question mark over it. The way I saw things, anything was possible! If David could slay Goliath and Moses could part the Red Sea, then I knew that I could bust out of prison.

The visits were not always pleasant experiences, like the time Tracey and the boys came to visit me and the local police were waiting at the prison gatehouse to strip-search Tracey and another prisoner's wife and children. The police and prison authorities were acting on a tip-off that our visitors were bringing drugs into the prison. Nothing was found as a result of this drastic and over-the-top action, and we formally protested to the Prison Governor. It is hard enough to get family and loved ones to visit you throughout a long prison sentence, let alone having the added humiliation and degradation of a strip-search on reaching the prison gate. We put the so-called tip-off down to an informant somewhere in the jail who'd most probably put a note in the mailbox, no doubt obviously bitter and jealous at us having lots of loving visits with our families.

Prison is a strange place indeed. It is a place, in my view, where as little as 5 per cent of the inhabitants are 'good gravy guys', and the rest are invariably nasty people who become embittered if they see you wearing a new T-shirt or a new pair of trainers. I realise that this is a bold and, some would say, cynical or controversial statement to make but, sadly, it is a fact. Not perhaps surprisingly, the close proximity of hundreds of prisoners living together becomes a fertile breeding ground for jealousy and rivalry. For example, many successful career criminals are, by their very nature, the living embodiment of extroversion. These colourful crooks love to brag and flaunt their natural style, flair and wealth. Unbeknown to them, however, silently and stealthily they are making enemies who would go to extraordinary lengths to bring pain and grief to them and their families, like the arrest and possible imprisonment of prisoners' wives at the prison gates by the police for possession of drugs. A classic example of this is the resentful and disaffected screw who is censoring the prisoners' mail and who switches letters to different girlfriends or mistresses in order to cause maximum distress to all parties. These sort of Machiavellian plots occur all the time in the complex and surreal hinterland of long-term imprisonment.

Nonetheless, I have always striven to see the best in people I have met in prison and, as a proactive act of self-protection against unjustified and unwarranted ill-will or malevolence, we would form close-knit social groups or cliques of like-minded individuals who felt safe and secure in their own company and could relax and socialise without any undue animosity or hostility.

As I have stated previously, Reggie Kray was on 'C' Wing and, although he mainly kept his own company with Steve Tulley, I found him to be a thorough gentleman. Providing that it was within his power, he would help anyone who was in need of support or advice.

I really got to know Reg when he spotted one of his old friends Lenny Carter visiting me. When Reg realised that I was close friends with some of the old-school villains such as Lenny, he use to pop up to my cell with his adopted son Steve Tulley for a cup of tea and a chat. At this time it had not been publicised that Reg was a homosexual – not that it mattered – as it appeared he did not see any value in socialising with old-school villains in prison who could only regurgitate fond memories *ad nauseum*. Reg much preferred the animated company of younger prisoners who encouraged him to train, made him smile and gave him some hope in a cold world of melancholy and hopelessness. I recall, in 1984, Reg invited Perry Terroni, Kevin Brown and me to his sixty-third birthday party but, because Reg was anti-drugs, we politely refused unless we would be allowed to have a joint in his cell. It was not a problem.

That evening, we all went to his immaculate cell and had a proper old knees-up, guzzling prison hooch and puffing away. About a month later, I said to Reg that I had had a vivid dream about him and that he had been released from prison and that we met in a shoe shop in Canning Town. His face beamed into a smile and he said, 'Thanks, Tel, I love to hear about those dreams ... you keep having those dreams!' As we are now aware, over a decade-and-a-half later, in the year 2000 Reggie Kray was finally released and, after a short spell of sweet liberty, he passed away with cancer. Words cannot express how I feel for this man who had served over 30 years of imprisonment in the worst of British prisons, while many of his contemporaries who had committed unspeakable crimes had been released before him.

We all know that the reluctant release of Reggie Kray was more to do with the Government's fear of losing political power and public support than judicial deterrence and retribution. In many respects, Reggie Kray was a victim of selfish politicians who would rather leave a man to rot in prison than compromise their comfortable political position or status.

In the short time – about 16 months – that I spent with Reg at Parkhurst, we all knew that he was serving a monstrously long and debilitating sentence, one that would crush and destroy any man, even a strong and resilient individual like Reg. Never once, however, did I hear Reg grumble or groan about his fate. To use a boxing analogy, Reg took every day of his soul-sapping sentence flush on his chin and, despite being the recipient of some terrible body blows over the years, he marched on relentlessly with real Mandela-esque dignity and pride. Some critics will no doubt proclaim that Reg deserved every day of his imprisonment, while others may claim that he was a fellow human being 'more sinned against than sinning'. Whatever the case, Reggie Kray will always be respected as one of the great oaks of East End folklore and villainy.

It was while I was at Parkhurst that Tracey and I decided to take the bold step and leap into wedlock. Like most lovers, we had planned to marry some time during our relationship and, although we could not be together physically, we knew that we possessed a unique spiritual bond that remains with us whenever we are apart. Even now, as I write this book inside a top-security cell at Belmarsh Prison, I know and sense that Tracey's spiritual presence is with me and it makes me glow with warmth and comfort. It was because of this strong sense of inner contentment and the desire for it to go on and on for ever that we decided to get married on the seventh anniversary of our first date, 6 June 1984.

The wedding ceremony was to be held outside the prison at the local registry office in Newport, Isle of Wight. Outwardly, I was overjoyed at the prospect of marrying my darling teenage sweetheart, but inwardly I was secretly hoping that my ultra-staunch and determined friends would use this golden opportunity to break me out. They had sent me several messages since my conviction in June 1983 to sit tight, keep focused and try to get allocated to a semi-secure prison where they would be able to help me escape, even if it required them coming over the wall to get me. This type of bone-deep help is rare, and you cannot buy it. Invariably, prison or courtroom escapes only occur due to the dedicated desire of family and friends to bust you out, because they like you, love you and miss you. No amount of money can buy this type of determined allegiance, it is earned through very close friendship, loyalty and respect.

It was absolutely imperative, therefore, that I told no one about a

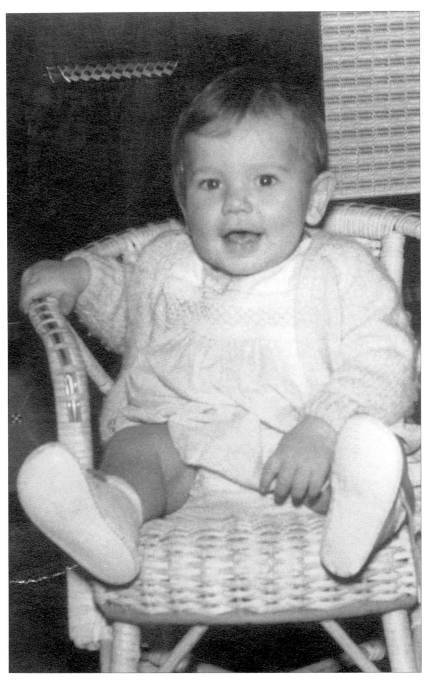

Me celebrating my first birthday in my best clobber in 1960.

Me with Lenny, my brother, aged three.

Top: My fiancée Tracey Etherden and I in 1980 enjoying a glass of champagne.

Bottom: (*left to right*) Boozy Freeman, Tracey Cox, Patsy Etherden, Tracey and I in the summer of 1980 at Clacton-on-Sea.

Top: The Canning Town crew as they are today. On the top row are Kevin Bryan, Paul Woolard, Ray Old, Dave Bailey, brother Lenny, Tony Bowers, Martin Bowers, Gary Ishmael and Steve Clark. On the bottom are Boozy Freeman and John Turner.

Bottom: Anyone for football? Me posing in 1980.

Top: Tracey's sister Patsy, me and Tracey down at the family caravan in 1980.

Bottom: Marrying the girl of my dreams on 6th June 1984 at Newport Registry Office on the Isle of Wight. I am flanked by my son Terence, my brother Lenny, Tommy Hole and my son Bradley. Note the handcuffs.

DAILY EXPRESS

Wednesday November 21 1984 ● 20p ● TV Pages 24 and 25   **THE VOICE OF BRITAIN**

THAT MAN MANILOW

LUCY EWING

NAKED MEN

DON'T MISS THE FIRST LADY OF FLEET STREET, Page 9

TODAY IS ALL ABOUT

Danger men sprung from prison truck

BMW gang wield axes in ambush

Express Reporter COLIN PRATT

TWO dangerous prisoners were on the run last night after being sprung in an elaborate underworld plot.

London gangsters armed with axes snatched them from a prison van in a rush-hour ambush and raced to freedom in a stolen BMW car.

It took less than a minute. Police hunting the ong-term prisoners warned the public: "Don't approach them. They are very violent."

As road blocks were set up and a helicopter joined the search, it was revealed that the escape plan began with a staged punch-up in Kent's Maidstone jail.

The aim of the brawl was to provoke disciplinary action against the ringleaders, Terrence Smith, 25, and John Kendall, 33, and get them switched to a tougher prison.

It worked to perfection. For when the two thugs were being transferred to Parkhurst, Isle of Wight, their gangland friends on the outside had been tipped off and were waiting to pounce.

Bank robbers Smith, serving 15 years, and Kendall, 10 years, had been in Maidstone jail for only a few weeks. They had gone there for a course on business management. Instead they were plotting their escape.

They were handcuffed together after breakfast yesterday and driven from the jail in a yellow van. A third prisoner was with them. They were escorted by four prison officers and a fifth at the wheel.

FLARE-UP

Waiting en-route were the four-man ambush gang in two fast BMW cars stolen from Wanstead, East London. They launched their attack as the van turned off the A25 on to the A127 at Reigate, Surrey.

A silver green BMW cut in front of the van forcing it to hit a lamp post. The masked raiders, wielding axes and pick-axe handles, smashed the van windows and warned the warders: "Let these two men go or we'll beat you to pulp."

Smith and Kendall leapt out and were driven off in the getaway car, a blue BMW, registration A670 TRP. The third prisoner remained in the van and made no attempt to escape.

PUNCH-UP

Detective Superintendent Keith Portlock said: "We are dealing with violent and dangerous men. We understand this incident involves a London gang and it appears highly organised."

A prison official told of the jail punch-up that led to the escape. "Smith and Kendall deliberately engineered a violent flare-up at Maidstone," he said. "It seems now it was all part of the plan."

Smith, from Dagmar Road, Dagenham, was jailed last year at Chelmsford for his part in a £20,000 robbery.

Kendall, of King's Court, Plaistow, was part of a six-strong robbery gang sentenced at Snaresbrook.

The judge described the gang believed to be master-minded by Kendall, as "the scum of society." A massive manhunt for the men was under way last night.

FUGITIVE: Kendall 10-year sentence

FUGITIVE: Smith serving 15 years

NDETTA OF THE ROMEO RECTOR
Y WOMAN HE LOVED: SEE PAGE 5

What the *Daily Express* and the *Sun* had to say about my escape from Maidstone jail in 1984.

RUSH-HOUR GANGSTERS
FREE DANGER MEN

Prison van is ambushed

TWO dangerous prisoners were sprung to freedom yesterday in a daring rush-hour ambush in a busy town centre.

An underworld rescue gang in two stolen BMW cars pounced on a yellow prison van containing the two men and another convict.

As horrified drivers watched, the van was forced off the road and into a lamp-post.

Terence Smith   *John Kendall*

Then four hooded thugs armed with pick-axe handles jumped from the BMWs and hurled a sledgehammer through the van's windscreen.

Four prison officers on escort duty were brutally attacked by the gang while the two criminals — handcuffed together — jumped into the street.

The convicts and their rescuers dived into one BMW and roared off through the centre of Reigate, Surrey. The third man did not try to escape.

Last night police swooped on addresses in East London and Essex in a bid to find the fugitives.

Snatch

Worried detectives believe the pair were sprung by a London gang to take part in an armed robbery now being planned.

The snatch happened while the convicts were being taken from Maidstone Prison in Kent to Parkhurst, the top-security jail on the Isle of Wight.

Freed were Londoners Terence "College Boy" Smith, 25, serving 15 years for armed robbery and John Kendall, 33, doing 10 years for robbery.

EMINGTON AP100.
HES IN SMELLS AND
BEFORE YOU DO.

How The Sun exposed the shirkers yesterday

City's dozy sweepers on the carpet!

DOZY street cleaners caught napping by The Sun were last night carpeted by their angry bosses.

And the fate of the £140-a-week shirkers will be decided today.

By ANDREW PARKER

Five cleaners and several of their supervisors were hauled in front of a disciplinary committee. It follows the story in yesterday's Sun which blew the whistle on their forty winks.

Demanded

Coventry's Labour-controlled council was stunned when we

miracle" if cleaners worked four hours of an eight-hour shift.

Coventry's chief engineer Brian Redknap said last night: "A report of the disciplinary hearing will go to a meeting of the Public Works Committee tomorrow morning."

Fire kills mum and two tots

A MOTHER and her two baby daughters died last night as a blaze swept through a guest house in London's West End.

Two more children were seriously ill in hospital after the inferno in busy Baker Street.

More than 80 residents fled —18 of them escorted down a fire escape by firemen—as flames tore through the City Guest House.

Ladder

Hero taxi driver Frank Baker, 45, stopped his cab and raced to the rescue when he saw smoke pouring from a second-floor window.

Frank, of Streatham Vale, South London, grabbed a handy ladder and scrambled up to reach a trapped woman and two youngsters.

The cabbie, who burned his hands pulling the youngsters clear said: "The woman was hysterical."

An elderly man rescued from the fire was early today in a serious condition". in the Middlesex Hospital.

WEATHER

MAINLY dull, rain spreading from W. Max 54F(13C). OUTLOOK: Colder.

Life on the run. *Top*: Bearded and with sons Terence and Bradley. And *bottom*, what better disguise on Christmas day 1985, than Father Christmas and an even bigger beard! Baby Jade is suitably impressed.

possible escape at my wedding. I was not 100 per cent sure that the escape plan was laid on, but the last thing I wanted to do was to jeopardise or compromise the ceremony or the safety of my close friends through inadvertently blabbing my mouth off in the prison. I decided to let things ride and, if the escape occurred, all well and good, and, if it didn't, I would still come away with the prize, a very beautiful and attractive wife. I simply could not lose.

On the day of the wedding, I was taken out of the jail under a heavy escort of six prison officers in a Category 'A' prison van and handcuffed to a screw throughout the short ceremony. As I walked into the rear entrance of the register office, the first thing I noticed was how stunningly beautiful my future wife looked. She was absolutely ravishing in her very ornate, cream-coloured wedding dress and matching accoutrements. As I surveyed the large upstairs room where the ceremony was to be held, I noticed my two young sons dressed as pageboys and the Best Man, young Tommy Hole, wearing his immaculate light grey suit. It was then that I knew that I could relax and that today was a non-runner in terms of a dramatic escape. Over 30-odd members of my family and friends had come to the island to share in this special day; many of them were to remain on the island for the rest of the week while they all took turns visiting me. On returning to Parkhurst straight after the ceremony, and divulging the good news that I had just got married, everyone was surprised that I had not told anyone about my plans. I made up some lame excuse that I wanted to keep it a private affair, as I did not want to make a fuss. I remember one particular screw asking me how long I was serving – as if he didn't know – and then asking how long I had served. When I replied two years, he looked at me with a derisory smirk on his face as if to say, 'It won't last.' Little did he know that his work pals nearly had a handgun poked up their nostrils and they'd nearly been one short on the official prison roll count. Moreover, little did he know that it wouldn't be long before I would be out and this would allow me to consummate the marriage. Little did he know that we would celebrate our twenty-fifth year of togetherness and seventeenth year of marriage, and still be going as strong as ever. Screws can be so cynical!

After the wedding, things returned to normal within the jail and, in order to activate the 'You help us and we'll help you' proposition from my robber friends, I kept up the education classes and elementary exams. My friend John Kendall was heavily into mathematics and had enrolled for an exceptional electronic educational course at Nottingham Prison. Places on the annual O-level course at Maidstone were severely vetted and restricted and I feared that, because of my offence of armed robbery and the length of sentence it incurred, plus the glaring fact that I had only served two years, if they had to drop anyone from the shortlist it would be me. This precarious situation was made worse when Kendall was refused a place on the electronics course at Nottingham Prison and now he wanted to jump ship mid-stream and enrol on the Maidstone course. In theory, he knew that this manoeuvre was likely to scupper my chances of going to Maidstone, but I could not explain to him the ulterior motive of my desire to get to Maidstone as I steadfastly refused to trust anyone. I was caught in a really awkward dilemma – either ask Kendall to drop out of the running for the Maidstone course, which I very much doubted he or his wife would consider, and thereby possibly jeopardise my security, or let things ride and hope and pray that I made the transfer list on merit.

In any event, I decided it did not matter, as I was informed that the Principal Education Officer at Maidstone Prison had accepted both Kendall and me and that we were to be transferred to the Kent prison in early September 1984, several weeks before the academic year.

11

On the Run

After saying a heartfelt goodbye to the many friends and acquaintances I'd made during my stay at Parkhurst, it was with some relief that Kendall and me and several others boarded the prison bus for Wandsworth Prison in South London. We were to spend one night on a stopover at the jail and then move on to our final destination of Maidstone Prison in Kent.

As far as the escape was concerned, stage one had been completed. I had managed against considerable odds to get to a semi-secure prison, and the difficulties of stage two now had to be confronted. Again, without letting anyone know about my intentions, I wanted to explore and evaluate any weaknesses in prison security, such as the location of the lowest wall. Would I need to cut my cell bars to get out at night, or could I brazenly escape during the exercise period while all the prisoners were on the yard?

All these issues would have to be resolved in due course, but first I had to get acquainted with the lads at Maidstone. Both Kendall and I were allocated to Kent Wing, where we were greeted by the sensible element on the wing, such as Joey Martin, who was very close friends with Reggie Kray, Johnny White, Tony Ash and Billy Haywood.

They all made us feel very welcome and immediately enquired about old friends and acquaintances whom we had left behind at Parkhurst. It was then that I encountered my first obstacle; a black guy up on the threes landing was asking if I was on the wing. I asked his name and quickly realised that it was a guy who'd had a row with Perry Terroni on the basketball court at Parkhurst. Perry could not fight to save his life and was getting hurt, so I'd jumped in and stopped the row. Later, the row developed on the wing and the fellow got bashed. Perry was placed on Governor's Report and the case was later dismissed due to the lack of evidence. The black guy was transferred to Albany Prison and was bad-mouthing both Perry and me.

The last thing I wanted was a violent confrontation with the guy in full view of everyone on the first day on the wing, so I slipped up to his cell alone and fronted him. Like men in an adult world, we vented our differences and shook hands and reassured each other that there was no value in carrying on the conflict in this new jail.

What I did notice about Kent Wing, though, apart from the ubiquitous group of Cockney robbers and professional villains, was that there appeared to be a very large contingent of ethnic prisoners who seemed to hog the cookers during evening association and cook the screws exotic curries. As Johnny White informed us, the ethnics were all right and no one bothered them, but they were very sycophantic towards the screws and, in return, they had monopolised most of the best jobs on the wing.

It was not long before we started the education course under the aegis of Miss Jackman, the Deputy Head of the Education Centre. Also on other courses were two long-standing friends of mine, Tony Yellop, a fellow Towner who had been sentenced to ten years for a building society robbery, and Egan Blackford, my old black Borstal friend who was now serving a life sentence for fatally stabbing a person during a bungled robbery. Indeed, Tony Yellop was a very good friend, as I knew his dear mother Stella and all his family, and, therefore, contrary to previous concerns and anxieties, I knew that I could trust him.

Tony informed me that, three months before my arrival, two prisoners, one called Frannie Pope, had indeed escaped from

Maidstone Prison by going over the wall and the security had been considerably tightened up in the jail. Not only had all movement of prisoners been heavily supervised and new wire fences been erected, but during the daily exercise period a burly bouncer-looking gym screw stood guard at the lowest point of the prison wall. Put bluntly, I was gutted! I had come all this way and things were not going to plan. Nonetheless, I was still very much determined to escape.

The plan that I had in mind was to get my close and loyal friend young Tom to sit on top of the prison wall with a mask and shotgun, fire a warning shot to let the screws know that we meant business and chuck me down a lifeline. The escape route would be meticulously planned and involved several change-over vehicles, so that we could get well clear of the Maidstone area and, all being well, we would be home before nightfall. All I had to do was to get my pals up on a visit using fictitious names and fill them in on the details. As things stood, my side of the bargain had been achieved; I had got to a semi-secure jail, now it was their turn to fulfil their promises and, being men of unswerving loyalty, it was only a matter of time before I would be home.

Several inexplicable events occurred to me at Maidstone, however, that made me think that someone may have been on to my escape. First, whenever you enter a new prison, one of the first things the reception screws do is to take head-and-shoulders shots of all new prisoners. During this reception photograph, I left my glasses off, knowing that, when I escaped, the screws would give the police and media the most recent photo of me. Some weeks after my arrival at Maidstone, some screws visited the Education Centre and asked to take some new photos of me. Although this is not unusual, it is far from normal. It set the alarm bell ringing in my head.

Second, about the same time as the new mugshots were being taken, the Principal Officer (PO) of the wing called me to his office and suspiciously proclaimed, 'What are you doing here, Smith? A prisoner of your length of sentence should not be here,' to which I casually replied, 'I'm only here for the education course, Guv'nor. I don't particularly like your jail and, once the education course is over, I can't wait to get back to Parkhurst!' I sensed that he was on to something and yet I knew that it couldn't have been an informant because I never told anyone about my plans to save Tony Yellop, whom I trusted implicitly. It may have been the earlier escape by Frannie Pope that had compelled the security screws to scrutinise all possible escapees. Whatever the case, I had to tread carefully, as any infringement of prison rules and regulations would provide the screws with the ideal excuse to swag me back to Parkhurst.

Back on Kent Wing, we used to get up every morning and visit the ablutions and wash and shave in the sinks provided, but the cons of ethnic origin who were predominantly Muslim used to wash their feet in the sinks where we had to shave. A dispute arose, in which I pointed out that, if the prison had made sinks to wash our feet in, they would have put them on the floor. In short, the excessive hygiene and cleanliness of the Muslims was at the detriment of those wishing to shave. Therefore, to their chagrin, several of us told the Muslims to wash their feet in the showers provided. No doubt the Muslims had a pow-wow about this new development and planned a response. The dispute came to a head when one disgruntled prisoner smashed all the porcelain sinks in the washroom opposite my cell so the foot washing could not continue. This is a common response in prison between two or more disputing prisoners where, if one prisoner cannot get his own way, he would rather destroy the object of dispute – a TV or video, for example – rather than let the other person succeed in his wishes. This type of displacement violence or vandalism is also replicated when screws introduce new and unfair prison rules. Rather than embark upon a full-scale riot, prisoners initially express their discontent by setting fire to TV rooms, the hotplate or cleaning cupboards, anything to warn the Prison Governor that there is significant disquiet and disaffection brewing in the jail.

As far as the 'Battle of the Sinks' was concerned, the foot-washers recruited a large Spanish guy called Hernandez to pursue and protect their interests. Hernandez kept having sly pops at me and obviously wanted a showdown. Several times I had to bite my lip and swallow my pride without losing too much face, but I simply couldn't tell anyone about the silent conflict I was enduring in order to keep my long-term plans alive. As far as I was concerned, the overriding reason why I was at Maidstone was to escape.

Hernandez must have sensed my reluctance to confront him and mistook it for a weakness and, in true bully fashion, he tried to intimidate me further. Normally, I would not let such a conflict go beyond the very first insult, as I would have chinned him there and then and be done with it, but this arsehole thought that I was a paper tiger and pushed and pushed me into a corner. One day I had had enough and stupidly mentioned it to my friend Kendall, which was the worst thing I could have done, as he immediately stormed off to confront the guy. I quickly caught up with him and grabbed him and said, 'Stop! This is my row, leave it to me!' I copped for the geezer in front of his ethnic pals and offered him the opportunity of a good old-fashioned straightener in the bogs.

We went to the recess and steamed into each other. Outside the recess, a small crowd gathered, including Johnny White, Kendall and a horde of ethnic onlookers. What we did not know was that Hernandez was a 6ft 2in strapping Spanish guy who had a deformity of his right arm which he concealed very well. He grabbed on to me like a mechanical claw and we rolled about the recess floor like lovers in the snow. It was the most comical fight I have ever had. I was trying to break away so that we could trade some decent blows at each other but he had me in a vice-like grip. In the end, Johnny White had had enough and clumped him a couple of times with a lump of wood, as did Kendall. The hilarious thing was, however, that we all wore thick prescription-type glasses and, while I was on the floor with this geezer, we were bashing each other up, too.

Without further ado, the ethnic cons went straight down to the ground floor and lay siege to the Wing Governor's office. As far as he was concerned, this was a serious incident and Kendall and I were swagged to the jail's punishment block. I knew immediately that I had blown my one and only chance to escape. We were not placed on Governor's adjudication for the fight, but we were to be transferred back to Parkhurst at the earliest opportunity. Miss Jackman came to visit us in the punishment block and we tried earnestly to argue that it was not our fault and could she possibly persuade the Governor to give us another chance, but it was to no avail, the Governor was adamant, we were *personae non grata*.

In spite of what has happened throughout my adventurous and eventful life, I always return to the paradox that 'some bad things happen for the best'. I therefore quickly got a message to my pals, telling them that things had changed and, because of the fight, I was now being transferred back to Parkhurst the following Tuesday, 20 November 1984. Young Tommy Hole came and visited me on the next visit and we decided that the best way to succeed in our endeavours was to break me out of the prison van en route to the island.

As always, I kept all the plans close to my chest, without even telling Kendall, as I was still unable to trust anyone. On the exercise yard in the punishment block, though, Kendall nearly jeopardised the plans when he asked the supervising screw, 'What time in the morning are we leaving on Tuesday, Guv?'

The screw replied, 'It will be early about 7.30am.'

This annoyed me, as it was stupid questions like that which could put my friends in jeopardy, but I felt that it was best not to tell Kendall anything.

On the day of the transfer itself, we were unlocked early for a shower and Kendall, who had been suspicious of my visit with young Tommy Hole, asked, 'Is anything going to happen today?'

I answered, 'I am not sure but, if there is and we are cuffed together, just hold your arms out and they will be bolt-cropped!'

Thereafter, until we were loaded into the prison van at the entrance of the punishment block, I followed Kendall around like a hawk, making sure that he did not rat on my friends. By all accounts, Kendall had an impeccable history and was reputedly proper stuff, but I had been taught by the old-school, whose cardinal watchword was 'Never trust anyone you do not need to'. There was never any suggestion that Kendall would do anyone any harm, but I had to watch him closely all the same.

At about 7.30am, I was handcuffed to Kendall and a Turkish prisoner also being transferred was handcuffed to a screw. In addition, there was a Senior Officer (SO) in the front of the van with the driver and three other screws in the rear with us, making a total of five screws and three prisoners. The prison van itself was a yellow Bedford minibus-type vehicle with bars on the windows and, surprisingly, the passengers in the rear had access to the front passenger side of the van where the SO was sitting. I purposely wore a traditional blue-striped prison shirt as I wanted my friends to see that prisoners were inside the vehicle as they drove past.

As the prison van pulled out of the large prison gates of Maidstone, I casually looked up and down County Road to see if my friends were on the plot. As I looked up and down the road, the screw directly opposite me did so as well to see what I was looking at, but fortunately the road was clear. We drove a short distance and, unbelievably, the prison van stopped at a newsagent's and the SO darted into the shop and bought a newspaper. Unbeknown to me, a new BMW 3 series pulled up in front of the prison van. The male passenger got out and went into the paper shop and when he came out he looked right at me in the prison van to verify that I was indeed on board the vehicle. Brilliant! This was the confirmation that I needed that things were going to happen today. All I had to do was sit tight and wait until they initiated the escape and I would do all I could to help them from inside the van.

We drove away from the paper shop and quickly linked up with the M20 motorway heading towards the M25. It was a very cold November morning with thick patches of mist and fog in places. This would dissolve as the bright morning sun broke through. As the bright yellow prison van motored serenely down the M20 and on to the M25, little did the screws know that two freshly stolen BMWs from a dealership in Wanstead, East London, with three occupants were lurking up to a mile or two behind them. My pals were highly professional robbers and one of the skills of the trade was how to follow security vans at a sensible distance without being spotted. This may sound easy to do, but as any diligent and determined armed robber will tell you, it is an art that requires excellent judgement and concentration. One slip-up and it could mean a 'conspiracy to rob' charge at the Crown Court or, worse still, a life-threatening 'ready-eye', in which armed police would shoot to kill their targets. It is no game, it's a serious business.

As the prison van drove along the motorway, my pals decided that the best place to conduct an attack on the vehicle would be once it had left the M25, otherwise we would travel too far away from the urban areas and possibly hamper our chances of escape from the scene. At about 8.30am, their chance came sooner than expected. The prison van left the M25 at junction 8 and, as it turned left down the A217 towards Reigate, a BMW 5 series screamed up and overtook the prison van and smashed into the front driver's side of the vehicle, forcing it to career off the road and on to a grassy verge. At the same time, a second BMW 3 series blocked the rear of the prison van so it could not escape. Two masked men, one carrying large bolt-croppers and the other a pick-axe handle, alighted from the leading BMW. The masked raider with the pick-axe handle crashed it into the prison van's windscreen, shattering it, while the other raider with the bolt-croppers retrieved the van's keys from the driver and went to the back of the vehicle to open the rear doors.

Meanwhile, I dived over the front passenger seat and grabbed the SO. The screw behind me, in turn, grabbed my legs in a tight grip and, as I was wriggling and wrestling to get out of his grip, my jeans came down and my bare bum was in his face. The SO in the front seat quickly realised that this was a no-win situation and that it was no time for heroism. He ordered his staff to let the prisoners go. I dragged Kendall still handcuffed to me across the front passenger seat and out of the front passenger door. By that time, one of my pals had undone the rear doors to the prison van and had entered with the bolt-croppers, but it was too late as I had already dragged a bemused Kendall to the back seat of the waiting BMW. Eventually, we all piled into the BMW and did a spectacular U-turn and sped off past the prison van and long queue of traffic that had built up behind the rammed vehicle. We then shot across the elevated roundabout over the M25 and chucked a right down the first country lane. The driver of the BMW pushed the vehicle to its limits as it negotiated the treacherous country lanes. One slight mistake and we could easily find ourselves in a field or ditch as the roads were still covered with ice and frost. Then Kendall said something very embarrassing that revealed that he was out of his depth. He exclaimed, 'Is there going to be a shoot-out?' My pal in the front, who did not know Kendall, replied, 'Chuck that cunt out!' But I intervened and said we should let him be, as he was OK.

We continued to drive for several miles down country lanes and then we all knew that we had to abandon the BMW, as the police would by now be putting the registration number of the car over the airwaves. We reached a little village called Couslden in Surrey. There we split up; young Tom, Kendall and me jumped on a British Rail commuter train to Victoria Station, central London, while my other two pals made their own way home.

When we reached London, we went to Wanstead Flats and fed the ducks in the pond while young Tom went to sort out a safe house for us to stay in. I quickly phoned my wife Tracey before the police had time to set up a police operation, and told her that I was out and I would not be able to contact her for several weeks. When young Tom came back to us, he said that there was a problem. My pals had a very good safe house for me to go to but, because they did not know or trust Kendall, he could not go there. Basically, I pointed out that we could not really dump him and that he would have to come with me to the alternative accommodation.

Once we were settled into our sub-standard bolt-hole, I put it to Kendall that, if he wanted to, I would give him some money and he could give himself up. He did not want to do this as he said that, if he gave himself up, he would be returned to Wandsworth Prison where the screws would give him a bad time. This was, in fact, true, as all prisoners who'd escaped and were then recaptured were indeed taken to Wandsworth and recategorised as 'Escape Risk' prisoners. These prisoners were subjected to a whole catalogue of senseless punitive rules and regulations, such as being continuously checked every 15 minutes throughout the day and night, forced to wear distinctive yellow prison clothing and had a subdued red light on all through the night. Kendall was 100 per cent right; why sacrifice the beautiful world of freedom, individuality and choice for a Stalinesque mini-State of screws who abhorred and detested all successful villains and wanted them under their iron feet of oppression and control? He was right – there was no choice to be made.

Obviously, we all knew that the dramatic escape of two long-term Category 'B' prisoners would be of some interest to the media and that the police would mobilise and activate all their resources to recapture us, but the subsequent news coverage of the event was astounding. Even before the day was over, the *Evening Standard* newspaper had included the dramatic escape as its main story and put our mugshots on the front page of the late edition. We could not believe the attention that we were getting as even the national and local TV news programmes ran the story.

The very next day, the tabloids milked the story for all it was worth, claiming that 'an underworld rescue gang' had busted us out 'to take part in armed robberies now being planned'. Ironically, the *Star* newspaper came closest to getting the facts right when it ran the headline CUFF LUCK! and alluded to Kendall's fortunate role in the escape. Henceforth, we were sensationalised and demonised by the press in general as extremely dangerous and violent criminals who were not to be approached. To some degree, the *News of the World* came to my rescue when it referred to me as 'College-Boy Smith' due to my penchant for learning and clean-cut persona. Well, I suppose it was better than being called 'Scar-Face Smith' or something equally derogatory.

To exacerbate our situation, two days after our spectacular escape a well-organised gang of armed robbers ambushed a Brinks Mat security truck on a slip road near where we escaped and they used a mechanical digger with a large shovel on the back of a low-loader lorry to peel the roof off of the security truck. The robbers escaped with a substantial amount of cash and the police were working on the theory that we had been broken out of prison specifically to take part in this major robbery. Of course, it was all nonsense, but it pushed us up another couple of rungs on the ladder of criminal demonology. Even the local East London newspaper, the *Newham Recorder*, warned the public to be vigilant as we could be planning robberies in the borough. It appeared that the propagandist and sensationalist media machine was running on all cylinders; it was unstoppable. It became a place where the lines between fact and fiction, myth and reality were blurred to such an extent that anything could be written about us and believed by the vast majority of the public.

Over the next three weeks, we sat in our little safe house somewhere in Canning Town and we watched the media gradually lose interest in us. We never left the safe house once. We couldn't, as the area was crawling with plain-clothes undercover police officers walking the streets in a vain attempt at spotting us. My friends were visiting us every other night to bring us food, clothes and essential goods. They were feeling the pressure, too, as our wives and other members of our families had been arrested and taken to Reigate Police Station for interrogation. They had my wife Tracey for three days, pumping her for information, but the poor girl could not tell them anything as she didn't know where I was staying; no one did. As they maintained the pressure on our families, Surrey Police sent a significant detachment of determined detectives to the East End to help in the search and our apprehension, but we managed to remain underground for a month before we were finally forced to move from our safe house as two uniformed cozzers knocked on our front door. We told our helpers that night and we were moved to a hotel in Essex and then on to a plush flat in one of London's most stylish locations, Chelsea.

It was a great relief to move away from the East London address as, although the neighbours knew that someone was inside the house, they never saw anybody and this would make them extremely suspicious over the course of time. The little flat in Chelsea was a breath of fresh air and, over the intervening weeks since the escape, we had adopted new identities and facial disguises by growing beards, moustaches and long hair. To complement Kendall's disguise, he bought a top-of-the-range wig from a reputable wig-maker as he was easily recognisable walking up and down the King's Road without any decent disguise.

Fortunately for us, our self-contained flat in Chelsea was adjacent to the premises of our landlord. I mention this because, in spite of the decrease in daily coverage of the escape, we were allotted high-profile status on both Shaw Taylor's *Police Five* and the newly introduced *Crimewatch* TV programmes. Whenever we were on these programmes, we could go into our bathroom and listen to what TV channel our landlord was watching through an empty glass put against the bathroom wall. Luckily, on each occasion they were watching different channels to us.

As the police search for us intensified in the East End of London, my friends provided me with a large chunk of cash and pointed out the dangers of visiting us in case surveillance teams were following them. There was one urgent problem, however, because we had not contacted our wives or families over the last four or five weeks. Kendall's wife was going around East London claiming, 'I know they've killed my John, he would have contacted me by now, they've killed him, I bet they've killed him!' In order to shut her up, we got Kendall to write her a personal letter, telling her to sit tight, keep quiet and, once we were out of the limelight and the police could not continue to fund such a non-productive operation, we would be able to see our families again. We both knew that this could take anything up to three months. Already, the *News of the World* was claiming that College-Boy Smith had been smuggled out of the country to Tenerife in a refrigerated lorry.

A crucial time for us would be the forthcoming Christmas period. No doubt, if the police intelligence reports did not come up with anything over the festive period, then there was a strong likelihood that we were, indeed, somewhere abroad. I recall, despite being unlawfully at large, Kendall kept pestering me about his forthcoming appeal against his sentence. Contrary to our rigid policy of non-contact with our families and friends, I agreed that he could phone his brief, providing he caught a train outside London and made the call from there. So one day he set off early in the morning and returned later that evening.

At the time, he was serving ten years for burglary and, because his co-defendants had their sentences reduced, Kendall also qualified for a reduction. When Kendall returned, he said that his sentence had been slashed by two years and that he was now serving eight years' imprisonment. I pointed out that there were not many appellants who had had their prison sentences cut while they were already out of jail. To celebrate, he donned his wig and we went out and guzzled several bottles of bubbly in a nearby public house on the King's Road. I must admit, Kendall may have been a bit of a panic-artist, but he was excellent company and always looked on the humorous side of things with his attendant infectious laughter. On one occasion, we were having lunch in a cosy little restaurant in the back streets of Kensington and Kendall was in hysterics because the TV presenter David Frost was sitting at a nearby table and he did not know that he was within spitting distance of two of London's most wanted fugitives. This really tickled Kendall.

Initially, we did not purchase a car, as parking in the London Borough of Kensington and Chelsea was horrendous. It meant finding a parking meter and keeping it topped up every four hours. We opted for black taxis and public transport to get us about. But then again, we were told, rightly or wrongly, that black taxi drivers were privy to photographic lists of wanted people supplied by the Metropolitan Police. We therefore opted for the London Underground tube service. We used to walk from our cosy flat to South Kensington Station and, on our way, we used to pass marching columns of uniformed police constables on their way to their beats along the King's Road. We use to laugh inwardly to ourselves that, even if one of the policemen thought that we looked suspicious, he could not break ranks and confront us. Outwardly, though, it was no laughing matter, as every cozzer in the land wanted to jump on our backs and return us to prison. It was important for us to maintain and sustain the highest level of security and anonymity. That was the beauty of living in such a cosmopolitan area as Chelsea, as no one asked questions, no one enquired as to who you were and what you were doing. They were all too busy getting on with their own lives and wanted as little interruption or interference as possible.

Living in Chelsea was a real revelation, as it opened my eyes to how the other half lived – the rich half – and it forged within me a bone-deep desire to be successful and to have a taste of what they had – the wealth, possessions, security and comfort. I know that it sounds incredibly materialistic, but I viewed myself at this time as a pauperised East End villain who'd had to drag himself out of the gutter of deprivation and destitution with a mask and a gun. No one had put a silver spoon of inheritance or wealth in my mouth; therefore, inadvertently, Chelsea came to symbolise the promise of ambition and affluence for me. I wanted what I viewed as my share of the country's opulence and wealth. I had seen many honest labourers in the East End work their fingers to the bone for a pittance. This was not for me. Living in Chelsea only compounded the Marxist notion that the capitalist economic system of the distribution of wealth was fundamentally unfair and, therefore, no security van was safe. Henceforth, it was work, work and more work.

Before I began to work, however, I had to resolve several significant issues. First, we had to find new accommodation, preferably in Chelsea; and second, I had to inform Kendall that my friends were not prepared to let him work with them. They were already very successful robbers and refused to compromise their safety by letting a relative stranger into the firm. The price for the folly of such decisions was still being paid by those incarcerated for decades due to the supergrass era of the 1970s. The new breed of close family-orientated robbers were not prepared to let circumstances dictate events. Kendall may have been good stuff, but he was surplus to requirements and therefore not worth the risk.

One of the first things I had done at the beginning of 1985 was to purchase a powerful motorbike. It was acceptable to some degree to use public transport to visit my friends but the anonymity of wearing a crash helmet made the motorbike an excellent choice of transport to get around London and the surrounding areas. As long as I kept my speed down it was quick, reliable and anonymous.

The next stage was to see our wives and children. It was essential to wait such a long time before we saw them as, in many respects, as far as the super sleuths at Scotland Yard were concerned, our wives were our Achille's heels. Some cynics would say that it was abnormal to put off seeing our wives for so long. My answer is that being a fugitive is not a game. I wanted to remain at large for a lot longer than a couple of months. I had heard of some well-known East End fugitives, such as Jimmy Moody, who escaped from Brixton Prison in 1980 along with Stan Thompson and a member of the IRA, being 'on their toes' for years and years. It was my aim to reign for a decade or more and the only way to succeed in this endeavour was to do it the right way.

The first time I saw Tracey after the dramatic prison escape, I drove to a pre-arranged meet on my motorbike. I'll never forget it, as it was pouring with rain and along came Tracey dressed like she was going to a glitzy ball at the Ritz. I gave her a big hug and kiss and asked her quickly to put on some wet skins and a crash helmet and we roared off for a romantic weekend at a secret hotel in the wilds of Essex.

We were incredibly nervous at first, as we had not slept together for over two years, and it was a terrible shock for me to see how much body weight Tracey had lost over that time, for, some years earlier, Tracey had been diagnosed as having Crohn's Disease, an incurable ailment which affects and irritates the digestive tract and colon. I was to learn that Crohn's Disease is a psychosomatic illness which is aggravated at times of physical and emotional stress and worry. Over the last two years, it goes without saying, I had put my wife through a lot of stress and tension and I take most of the blame for her poor physical condition and health. The only remedy I knew to overcome this was copious amounts of love, laughter and togetherness.

It was not long before Tracey's body weight began to rise and she fell pregnant with our third child. This was the best thing that could have happened to us, as our plans to have another child while I'd been in Parkhurst were coming true and the thought of all those natural proteins and vitamins running riot inside Tracey's petite body would no doubt aid her in her recovery from the vicious symptoms of her illness. Almost immediately upon hearing the splendid news of the conception, we went out to celebrate and drank several bottles of champagne. The next day, now that Tracey was confirmed pregnant, she became as temperate as a nun. Henceforth, her only cravings would be Slush Puppies and gherkins.

Not long after this uplifting news, Kendall and I moved to a larger basement flat on the other side of the King's Road. The rent was £1,000 per month, but it was well worth it as, not only did it have a massive circular bath, but it was also several doors away from the residence of Paula Yates and Bob Geldof. I had always been an admirer of Paula, particularly when she first introduced music lovers to *The Tube* on Channel 4 in the early 1980s. Early every morning, I used to see either Bob waiting for his driver outside his house or Paula taking their daughter Fifi to the nursery. I felt quite safe in the knowledge that we were living in the midst of music and TV celebrities ... until there was an almighty drunken row in the flat above us and the occupants stormed out of the house. Then there was a knock at the door and I was just about to open it when I noticed the shape of a uniformed policeman. He rang several times and, to my amazement, a third person came down the stairs from the flat on the third floor. There I was, listening to him grassing up his neighbours who lived in the middle flat who were having a typical domestic row over family and money issues. The grass, I thought, we will have to watch it around here, especially if we were put on *Crimewatch* again.

We stayed at this plush address for about six months and, because of the exorbitant rent and the desire to start doing what I was good at, robbing security vans, I decided to seek another flat, only this time in Putney, South-West London. I felt a bit awkward, really, as I had to park Kendall up in order to start robbing again with my close friends. As I have said before, there was no way that they would entertain Kendall on a bit of work, so we had to split up. I did have some serious reservations about moving from Chelsea, as I had grown to love the area, the thrill of accidentally bumping into celebrities, the cosmopolitan clientele on the fashionable King's Road, the swanky and stylish restaurants, and the all-pervasive aroma of wealth and decadence. They were exciting times for us all, and I would go so far as to claim that it was the best time of my life. Chelsea had become the centre of the universe, it was the *ne plus ultra* of existence, it was Bird's creamy custard mixed lovingly with Ambrosia rice, cloying, thick indulgent yumminess. It was definitely me.

On a geographical level, the move to Putney was ideal as it put me further away from the temptations of returning to East London and it provided me with a new fertile area to plunder. Absolutely no security van was safe when I was about. I would set off early in the morning on my motorbike and scour the corpulent capital in search of a big fat security van. The first bit of work that I had after the escape was with young Tommy Hole. As I have said before, we used to argue over who was going to seize the prize off the security guard. Seeing as this was my first bit of work since busting out of the prison van, I beseeched him to let me seize the prize. I said to him, 'You sit in the car and I will do the honours.' As the security guard collected the canvas sack of cash from the chute of the security van, I pounced on him too eagerly and, because I surprised him, he put up a terrible fight. Unlike some callous armed robbers who I know, I would not 'ping a guard' for nothing. I would let off warning shots if necessary to control the surroundings and get my own way through the manipulation of terror and fear, but to 'ping a guard' cold-bloodedly in the leg for nothing was not my style. On this occasion, I ended up letting off a few rounds and clumping the security guard with the gun. Of course, I came away with the £20,000 prize; after all, that's what I was there for.

Thereafter, I would creep out and about with young Tom and go to work about once a month. To a great degree, the overriding reason why I escaped from prison was to be with my family and I believe, if I had been released from prison under normal conditions and circumstances, I would not have been so audacious or eager to continue robbing. But our social and economic circumstances were far from normal. The sensationalist media had portrayed me as a violent fugitive who had only served two years out of a 15-year sentence. As any decent villain would claim, being a well-publicised fugitive requires lorry-loads of cash to remain successfully at large. Inevitably, money would be splashed out on exorbitant rent, cars, clothes, food and general living expenses. Therefore, the target of robbing at least one security van a month would cover the cost of these expenses and also satisfy my devilish cultural addiction to rob what I perceived as justifiable and legitimate financial targets.

It was important for me, though, not to get pulled down by the very awkward dilemma in which I found myself – either I stopped committing robberies and was eventually captured through a radical dearth of resources, or I continued to rob and remained at large to be with, however periodically, my loving family. Some critics will claim that I was selfish and, if I was really concerned about my family, I should have stopped robbing. Alas, this may be true, and it came to light many years later, through specialist assistance, that I learnt that I was indeed addicted to risk-taking. Like the free-fall parachutist, bungee-jumper or dare-devil motorcyclist, I needed to have my fix of adrenalin-pumping adventure, and the fix for me was the thrill and excitement of stealing large chunks of cash from security vans and leaving very little evidence behind for the police forensic teams to sift through. In my view, there was nothing better than reading about a successful blag in the newspapers in which masked raiders were indirectly praised for committing a dramatic robbery with military precision and coming away with the prize.

Alternatively, I was acutely aware of the very real pitfalls of being an armed robber, such as being shot dead by armed police, suffering permanent injury, spending life in prison or, at the very least, having to endure a decade or more at the mercy of the British penal system. Perhaps that was what made armed robbery so exciting, as it was a bare-faced gamble with one's life, a gamble in which the robber had to be lucky all of the time and the police only had to be lucky once.

With so much spare time on my hands, when I was not socialising with my family I turned to keeping fit, which had always played a large part in my life anyway, by regularly jogging between three and five miles around Wimbledon Common and also playing badminton at a local evening class. The social and cultural constitution of the badminton class was quite fascinating as, in one section, we had the professional clientele of insurance consultants, accountants, lawyers and even a circuit judge, and at the lower echelons of income we had the middle- and working-class wage-earners. I was quite an enigma to them as, although I spoke with a Cockney accent, the expensive car and the clothes I wore definitely put me in the professional sphere. Either way, we played excellent badminton, mainly doubles, but I did play their best player at a game of singles in which I beat him. He was so impressed with my standard of play, that he invited me to join Wimbledon Badminton and Tennis Club to become graded as a serious competitive player. I was eager to do this but I envisaged signing loads of forms and being checked out by some high-ranking cozzer on the board, so I reluctantly had to reject the idea.

As the months of 1985 slipped by, my life revolved around the monthly bit of work, some quality time with Tracey and my beautiful boys, now aged two and three, and a strong desire to do all the things that I had wanted to do but were put off for some reason or another. A comical event occurred when I picked up my boys for the first time after the escape. As they got into the car and I'd started driving through the back streets of the East End, my oldest son Terence said, 'Mum, I didn't know that we've got two dads.' Obviously, Tel-boy didn't recognise me, due to the radical facial transformation that I'd undergone.

At this time, I was seeing quite a lot of my elder brother Lenny who had followed my career choice of armed robbery and, despite working with other groups of robbers while I was away in prison, he decided to link up with me and young Tom as we were, to put it mildly, not only well-organised and respected robbers, but we were also prolific and forever chasing the holy grail of robberies, the modern-day quest for the 'big one'. There is some evidence to suggest, however, that professional, high-profile robberies, such as the largest cash robbery in British history at the Security Express depot in Shoreditch in 1983, and the gold bullion robbery at the Brinks Mat depot near Heathrow in 1984, have been disastrous for those who took part in them, in that the robbers in these high-profile crimes have been pursued, persecuted and imprisoned in some form or another. The professional robbers I mixed with preferred to commit one or two major robberies a year, pocketing about £100,000 each and then slipped back into their anonymous social life without all the hullabaloo of a high-profile police investigation. In short, it is better to lie dormant and be active every once in a while than to draw too much attention to yourself, to the extent that you can't even go up to the newsagent's without being bottled by SO11, the surveillance mob.

While I was living in Putney, I had a couple of close scares with the police. The first one occurred when I went to watch a Simple Minds concert at Wembley arena with my brother Lenny. We arrived and bought some tickets from the touts outside the arena and, after drinking countless glasses of wine, we made our way to our seats near the front row only to find a group of women in them. We ordered them out of our seats, but they had pulled a classic scam whereby they had reported their tickets stolen to the management and had had them replaced. The argument grew until we had to settle the dispute outside the auditorium with the manager who threatened to call the police to settle the dispute. We had been well rumped and, against our wishes, we had to swallow or else get arrested and be returned to prison. We immediately slipped outside to collar the tout but he had disappeared, too, so, in the end, we resolved to take it out on Group 4, Security Express or Securicor the next time we were active. They would pay for it as they always did!

Another scare occurred when I returned home one day on my motorbike to find my road blocked off by marked police cars and policemen evacuating all the occupants of the flats where I lived. God, I thought, they've tumbled the flat. God knows how, as no one, not even close working friends, knew where I lived. As I stood at the bottom of the road in the rain, debating whether to see if any more developments occurred, a bolt of lightning flashed in the foreground, which I took as a divine message to get the hell out of there. I returned several days later to see if I could piece together what had happened and I spoke to a neighbour who said that there had been a gas scare in the flats and they'd all been evacuated for their own safety. It was a relief, as I had stashed all sorts of robbing equipment in the flat.

With regard to my brother Lenny, he had become a trusted member of our group of robbers. Lenny was not a planner or organiser, but nonetheless he became a reliable and resolute member of the team. If I said to Lenny, I want you to stand there and do this or do that, he would do it exactly to the nth degree. He would never let you down and that is all one requires in any trade. If there was one major failing with Lenny, he had all the social skills of a club hammer. For example, Lenny was invited to a family wedding and, at the reception, a distant member of the bride's family sidled over to him and said, 'Hello, Len, you don't remember me, do you?'

'No' replied Lenny.

'I was in Albany Prison with you,' the fellow said.

'Oh yeah?' said Lenny. 'What wing was you on?'

'No ... I was a prison officer!'

Lenny immediately chinned the screw there and then, sending him crashing into the sandwich table. When Lenny told me the story, I said to him, 'Why didn't you have a chat with the fellow as he may prove double handy later on?' Lenny said that he couldn't help it, that he just hated screws and we burst out laughing. Perhaps that forthright episode of tact and diplomacy sums up Lenny precisely. There are no grey areas with Lenny, everything is translated into black and white and, hence, much to his chagrin, I nicknamed him 'The Soldier'. He would never make a five-star general, but with soldiers like Lenny on the front line, he made the work of the planners and organisers much easier.

During this period of being unlawfully at large, I heard some sad news that one of my cherished mentors in the art of armed robbery, Lenny Carter, had fatally shot himself. Because of my low-profile status, I had not seen Lenny since the prison van escape and, as far as I was aware, he had made no attempt to see me. Apparently, Lenny had travelled to the outskirts of Epping Forest at Whipp's Cross and shot himself through the heart with a handgun. Although deeply saddened by this when I heard it, it did not surprise me that this had happened. I recall that, during my closest period with Lenny, he always said that he could not face another lengthy period in prison and that he would rather top himself than go back inside. At the time of his death, I don't know if Lenny was wanted by the police or if he felt in some way that he would be returning to prison but, whatever the case, it's alleged that he took his own life. I had many good times with Lenny, both on a social level and on the pavement, and for that reason, in my heart and spirit, he remains a true friend.

As the months of 1985 drifted by, I began to feel more at ease with my fugitive status and its attendant shortcomings, such as the ever-present fear of capture, loneliness and the uncertainty of what the future had in store for me. I was becoming increasingly comfortable with the idea that I had to keep looking over my shoulder for, provided that I did not see or visit anybody over and above those who I already trusted, I felt that I could reign for ever. Just as the spotlight of police attention began to focus upon more accessible and topical villains, my brother Lenny was involved in a very violent fracas at a nightclub called Reflections in Stratford where a young local man was fatally stabbed. Evidently, the row began due to a dispute between the Towners and the Stratford lads. Blows were thrown, ammonia squirted, knives plunged and even a shotgun was discharged. Alas, in the nightmarish battle, Lenny and several others had to barricade themselves in an upstairs room. As the police got to grips with the case, the Murder Squad detectives started to build their case around one man – yes, you've guessed it, Lenny Smith!

Very soon after the incident, Lenny came to see me and I asked him all about it, whereupon he swore on his children's lives that he hadn't stabbed anyone. In fact, I did know that Lenny occasionally carried a weapon, but it was not a knife. Later, we learnt that a barmaid had written a statement claiming that she had seen a large, fat man with a long-bladed knife, which did not fit Lenny's description at all.

As a result of the incident, I made some enquiries through a well-connected go-between with the police to see exactly what the case was against Lenny in exchange for money, and the message came back, 'You're too late, someone has already beaten you to it and the paperwork has already been written up on Lenny!' It transpired that there had to be a scapegoat and it was going to be my brother. Over the next year or two, Lenny stayed out of the way and fled abroad. While he was away, a certain detective badgered and pestered the barmaid witness in the case to say that she saw Lenny with the knife and *not* the 'large, fat man'. By the time the case had reached Lambeth Magistrates' Court for committal proceedings, the barmaid in open court had made a formal complaint about the treatment and persecution that she had received from the detective and the case was dismissed, and rightly so!

At about the time of the Reflections nightclub incident in

September 1985, I was called to a meet by a pal of mine who was planning a major robbery in Essex. He said that he and some other prominent South and East London robbers were joining forces for a tasty bit of work and, if there was a space for me, he would try to get me involved. The only problem was that, some of the other robbers were apprehensive about working with a high-profile fugitive like me, as it might bring it on top for them.

Several weeks later, however – alas, without me – five robbers stopped a Brinks Mat security truck on the A128 which was delivering cash to banks throughout the Essex region. They stopped the security truck by using a lorry and rammed its back doors using a stolen mobile crane. The masked gunmen then escaped with over £500,000 in a Range Rover which made its escape over nearby fields. In the process of the police manhunt, two of the suspected robbers were captured – Johnny Read and Peter Mitchell. They'd abandoned a stolen Bedford camper van with the cash from the robbery in it. Later, at the Central Criminal Court, they were both convicted and sentenced to 22 years' imprisonment each and, to this day, they protest their innocence, despite being released from prison several years ago.

On 29 October 1985, I received a rare phone call at the Putney flat informing me that Tracey had not long given birth to a 6lb 2oz baby girl, Jade Nadine Smith, at Barking Maternity Hospital. I desperately wanted to be present at the birth but it was not feasible, as the police may have been expecting this. I recall sitting alone in the flat and wanting to go out and celebrate the birth of our 'miracle baby', but, sadly, the very people I wanted to celebrate with I could not see. Several days later, though, Tony Colson, Kevin Brown, my brother Lenny and I celebrated in style at a famous central London nightspot by singing Jade's anthem, the newly released Simple Minds track 'Alive and Kicking'. I recall us drunkenly swaying in each other's arms in blissful boisterousness and brotherhood, a moment to savour for ever.

Before we knew it, Christmas was upon us and it was imperative that all our family, including our newborn baby daughter, spent the festive season together. It was our first Christmas together as a family since 1981 and I was determined to make it the most memorable one for all of us. By that, I mean I bought a Father Christmas outfit from a fancy dress shop and put it on early on Christmas morning. I went into the boys' bedroom and gave them a brilliantly realistic portrayal of Father Christmas, even down to the deep booming voice. Leaving the children to open their presents, I quickly slipped off the outfit and the boys eagerly said, 'Dad, Dad, Father Christmas has been here and he gave us our presents!'

'Yeah,' I replied, remembering to alter my voice, 'I just saw him pulling away on his sleigh outside and he said that he was coming back later on to take you down the shops!'

After a couple of hours playing with the children. I slipped the outfit back on and walked the boys to the newspaper shop along Upper Richmond Road. What started as a comical festive stunt turned into a veritable dramatic performance for, as soon as I opened the front door of my flat, people started to pop their heads out of their upper windows and shout at me, 'Look, there's Father Christmas!' It was like being a famous politician or pop star. Cars started to beep their horns, attracting even more attention. I only had to walk 200 yards to the shop and back with my two young sons and it felt like I was the most sought-after and most popular character in the world. As I reached Upper Richmond Road, the inevitable occurred; a marked police car with three cozzers in it came along with tinsel tied to their aerial. They blasted their siren and I gave them a courtesy wave, thinking, If only they knew that I was one of London's most wanted fugitives.

When I got back to the flat and told Tracey about the unforgettable experience we began to laugh hysterically. We spent a fabulous Christmas together, one that had profound significance, as we were not supposed to be together. It was like stealing Christmas off the police, judiciary and the penal system all in one. On New Year's Eve, I arranged to spend it alone with Tracey at a West End nightclub called The Hippodrome. Surprisingly, not many East Londoners visited this particular nightclub at the time so it was relatively safe to enjoy the celebrations there. As we got progressively sozzled on Buck's Fizzes, it was not long before the chimes of Big Ben began to echo around the auditorium. As we welcomed in the New Year in the middle of the dance floor, I picked Tracey up in my arms and gave her a red rose that I had secretly bought earlier. I wished her happy New Year and we danced the night away. It was a very special night for us, as we had been through a lot of stress and hardship over the previous couple of years, what with my arrest, trial, conviction, long prison sentence and Tracey's debilitating illness. For a short moment, it seemed that all our troubles had evaporated and we were caught up in an exquisite explosion of love and togetherness. We'd done it! Against all the odds and obstacles, we'd both pulled through with a beautiful baby daughter as well.

Lurking in the back of my mind, however, was the dark fact that one day I would have to return to prison and confront and overcome the corrosive effects of long-term imprisonment. It was a daunting thought, but one that I felt I could face with some sort of equanimity in that I would not be serving 15 years for 'one poxy bag of cash' as I had snatched another bite of the cherry and, boy, were they paying for it now.

Everyone must have one definitive moment in their life when they visualise or witness, almost in slow motion, something incomprehensibly terrifying that is about to happen. This occurred to me when I took my two sons, Tracey and her parents to Wimbledon Common in early 1986. It was a particularly cold Sunday afternoon and we had just had lunch and we all decided to take a leisurely walk over the nearby common. On reaching the lake in the forest, we noticed that it had been frozen over with a thick layer of ice and lots of people were playing on it, running and sliding, falling over, to whoops of delight and laughter. Of course, it was not long before we were on the ice enjoying the comic thrill of slipping, sliding, skating and falling on the treacherous, magical surface. I recall chasing my son Bradley at one end of the lake and spontaneously saying, 'Where is Tel-boy?' As I turned round, I saw Tel-boy fall through the ice at the shallow end of the lake. I recall an equally vigilant father about to go to Tel-boy's assistance at about the same time as me, but he saw me react. As quick as humanly possible, I raced over to him and pulled him out of the waist-high freezing water. Thereafter, we abandoned the frolics on the ice and went home. It was quite simply the fright of a lifetime and one that I find hard to write about even now.

Due to the social and economic upheaval of the festive and New Year period, it takes several weeks for the security vans to settle down and get into their regular collection and delivery patterns. Some security cash-in-transit companies are more complicated than others, as they vary their collection and delivery schedules, but most with some diligent and dedicated scrutiny can be tied down to a specific timescale or pattern. I recall one particular security van that I robbed had outfoxed me for months on end, but then I tumbled its enigmatic delivery system and waited three months for its next potential delivery time. As I waited on the High Street some distance away from the target and saw the familiar colours of the security van coming along in the traffic, I felt a frisson of self-satisfaction that I was spot on with my judgement. As the security van pulled up and its occupants began to chaperone its contents across the narrow pavement, I was there to greet them. Thank you very much, and off I went in a stolen waiting get-away vehicle. Another feather in my cap!

In robber's parlance, I was what you'd call a 'front-runner'; invariably, I was the one who had studied the behavioural traits of the security guards and had acquired almost perfect judgement at getting close to the ones with the prize in order to rob them. After all, security guards were only human and were susceptible to the use and abuse of habits which could be discerned in their daily routes and delivery strategies. Not only would I invariably be the first robber to confront the guard, I would also normally be the one to drive the get-away vehicle as well, albeit a motorbike, car, lorry or van. Don't ask me why, but I felt extremely confident in my own ability to do the job correctly without undue drama or mayhem. Moreover, even if there was an unplanned incident or impending disaster, I always knew that we were in total control and knew exactly how to deal with the problem.

There came a time during this period that I saw myself as invincible. Apart from an unfortunate 'ready-eye', I thought that it would be extremely hard to catch me on a robbery. I knew that, if I did get caught, it would be due to something inexplicable.

As I have explained before, most serious professional robbers aim for one big job that will enable them to hang up their guns for a year or two or, in some rare cases, for ever. In this, I was no different. I had progressed from running up to security guards making deliveries or collecting from High Street banks and relieving them of their sacks of cash, to dragging guards back to their vans and making them 'chuck 'em out'. I'd also climbed inside security vans and emptied them, or rammed them while in transit on public roads. In spite of all the investigative resources that would be employed on a high-profile, daredevil raid, I still wanted the big one. I wanted a million-pound blag.

In the spring of 1986, I thought that I had found the perfect security truck to rob as it drove from a new security depot to the best bank in the world, the Bank of England. As soon as I saw this bit of work, I knew that I had to have it. It would 'go' as it was a natural progression for me to attack this monster of a security vehicle and offload its succulent contents. This particular bit of work would require some serious planning and my most effective organisational skills. First, I would need more manpower. I already had young Tom, my brother Lenny and me, but I needed three more. Therefore, I recruited one robber from North London and two from South London.

We all met up at a West End bar and I outlined the plan. We were to stop this armoured beast of a truck with a sizeable lorry and ram its back doors with a specially converted JCB digger. I left nothing to chance in preparing this bold and daring blag, so I went out and stole all the vehicles required – two trucks, two vans, several cars and a motorbike. I left the JCB until last, which I had no problem in obtaining. The only difficulty with this bit of work was that, when it left the security depot, it had to take a short-cut down a certain road and sometimes, contrary to habit, it would stick to the main road. I pointed this out to the others and we all decided to get ready for it and wait in ambush for up to four consecutive weeks.

The first two weeks, the beautiful beast came out of the depot and went down the main road. We were all gutted and, to keep everyone happy and focused upon this particular piece of work, another robber and myself decided to pop out on the motorbike and have a bit of work 'on spec' in order to share it out among all the others.

As the other members of the team were returning the stolen vehicles to their safe parking places, I jumped on to the powerful motorbike and headed for the City of London looking for a suitable security van to rob. In many respects, this was contrary to the way I worked, as it was very dangerous and unprofessional. For instance, there is a higher ratio of armed police in the City due to the all-pervasive threat of terrorist attacks and, being an inveterate planner and organiser of the perfect armed robbery, suddenly becoming a 'Specko', or going to work without any particular knowledge of events and escape routes, was foolish. But my co-robber on the motorbike had done this before and I could see why he enjoyed it so much. It was so exciting, the adrenalin was surging through my body by the bucketload as we cruised through the City in search of a suitable target. It was not long before we found what we were looking for, as security vans are as common as pigeons in the City; they flock there like creatures of habit, making deliveries and collections by the hundreds. And if the security vans were well-fed pigeons, we were the hawks swooping in for the kill.

Bang ... bang ... a couple of warning shots rang out on the High Street as my partner cornered a guard delivering the cash to a bank. Before anyone had a clue what was happening, we were roaring away from the scene. God, it was such a buzz, but deep down I knew that this type of unplanned and arbitrary work was perilous. Perhaps the only advantage in committing this type of robbery was that the crash helmet covered your face at all times and it was very difficult to get ambushed on a police 'ready-eye' because the robbers did not even know their target, so how on earth were the police going to know? Nonetheless, the powerful frisson of robbing 'on spec' could not outweigh the underlying anxieties of getting caught through unplanned events or freak circumstances. It was a dangerous game indeed.

That aside, it was a successful mission. We cut up about £30,000 with our partners, which helped to alleviate the itch to drop the larger robbery in favour of smaller touches. We were about to pull the monster truck robbery the following week, when I heard that one of the South London robbers, the motivating force behind the recruited trio, had been arrested for an assault charge. The assault charge was not the issue; it was the outstanding warrant for his return to prison that was the real problem. I knew that, once I had lost this valuable partner, it would be hard to motivate the others and the impetus to continue would be lost. Then we lost one of our lorries. I quickly the lorry replaced, but the irreplaceable loss of my alter-ego consigned the plan of robbing the beast to the graveyard of good ideas and, sadly, it was not to be.

In the interim, I had purchased a new caravan on a holiday camp down on the south coast. I did this as it served as another summer bolt-hole for me to escape to if I felt like a break. Moreover, with three young children, it was the perfect spot to create and develop some 'quality time' with my young family. At this particular time, I began to analyse and evaluate the direction my life was taking and concluded that, as long as I was unlawfully at large, there was no point in stopping robbing. I was still embittered at the way I'd been convicted for the Corringham robbery and its excessive sentence. In my view, I knew that one day I had to return to prison to complete the remainder of my sentence, but, in the meantime, I was going to rob as many security vans as I could so that, when I returned to prison, I could claim that I had had a good run and that at least I would in prison for something.

By now, 'Specko' had become a major feature of my life, and I was on a self-destructive mission as I was going out on the motorbike at least once a week. The more I did it, the more invincible and intrepid I felt and became. No part of our beautiful city was out of bounds. Providing the prize was right, if a security van was making a delivery outside Buckingham Palace, I would have robbed it. All the other robbers around me benefited from this as well; if they were not on a particular robbery with me, I would put some money aside for them. I called it 'indoor money', to help with the exorbitant living expenses, as we were all by now residing in the West End. We were like one huge family, robbing security vans in the week and meeting up at snazzy restaurants and eateries at the weekend.

Seemingly being blessed with the foresight or foreknowledge of impending danger, I predicted a week before my next excursion 'that we should stop going out on Specko otherwise we are going to have a terrible tear-up and one of us will get nicked'. I added that we should concentrate on our medium-sized robberies, the ones that required serious planning and organisation, reaping anything from £100,000 to £500,000. We all agreed to adhere to this philosophy ... that is, until the next day, when I received a call from an old friend.

12

Demise at Kensal Rise

Having decided to knock 'Specko' on the head, I had a message from John Kendall that he wanted to see me. I slipped over to East London on my motorbike to listen to what he had to say. Kendall claimed that he wasn't having much luck financially; in fact, he was in debt due to his heavy gambling habit and he asked me if he could come to work with me. I knew that my close friends would not entertain this idea, so I said that I would take him out for a bit of work 'on spec' the very next day. Before we went out, however, I explained to him the perilous pitfalls of 'Specko' and explained to him that it was a high-risk enterprise.

The next day, 11 June 1986, I met Kendall at the rear of Wormwood Scrubs Prison in West London ... a bad omen. We were on a Yamaha 1100cc motorbike, not my favourite bike ... another bad omen. My 'lucky mechanical horse', a Kawasaki 900 GPZ, was in the repair shop as it kept overheating. We were dressed in proper motorbike regalia, as we did not want to draw undue attention from the traffic police patrolling the streets of London. From experience, I had learnt that real bikers do not dress in casual clothes and are very rarely stopped by the police, therefore I had invested in some expensive and stylish black leather clobber from a shop on the King's Road, so that, once I was off the motorbike, it was hard to tell whether or not I was a biker. This tactic enabled me to get closer to security guards without drawing their attention.

In any event, I met Kendall at about 9.00am and checked that he had brought his own tool, a .22 pistol. I had my favourite silver snub-nosed .38 Smith and Wesson revolver. It was small and well balanced, but nonetheless deadly at close range. Thankfully, due to my own mental and physical confidence, I have never had to shoot anybody callously as I have always been in total control, and if a security guard did not respond to my demands or orders, I would either clump him with the gun or fire a few shells at the floor near his feet to create a real atmosphere of fear and terror. It always produced the response I required without the need for bloodshed and I never came away empty-handed. That is why robbers enjoyed working with me, as I was a serious cat and the streets of luscious London were my territory, where I would leave my mark.

At about 9.30am, as we rode through Paddington, I spotted a red non-descript Post Office security van making a delivery to a sub-post office. The three-man crew were active. Two were on the pavement and the custodian was inside the van, passing the cash out. I was not interested in the cash being transferred across the pavement, as I wanted to jump inside the security van and drive it away and then unload all its contents. But to do that it required a team of three robbers – two to get inside the van and take care of the crew, while the third robber follows the hijacked security van to a safe place to unload the cargo of cash. Seeing as we were on a motorbike, this idea was a bit of a non-starter. In addition, one of the security guards had already seen me walk past the security van and was feeling uneasy at the sight of a pedestrian dressed in black motorcycle clothing with a helmet. This did not bother me because, if I made a move on him, by the time his suspicions were confirmed, I would have my .38 handgun up his nostrils, checkmate, and the endgame would be complete, providing he did not want to annoy me.

As I walked past, I nodded to Kendall to leave the PO security van as there would be richer pickings later on. That is the beauty about robbing 'on spec', for, if the conditions or circumstances do not suit, you can always move on to another security van further along the road or even another area. We hopped back on to the motorbike and drove to a place called Kensal Rise, a cheeky little high street with a Barclay's Bank and a yellow Security Express van outside it, obviously doing what we called a 'bank run', as it was there so early. I decided that this was just right.

In order to prevent anyone following us on the motorbike, I parked it behind some concrete pillars that prevented traffic entering a nearby side-road. It was perfect, as I could create as much drama and commotion as I liked and no one could follow us down the sealed-off road. As I walked round to the high street, I was feeling very confident, like a centre-forward in an important football match in which I knew that I would score, and it would be a hat-trick! As I surveyed the high street, I noticed that the two security guards were already transporting the single bags of cash across the pavement. One guard was at the chute of the security van while the other was shuttling the cash bags to and from the bank.

As I walked up to the security van dressed in my intimidating motorbike leathers, I tried to judge my approach to catch the guard during one of his shuttle runs, but it was not to be as the security guard at the chute did not fancy me one little bit, so I confirmed his suspicions by putting my handgun to his head and ordered him to tell his colleague inside the security van to 'Chuck 'em out!' In the meantime, Kendall came over to support me. Then the other security guard came out of the bank and I copped for him, too, as experience had taught me that, if I copped for the custodian of the crew, the guard in the back of the security van was more likely to obey his orders.

As I ordered the security guard to 'Chuck 'em out!' the chute opened and I retrieved a large green bag of cash. Not content with this, I ordered that more cash bags be thrown out, but there was very little response. I knew that the security guards had been trained to delay the robbers for as long as possible, so I upgraded the fear factor by firing a couple of shots at the floor. The chute soon opened and I retrieved another cash bag. All in all, we had secured £35,000, not exactly a king's ransom, but enough for our basic needs. We ran off down the high street past some stationary traffic that had seen us flee the scene, and down the road near where our motorbike was parked. As we jumped on to the motorbike, the usual active witnesses came to the top of the turning to note the registration number plate of the get-away vehicle. No one, however, was brave or stupid enough to take us on, so we powered off down the blocked-off road.

About midway down this avenue, we came to a quiet crossroads. In many respects, these crossroads have come to embody or symbolise the crossroads of my life. I could have gone straight across, but I feared that, despite the distance, the witnesses would still be able to see us. I could have chucked a left, which would have taken me, in theory, further away from the safety and security of the city, or I could turn right, which would take get me back to my favourite escape route along the A40 Marlborough Road, the West Way viaduct at White City. As I turned right and was applying the power, an estate car came out of a parallel road and screeched around the corner towards me. I knew straight away that we were in trouble as, not only was the vehicle heading for me a Ford Granada estate, a car that has brought nothing but bad luck to me in the past, but it was also dark metallic green in colour, a colour through superstition that I avoid like the plague. The mysterious combination of these two factors occurring at the same time could only mean one thing ... unavoidable disaster.

As expected, the Ford Granada estate car pulled right across my path while I was travelling at about 35–40mph. This type of situation has happened to me before – security vans have chased me while on a motorbike – but I used to scoot up the pavement or around stationary traffic to avoid them. This time, however, there was no stationary traffic to hide behind, and trying to negotiate a 6in-high kerbstone at a very acute angle meant one thing: I would be thrown off the motorbike anyway.

The Ford Granada estate pulled right across my path and we hit his offside front wing. Kendall and I were immediately thrown through the air. I rolled along the pavement and, when I stopped, I did a strange thing. I took off my crash helmet. For a robber in crisis, this is odd behaviour, as I had to protect my facial features at all times. As I stood up and took a step with my right leg, nothing was there, so I did a shoulder roll to soften the impact with the pavement. As I did so, I landed in the gutter and then I noticed the reason why I could not walk. My right lower leg from the knee joint down was missing. I thought that my leg was in the road somewhere. All I could see were the two large bony protuberances of my thighbone. Unbeknown to me, I had suffered a complete dislocation of the lower leg but, fortunately for me, the vital blood veins, vessels and nerve fibres were still attached to the leg that was located somewhere up my back.

Quickly, I used my hands to stop the loss of blood by squeezing the end of the leg with all my might. By now, the driver of the Ford Granada had driven away and another have-a-go hero had arrived on the scene in the form of a Gas Board driver, an ex-soldier or something who had witnessed the attack on the security van and wrongly assumed that the security guards had been shot. Evidently, he had squeezed through the concrete pillars at the top of the road that we had driven down. Upon reaching the chaotic scene of the rammed motorbike and me lying seriously injured in the gutter, he pulled his Gas Board van right up to my head which was now under the front bumper of his vehicle. If he had wanted to run me over, he could have, but he chose not to, and for that I am grateful. Nevertheless, he leapt out of his van and, seeing that I was already incapacitated, he set about Kendall right in front of me. As the gasman walked towards Kendall to seize him, Kendall shot him three times, once in the groin, once in the zip of his trousers and the other in the chest. The gasman believed it to be a cap gun and overpowered Kendall, until the police arrived about three to four minutes later. Fortunately, for the gasman, Kendall was only armed with a .22 calibre pistol for, if he had had my .38 Smith and Wesson, he would have been in dire trouble. As people started to come out of nearby houses, some thought the gasman was a thug and ordered him to get off Kendall. The gasman earnestly replied, 'These two have just shot someone around by the bank!' This was not true, as the only person who'd been shot was the gasman for intervening in an otherwise injury-free robbery.

As I lay in the gutter, the gas van was removed from the scene, the police came, an ambulance was called and a lovely woman came over to give me some first aid advice. She applied a tourniquet around my upper thigh and told me to release my grip on my leg, but I wouldn't. I recall that it started to rain and some people were holding their umbrellas over me, but I asked them to remove them as the cold drizzle on my face felt good. I asked the kind woman for her name and she replied, 'Terri,' which was like having a house brick smashed in my face, as from then on I would have to discard my pseudonym of the previous 20 months and would be known as Terry Smith again. I also recall drifting in and out of consciousness and saying that I would never be able to play football again, a sport that had given me so much joy and pleasure. Then some more plain-clothes cozzers arrived, obviously from the Robbery Squad, as one had the face of a right slag as he looked over at me on the floor and smiled. This would be the easiest nicking of an armed robber that he would ever have. Then an ambulance woman arrived, only to declare that her ambulance had broken down several hundred yards up the road and that they were sending for another one. It just wasn't my day! By now Kendall had been taken to Kilburn Police Station and the gasman to hospital in a panda car. Apparently, while in the panda car the gasman noticed blood on his shirt and then panicked when he realised that he had indeed been shot.

After about 50 minutes in the gutter, I was taken to Central Middlesex Hospital. The severed leg began to shake uncontrollably and, although I was going into shock, I still felt alert and aware of all the events that were going on around me. The ambulance crew took me into a cubicle where the nurses began to cut my clothes from me. Earlier, the police were asking me for my name but I said that I could not remember and now they were asking the nurses to ask me. Soon, an ethnic doctor arrived, a Dr Mizra, and he began to examine me. I recall him asking, 'Can you feel this? ... Can you feel that?' as he pricked my toes with what seemed like a pin. I kept saying 'Yes' to all his questions, as I did not want to lose the leg. Dr Mizra then said that he could save my leg but I would not be able to bend it at the knee. I recall saying, 'Please save my leg, doctor', for, as far as I knew, the lower leg was still detached from my body. In my view, to save the leg would be a remarkable exercise in itself.

I was then carted off to the operating theatre where they began to prepare me for surgery. I recall saying to them, 'Come on, put me out,' as it was like a living nightmare in which only one needle would end it. When I was in the gutter at the scene of the crash, I remember thinking what it was like for all those valiant soldiers on the battlefield in World War I and II, where many of the wounded were stranded in no-man's land and could not receive the treatment that I was now experiencing. I don't know what made me think of this, perhaps it was an experience that had happened to me before in a previous life. Whatever it was, it was undeniably moving.

I was in the operating theatre for about six hours. I recall coming round from the anaesthetic as the local London TV news programme was on in the recovery room, and I heard the newscaster talking about our incident earlier that morning. Then, as I gradually regained consciousness, a detective guarding me slipped over to me and began to quiz me about the whereabouts of my brother Lenny who was still wanted for the Reflections nightclub fatal stabbing. Talk about scraping the barrel! Are there no levels to which a cozzer won't stoop to secure information to gain an arrest? Naturally, being a streetwise villain, I was quickly on to this base ploy and had a sudden relapse into unconsciousness.

I was held in the hospital for a further two days, where I underwent another operation to cleanse the wounds. Then the police told the hospital that it was impractical to keep me at the hospital because it had been alleged that there was a threat on my life. Whether this was true is debatable, as I was never officially told and it might have been a ruse to get me back into custody as quickly as possible. As far as I was concerned, my long, colourful and exciting period as a fun-loving fugitive had come to an abrupt end, and the next day I was returned under a heavy police escort to Wandsworth Prison in South-West London.

13

The Wendy House

Due to the prison van escape some 20 months earlier, the prison authorities at the Home Office decided to upgrade my security status from Category 'B' to Category 'A' and 'E'. Basically, being labelled Category 'A' meant that, if I was unlawfully at large, I would be considered a danger to the police and public. As for the Category 'E' status, it meant that I was considered an 'escape risk' and that I must endure a wide range of extra rules and restrictions in order to prevent me from attempting another escape. As far as I was concerned, it was academic as I was in no fit state to get out of bed, let alone escape. At that time, I was on more painkillers and drugs than a heroin addict and a rock star put together and, as far as I was concerned, I was not going anywhere.

The orthopaedic surgeons at the hospital had put an external metal apparatus on my right leg. In effect, it was like a ladder inserted through my upper and lower leg to give the leg stability and encourage growth. Every day, the leg had to be cleansed with hydrogen peroxide and saline solution and then have clean dressings applied.

The screws at Wandsworth Prison at this time in 1986 were still notorious for being ruthlessly authoritarian. Their overwhelming attitude and demeanour was one of 'We don't want prisoners under our thumb, we want them under our heel'. As it was a Prison Officers Association (POA) union stronghold in London, any type of reform or improvement of the prison regime, conditions or visits were swiftly opposed as unworkable by the POA, through the lack of staff and resources. Thus, the overriding power structure of the POA managed to keep Wandsworth Prison firmly ensconced in the Victorian era.

As far as the prison hospital was concerned, it was contained in a separate building situated at the bottom of 'E' Wing and it would be best described as an annexed asylum, where those with serious psychotic problems, drug addictions and a penchant for self-mutilation would endure their harrowing hallucinations and nightmares. Piercing screams and continuous mumbling would echo throughout the lower and upper floors of the prison hospital all through the night. It was a real karzy, in which I drifted in and out of consciousness for months on end until I began to make some progress.

Due to the seriousness of my leg injuries, it became an unexpected opportunity for the medical screws to do some real nursing, instead of being the mere purveyors of tablets and liquid medication. I quickly became aware that, although the lower right leg had been reattached, I still had to overcome the everpresent dangers of infection through the dirt and grit that still may have been present inside the leg. To give credit where it is due, the medical screws were excellent nurses, except on one occasion where they left the hydrogen peroxide on the wound until the following day without wiping it away with the saline solution. When they examined the wound the next day, it had burned and blistered some of the good flesh around the wound. I did not feel any discomfort because the nerve endings around that particular area had not recovered yet. I decided not to report this lapse in concentration by the medics, as quite clearly I was not in any position to complain and neither did I want to bite the hand that was helping me to get better.

Once the leg was reattached, I was never in doubt about its viability, although several screws were split on the decision about whether I would keep the leg or not. I recall two screws having a £5 bet on whether it would survive the trauma that it had suffered. It appeared that the powerful antibiotics I was taking were not winning the battle against the infection. The senior medical officer, Dr Chang, kept sending away samples of the infection for analysis to determine exactly which antibiotics would deal best with the problem, but with little joy. Dr Chang was so concerned by this medical problem that I recall that, late one Saturday evening, after collecting his parents from Heathrow Airport, he went to the local hospital to secure a special batch of powerful antibiotics on my behalf. He came into the prison late the same evening to start me on this new course of treatment. Thankfully, the new antibiotics were successful and we beat the infection.

As the leg began its painful process of healing, I was on my back in the hospital bed for the best part of three months. To search for an apt analogy, I would say that the pain was like a city of ants marching along the nerve endings on a 24-hour basis. I have suffered the agonising effects of pain before, but not at such an unremitting level, where it consumes one's consciousness by the minute. In comparison, the gasman who had been shot by Kendall was out of hospital the next day and was being proclaimed a hero by the media. Little did the media realise that it was the unnamed and unpublicised driver of the green Ford Granada estate vehicle who'd initially rammed us on the motorbike who should have been praised. For, if it had not been for him, we would not have been arrested at all.

Opposite my cell in the hospital wing was a minor IRA recruit called Donald Craig, who was suffering from deep and disturbing bouts of depression. Through adversity with a common enemy, we became friends and he was delegated the responsibility of cleaning my cell and emptying the contents of my bedpan. Interestingly, when Donald was arrested, he claimed that the Anti-Terrorist Squad took him to a remote hospital in West London and wired him up for electric shock treatment to combat his depression. He felt that this was like a torture mission through which they tried to extract confessions from him. I had no reason to disbelieve him as he did receive a five-year sentence for his crimes, and he was sent to Maidstone Prison, whereas under normal circumstances anybody associated with the IRA was given an indeterminate sentence of hopeless proportions and placed in top-security prisons.

After 20 weeks in the prison hospital, the novelty of catering for a physically injured prisoner began to wear off and, despite still being bedridden, the screws began to insist that I should have the subdued red light on all night long. It was hard enough to sleep with the combined effects of never-ending pain, bedsores and the psychotic screams and wails of the lunatics, without having a red light on all night as well.

The night it was first put on, I managed to smash it and was placed on Governor's Report. Due to my bedridden state, the adjudication was held in my cell and, despite powerful arguments, I was found guilty and given a caution. Similarly, the prison visits were equally punitive. I was only allowed one visit per month for 30 minutes at a time. Normally, if a semi-decent screw was on duty, I could expect 40 or 50 minutes, but, all in all, it was not entirely conducive to maintaining strong family bonds.

On a physical and psychological level, these were testing times for me, as not only had I to contend with the traumatic experience of having my leg lopped off and put back on, but I was also in a hostile and dehumanising prison with inadequate contact with my family and loved ones. This was further exacerbated by the forthcoming trial and sentence for the Kensal Rise robbery. When the grey clouds of depression and despondency used to appear over me, I used to think of our miracle baby daughter, Jade, and the love that I had for Tracey. I derived so much strength and inspiration from this source that I knew I could confront and overcome almost anything.

As a result of my extended stay at Wandsworth Prison hospital, and the fact that the external contraption – the metal rods – were still in my leg, which were causing me pain and discomfort, I decided to write a petition to the Home Office asking for a transfer to Parkhurst Prison hospital, where they had the facilities to remove the metal rods. Usually, the external metal frame would be removed after 12 weeks, but here I was in my twentieth week and still enduring pain. After submitting the petition, Dr Chang came into my cell and said that, if I withdrew the petition, he would ensure that I would be transferred to Parkhurst Prison hospital very shortly.

It did the trick as, several days later, in November 1986, I was transferred. Due to my poor condition, circumstances dictated that I had to be transferred in an ambulance with an armed police escort. During the short journey down the A3 to Portsmouth ferry, at different stages there were anything up to three to six police vehicles and motorcycle outriders. As the ambulance and accompanying entourage of police vehicles motored through Portsmouth, the traffic police manned every roundabout and crossroads until we reached the Isle of Wight ferry. Later that day, on the local Solent Radio Station, it was wrongly claimed that the notorious Middle-East terrorist Hindawi, who'd tried to put his pregnant Irish girlfriend on an aircraft with a bomb hidden in her luggage, had been taken to Albany Prison on the Isle of Wight.

The anticipated return to the ominous portals of Parkhurst Prison was tinged with an element of apprehension and concern because I was not returning to the main wings of the prison where the camaraderie of the Londoners was strong and convivial, but once through the prison gates I was escorted to the prison hospital, an innocuous-looking Victorian building which was, in fact, a prison within a prison. The prison hospital itself was not very large. It held about 50–60 prisoners, many of whom were mentally deranged or criminally insane and were kept locked in single cells. Others with physical problems or injuries were housed in a separate section of the building. The seemingly deranged or demented prisoners were held on the infamous F2 ground-floor landing, where up to four white-jacketed medical screws would unlock one prisoner at a time for meals and slop-out. The more manageable 'patients', as they were called, were located on the upper F3 landing. As for me, because of my Category 'A' top-security status, I was placed in a separate cell near the clinical ward, where patients were kept after an operation. All types of surgery were undertaken at Parkhurst Prison hospital, ranging from sinus problems, gallstones, ulcers, bone injuries and even male breast deformities.

Almost immediately on my arrival at the hospital, I could feel a palpable air of animosity towards me, as it was only two years earlier that I had escaped while being brought back to Parkhurst. The overall supremo at the hospital was Dr Cooper, along with his understudy, Dr Stuart. These professionals were supported by one of the last Prison Chief Officers in the Prison Service. No doubt he was at the fag end of his career and, once he retired, the Prison Governors could once again regain the power to run the jails from the POA. Whatever the case, the prison hospital was Dr Cooper's very own domain. All in all, the prison hospital, or 'Wendy House', was a perverse pit-stop for the detritus of humanity that had succumbed to the mental stresses and strains of modern-day criminality and drug abuse. Some of these pathetic characters were, of course, eminently salvageable, through powerful psychotropic drugs and medication, whereas some were, no doubt, consigned to the scrap-heap of long-term insanity and mental care.

At first, the novelty of living in close proximity to the criminally insane was both fascinating and intriguing. Little did I know, however, that, in spite of having a physical injury, I would spend a year of my life alongside these nutters and lunatics. Perhaps the most glaring observation that I made during this time was the way the prison medical screws interacted with their charges. It appeared that, through continuous daily contact with these pathetic, almost subhuman, beings, the white-coated screws had adopted and embraced an enforced culture of contempt and disdain towards their charges. It seemed to me that many of the medical screws could not differentiate between those with serious mental deficiencies and those who were seemingly 'normal' prisoners. Inevitably, this led to a culturally constructed attitude of contempt and indifference towards everyone. In the long term, this process was so subtle that many of the prison staff had not even realised what had happened or indeed what was happening. It someone, an independent observer such as myself to acknowledge and record its existence.

Admittedly, not every prisoner on F1 and F2 was completely crackers. Some were incarcerated there for entirely different reasons, such as the IRA top-security prisoner who had lost significant sections of his arms and legs when a bomb he was transporting accidentally exploded. This particular IRA individual was so committed to the cause that he wanted to be recognised as a political prisoner and steadfastly refused to wear prison-issue clothing. Therefore, contrary to prison rules, he would only wear a prison blanket. As a direct result of this person's strong political belief and commitment, he was kept in the Wendy House with the lunatics for the best part of his 20-year sentence. At one stage, he was banged up in a cell next-door to me on F3 and I used to hear him using the weight of the metal bed to work out every day. Whenever I was feeling a little down or sorry for myself, I used to think of the pain and anguish that this noble prisoner was going through and it soon put things in perspective for me.

When I first arrived at the prison hospital and I was on ' "A" man alley' as we called it, I became friendly with Vincent Hickey who was campaigning against his conviction for the Carl Bridgewater murder case. Vinny was suffering from a very painful bowel complaint and, being a sensible chap, he began to educate me about the case and the terrible ordeal of serving a life sentence as an innocent man. At one stage in the hospital, I recall that he went on a hunger-strike for 45 days in order to highlight his plight and compel the Court of Appeal to reopen the case. I remember feeling so helpless sitting in my cell while this fellow human being was starving himself to death only several feet away from me. In many respects, I felt deeply obliged to do something and join the hunger-strike in support of his protest. It appeared absurd that here was a man going to great lengths to prove his innocence while the prison authorities sat by and watched the gradual deterioration of the man. Vinny told me that he had been seen several times by senior prison psychiatrists in order to ascertain whether or not his protestations of innocence were, in fact, a delusion, an act of self-deception in order to cope with the sentence. Fortunately, history absolved the Carl Bridgewater Four some years later when it was established that they had indeed been the victims of a police miscarriage of justice.

Not surprisingly, I had my own problems and the most pressing one was getting the legendary leg repaired. Before being transferred to Parkhurst, I had been told about the wonderful orthopaedic consultant at the prison hospital. During the first operation, Dr

Debelda – a veteran surgeon who had allegedly operated on numerous knee injuries in Northern Ireland – removed the painful metal rods from my leg. Then I had to endure the discomfort of intensive physiotherapy from a partially blind practitioner who was employed by the prison. The problem was, though, that during the initial operation to save the leg, the surgeon had rotated the lower part of the limb at an angle with a view to fusing the knee joint for stability at a later stage. Therefore, because the knee joint was not aligned properly, it was never going to bend again without radical surgery. The knee joint did have some movement – five degrees – and, although this was better than nothing, it was of very little use in walking. On the other hand, the physiotherapist kept trying to free up what he perceived as calcified bone and tissue in the knee joint. This created and developed a serious infection in the knee tissue and I had to undergo another operation to scrape the wound and try to release the knee from the perceived bony blockage. Naturally, the manipulation of the knee joint while under anaesthetic was unsuccessful and I was told by Dr Debelda to accept the leg as it was and be grateful that it had been saved.

Hugely disappointed, I refused to accept this bitter blow that I would never bend my knee again and sought an independent orthopaedic opinion. We contacted a well-known orthopaedic consultant, Dr Fari of Harley Street, London, who travelled down to the Isle of Wight to examine the injury. Not surprisingly, Dr Fari's diagnosis echoed that of Dr Debelda, that I was to accept the leg as it was. Moreover, Dr Debelda added that because I was a relatively young man of 28 and 'an aggressive sportsman', he would not consider giving me an artificial knee joint either. I was so disappointed, as I had heard so much about injured soldiers in the armed forces who had been given top-quality artificial knee joints. Musing on my predicament and with no offence intended, I began to ask what value there was for the prison or medical authorities in fixing the mangled leg of a common prisoner, a third-class citizen, a potentially dangerous armed robber who was being increasingly perceived as 'a menace to society'?

I had read and heard so much about the pioneering break-

YOU BLOODY HERO!

Shot Barry pins down gun raider

By MOHAMMED ILYAS

HAVE-A-GO hero Barry Smith was shot twice by a bank robber yesterday—yet still grabbed the gunman and held on to him until police arrived.

Van driver Barry, 43, was blasted in the chest and groin after chasing two raiders.

But as blood poured from his wounds, he found the strength to force the gunman to the ground.

And he clung on for **FIVE MINUTES** while police raced to the scene.

As soon as they arrived Barry, a British Gas driving instructor based at Bromley-by-Bow East London, was taken to hospital for emergency surgery. He is expected to make a full recovery.

The drama began when the robbers—one brandishing a .22 handgun—hijacked a security guard in Willesden, North London.

Agony

They snatched cash bags and fled on a motorbike, but were chased by Barry's van and another car. The pursuit ended when the car rammed the bike.

As one lay writhing with a leg injury, Barry charged the gunman.

Eye-witness Mrs Erna Wright said: "The gas man shouted 'Call the police, call the police.'"

Scene of gunfire . . . where Barry's van screeched to a halt beside the bank raiders' rammed motorbike

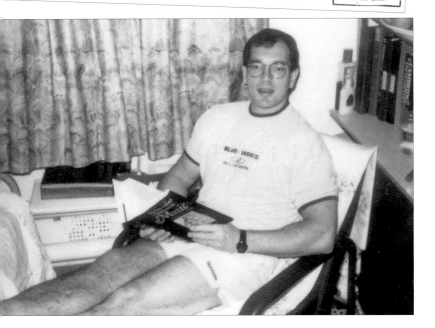

Top: The *Sun*'s take on the job that ended my lucky streak and nearly my life.

Bottom: On the inside again but supping at the font of knowledge. Studying in my cell at Long Lartin.

Top: Many thanks to Billy Bonds and Brian Storey of West Ham Utd for giving my sons an excellent match day in October 1990. West Ham routed Hull City 7-1.

Bottom: Fellow scholar and friend Andy Russell, who organised Kendall's dramatic escape from Gartree Prison in 1987.

My daughter Jade, Tracey and I pose for a rare photograph inside Long Lartin in 1992.

Top: Paul Gray, Joe Dupré, Peter Mitchell, Billy Adams, Charlie Tozer, me and Top Cat (Tony Colson) guzzling a post-meal bottle of prison hooch at Long Lartin in 1994.

Bottom: Perry Terroni, Kevin Brown and son on a joint prison visit in August 1993.

Top: Freedom at last! With my mother-in-law Iris Etherden, me, her husband Pat and Jade and Bradley.

Bottom: My wonderous Grandmother who played such an important part in my life. A truly remarkable woman.

Top: Gone but not forgotten. Darren Pearman in 1998 with his beautiful daughter Elle on holiday shortly before we lost him.

Bottom: Tracey and I soak up the sunshine in Tenerife in 2000.

From Padlock to Wedlock. My good friend Mark Blake's last day of bachelorhood in September 2002. *Inset*: His beautiful bride, Annette.

This Smith family on holiday and (*inset*), our newest addition, Sonny.

throughs in modern orthopaedic surgery, in particular regarding artificial replacement knee joints, that I thought it was only right and fair that I should reap the benefits of modern medical science, too. In fact, a close friend of ours, Gina Laveve, who had relatives in the USA, used to send me quarterly editions of a special medical magazine that focused solely on the knee joint and its manifold medical injuries and remedies. I still believe that, if I had been a member of the armed forces, the knee problem would have been resolved aeons ago. Someone out there could fix my knee, it was just a matter of finding that person, but first I had the huge problem of the forthcoming Kensal Rise robbery case.

As far as the case was concerned, it was a nightmare. We had been apprehended and arrested less than a quarter-of-a-mile away from the scene of the robbery with the money, motorbike, guns and so forth, but I still possessed a deep-down desire to fight the case. Sometimes, the case for the prosecution is so overwhelming that the police take it for granted that the defendants will plead guilty and they neglect to carry out the necessary evidential groundwork to secure the conviction. I had plenty of time to ruminate over the problem and, when I heard that my co-defendant was going guilty, I created a one-man defence to fight the case.

Basically, the defence was that three robbers set off on their motorbikes that morning to commit the robbery. On the way to the scene, my motorbike overheated and broke down. Subsequently, I caught a taxi to the scene and, as I updated my two accomplices about the broken-down motorbike, the security van pulled up at the bank. In a panic, they suggested that they commit the robbery on one motorbike and that I get out of the area as quickly as possible. I walked down a long road and, by the time I reached the scene of the crash, Kendall and his accomplice had committed the robbery. As they pulled up to talk to me, the Ford Granada estate came round the corner, lost control and smashed into the three of us. I received severe leg injuries in the crash. Kendall was badly shaken and disorientated by the crash and the third person who could be factually linked to the motorbike made good his escape.

Admittedly, this was a very tenuous defence, but it was feasible and one that I felt could work providing the jury was leaning towards the defendant. If we had been charged with conspiracy to rob, this defence would have been rendered useless, but seeing as we were charged with actual robbery and firearms offences, it was a 'goer'.

At the time, Kendall and I shared the same solicitor so I wrote out the defence in full detail and gave it to my brief. Kendall read it and changed his mind and then decided that he, too, wanted to fight the case, but he wanted to say that there were four of us, that the two real robbers ran off, leaving Kendall and me at the crash site. Moreover, my solicitor had acquired the services of a formidable legal team. I had Robin Simpson QC and Stephen Battern in my corner, while Kendall had Bill Denny QC and Stephen Solley representing him. Upon hearing this, Kendall decided that he wanted my QC, as he was the most sought-after defence counsel in the land. Not wishing to appear selfish, I concurred with Kendall's wishes and let him have Mr Simpson. Kendall was obviously not thinking straight because, if Simpson could win the case for me, it did not matter who had him in their corner, as he would by extension win it for both of us. This headstrong demand by Kendall revealed more about his selfish character and dearth of knowledge and intelligence than anything else. It was, in effect, an act of desperation: the ship was sinking and there was only one possible lifejacket and he wanted it at any cost. I should have seen the signs then.

During the spring of 1987, we both appeared at the Old Bailey for the commencement of the trial before His Honour Judge Mason QC. This was the first time I had seen Kendall since that terrible day in June nine months earlier. One of the things Kendall said to me was that he had been caught up in a terrible inner-conflict with himself over the way that he had let the gasman overpower him and arrest him. Kendall felt that he should have done more to escape from the scene. I did point out to allay these negative thoughts that he had shot the gasman three times and that should have ensured that he got away, but that he had selected the wrong calibre revolver. It was then that Kendall said that he wished that he had shot and killed the gasman and escaped. This emotional response was understandable, as any robber would have wanted to escape from the nightmare of being caught red-handed. Kendall was very surprised, however, when I said that I was glad that he hadn't killed the gasman. Kendall looked at me in amazement, as once again he had obviously not thought this one through, either. He was thinking of himself again and not the wider picture for, if Kendall had shot and killed the gasman, and escaped, leaving me totally incapacitated in the gutter, I would have been going up the steps at the Old Bailey to face a murder charge and would, most probably, be convicted through the legal concept of joint enterprise. I would have been given a mandatory sentence of life imprisonment with a recommendation to serve a minimum amount of years before consideration for release. I should have seen the signs!

After weighing up the pros and cons of our 'lambs to the slaughter' defence, I put a grave proposition to Kendall in the cells in the basement of the Old Bailey. Basically, I said to him that, if we continued with the defence that I'd created, which was only viable for one person, and we went upstairs and fought it, we would be like lemmings leaping off a cliff. I added that I was willing to put my hands up so that he could fight it solo or vice versa. Amazed, Kendall replied, 'Would ya be willing to do that?'

'Yes!' I said.

Once again, Kendall's reply spoke volumes, as he basically said, 'Bollocks ... I wouldn't do it for you!'

In my view, someone had to think rationally as this was not a game. Moreover, I still had seven years left to serve of my previous 15-year sentence, so whatever sentence I received it would overlap or run concurrent with the original sentence. Not surprisingly, Kendall's reply was, 'I want to fight it!'

Much to the astonishment of Kendall, we went upstairs and I pleaded guilty to all the counts and he pleaded not guilty. This meant another long adjournment for me which would not count towards my eventual sentence. Nonetheless, it was imperative that things were done right. I could not afford to do things any other way. I was taken back to Wandsworth Prison hospital and then back to Parkhurst Prison hospital a week later.

As the Category 'A' prison van pulled up to the main entrance to

Parkhurst Prison hospital, I was greeted by the Chief Prison Officer and several medical screws in the reception area. As I went to pick up my cardboard box with my personal possessions inside, a medical screw bent down and said, 'I'll carry that for you!' Immediately, I thought, Oh yeah? What's all this about ... room service? Then, as I walked through F2 landing to ' "A" man alley' where the top-security prisoners with physical ailments were housed, the screw said, 'You don't remember me, do you? I'm your uncle Tony's brother-in-law!'

Painful images of my brother Lenny chinning this screw and knocking him into the sandwich table at the wedding reception flashed through my mind and I sincerely replied, 'Listen, my name is Terry, not Lenny, and I am far more diplomatic than Lenny and I would like to apologise for my brother's stupid behaviour.'

The screw added, 'It doesn't matter, as I've reported our distant connection to the Prison Chief as I tried to get you transferred to another prison hospital, but this is the only top-security hospital in the south and you had to come here!'

I promptly added, 'Thanks very much.'

Obviously, the screw wanted to play it straight and had officially declared our distant relationship to the management. Although I could never blame my brother for chinning a screw, he had transformed a potential ally into a possible enemy out for vengeance, although this did not turn out to be the case. Thanks, bruv! As things turned out, because our distant relationship was out in the open and all the screws were aware of it, it made it increasingly difficult and embarrassing for the dog screws to dig me out and prevent me from enjoying simple privileges like an extra shower or hot water for a cup of tea.

A prime example of the underlying animosity and resentment towards peer-group prisoners like myself could be seen over the previous Christmas period of 1986 when all the London lads on the main wing of the jail had a whipround for me and contributed some canteen items, such as tea bags, milk, sugar, coffee, tins of salmon, tuna, peaches and pears. Reggie Kray and John Laveve sent the items over to me in a huge cardboard box and I must say it was one of the most poignant Christmas gifts that I have ever had. The cardboard box was absolutely overbrimming with goodies, much to the chagrin of the medical screws. At first they refused to accept the goodies, claiming that they were not allowed. But all the London lads on the main wing said that, if Terry Smith didn't get their Christmas gift, they'd refuse to go behind their cell doors at bang-up. The screws like nothing better than to clock off ten or fifteen minutes early, and now it looked like they would have to remain in the jail on standby possibly all night over an insensitive decision made in the prison hospital.

A compromise was soon reached. The official hierarchy of the hospital wing agreed to accept the goodies on condition that I left them with the orderly in the servery and the items would be given to me as I required them. The orderly, an ethnic guy, was well sweet as I had been giving him plenty of 'nightcaps' – prison terminology for a cannabis joint – to enable him to sleep more easily at night. Words cannot express the way I felt about this very generous gesture by all the Londoners on the main wing who knew me. It was a supreme act of friendship and loyalty at a time when I was being held in very hostile and intimidating environment. Thanks, lads!

As the weeks merged into months and Dr Debelda had stated that there was nothing that he could do for my leg injury, I was again placed on F3 landing with the lunatics. Inwardly, I was hoping that the Prison Governor would allocate me to the main wing with the other Londoners, but the slags had other plans for me. The Prison Service has a long memory, as it never forgets when a prisoner escapes or wins a court case against the prison system. Not knowing my fate, I found myself living alongside demented mass murderers, such as Childs, who along with Big H McKenna had killed several people in East London in the 1980s and burned their bodies in a council flat in Poplar. There were also mass poisoners like the infamous Graham Young and other deranged killers, such as the besotted train-spotter who had a perverse predilection for taking photographs of vulnerable and helpless young ladies dressed in black, standing on a chair with a noose around their neck. The only thing wrong with this weird fantasy was that he liked to kick the chair away from under their feet and watch them asphyxiate until their lives had been extinguished. These abnormal and deranged killers were my new neighbours.

I used to talk to some of the less serious nutters about their real or perceived problems. One quasi-sensible prisoner, who had been sent over from Albany Prison, claimed that he was being persecuted by the State and exhibited all the classic symptoms of paranoia. He claimed that he could hear screws creeping about at night in the loft above his cell. He claimed that the screws had made small holes in his ceiling and that they could look down at him at night. This sensible prisoner was deadly serious, so I said, 'Let's go to your cell and you can show me.' When we got to his cell, he pointed to the ceiling and said, 'Look there, there and there.' I looked up at the ceiling and there was absolutely nothing there! I turned to the demented nutcase and said, 'Yeah, you are right, it's a fucking liberty!' The geezer was stone raving bonkers, so I reasoned that it was better to agree with him than to upset his obvious delusions.

Perhaps the most vivid or exciting experience at the prison hospital occurred in the early hours of one morning when there was an almighty, violent thunderstorm with bolts of lightning flashing over the top of the jail. It was like a Hammer House of Horror film that not even Count Dracula or Frankenstein could have matched for excitement and suspense. As I lay on my bed in the dark cell and peered through the cell bars at the sky, I could see the grotesque, towering brick chimneys of the main wings looming menacingly over me with their lightning conductors reaching up like outstretched hands into the blackness. As the lightning flashed and the thunderclaps reverberated around the jail, it resembled the living embodiment of Hades. Almost immediately, all the lunatics in the prison hospital stirred like a sleeping monster and began to howl and cry like wounded wolves. It was as though they all had some long-lost affinity with the bottomless depths of Mother Nature. Like a magnet, we were drawn to the dancing drama of the night and its elements venting its wicked will. Even the screws, who were always in control of their medicated charges, were at a loss as to how to cope with the maniacal mayhem and chaos of the lunatics howling and banging on their cell doors. One demented demon got so carried away that four burly screws rushed him in his cell and swagged him down to the dreaded 'back rooms', where your only friends were isolation and silence. A place where rampant introspection forced one to believe that everyone is the enemy. A place where the prison authorities have constructed a white-coated dam to stop you reaching out to all those who love you and where you are divested of all dignity but where the powerful rock of pride prevents the abandonment of hope and survival.

The raging storm was, without doubt, the best party I have ever been to, where everyone was intoxicated on the rapturous atmosphere of nature alone. It may well be that, given the humdrum routine of our daily existence in the prison hospital, we magnified this quirk of nature out of all proportion, or that we began to appreciate what others on the outside took for granted. Either way, on that memorable night I sensed a tangible association between the thunderstorm and insanity in human nature. Who knows, it may have even touched me!

On another noteworthy occasion, it was about 9.00pm and the hospital was settling down for the night, so I decided to roll myself a big fat joint and read my latest novel. Just as I finished the joint, the medical flap on the cell door opened and a screw from the main wing who remembered me prior to the escape in 1984 started to speak to me. After the usual small-talk and pleasantries, the screw suddenly said, 'By the way, I phoned you up when you was out.'

'Pardon,' I replied, 'you phoned me up?'

'No,' said the screw, 'I phoned the *Crimewatch* programme up about you, as there was some well-dressed, studious-looking robber going around London robbing building societies on his own. He looked a bit like you as he also wore glasses like you, so I phoned them up.'

Amazed, I replied, 'Thank you very much, you are a nice fellow.'

He then added, 'No, they phoned me back and said it couldn't have been you as some of the robberies had occurred before you'd escaped!'

I had heard about this very efficient and effective robber who preferred to work alone. Rumour had it that he was never caught or prosecuted. Rumour also had it that he was driving through central London on his motorbike when he was involved in a fatal accident with police vehicles that were escorting a royal party to their destination.

After the charming screw had closed the medical flap and departed, I settled down to read my novel when the flap opened again and there stood in front of me a gross, fat dog of a screw we called Piggy. He took a couple of sniffs with his protruding, porcine snout and demanded, 'Is there anything burning in here?'

'No,' I replied politely.

'Are you sure, Smith?' he said.

I then lost my temper and stormed, 'Look here, I am sitting here reading my book minding my own business and you have come to my cell to antagonise me, now fuck off out of here!'

His piggy face went dark crimson and he sputtered like an irate parent chastising a mischievous child. 'Right!' he boomed. 'There will be no TV for you this week and you will be seeing Dr Cooper tomorrow!'

I added, 'Go on, fuck off, you fat cunt!'

The very next morning, the screws refused to let me out of my cell to do the routine ablutions. This was a clever ploy by the screws so that, by the time Dr Cooper had done his daily rounds, he was confronted by a dishevelled and unshaven prisoner. The inference was that a potentially violent Category 'A' prisoner, who has smoked cannabis, has become extremely violent and abusive. Action? No association, isolation and the screws go away and snigger to themselves in the Officers' Mess, another successful stitch-up.

Realising the ploy, I remembered that I had enough hot water in my flask and water jug to have a wash and shave. Quickly, I spruced myself up and waited for Dr Cooper to do his tour of the estate. As it was, Dr Cooper missed his rounds that day and I never heard any more about it until six years later, when a new prison rule was introduced whereby all prisoners were allowed on request to view their prison medical file. This was done in the presence of a medical prison officer who was allowed to sit next to you while you read it. I did this, expecting the file to be heavily edited or censored before I read it.

When I did get to view it, it proclaimed in bright red ink, 'There is some evidence to suggest that this prisoner smokes cannabis as he became extremely violent towards a member of staff during a routine check!' What a load of bollocks. Here we have a classic example of a basic prison medical screw who has transformed into a behavioural psychologist and who is able to establish a strong correlation between the use of cannabis and violence. The facts were that Piggy came to my cell and provoked me into an aggressive reaction. He then concluded that there was some evidence – a sniff with his truffle-seeking snout proved that I was a cannabis user and abuser.

Seeing as I was no longer under the auspices of the orthopaedic consultant Dr Debelda, I wanted to get out of the oppressive and dehumanising regime of the prison hospital, so I started to give some of the lunatics the occasional joint or two. They all loved it and preferred it to the official medication from the doctors. Obviously, this annoyed the doctors and, one day on his daily rounds, the cell door swung open and there stood Dr Stuart and his white-coated assistants. He sternly proclaimed, 'If you carry on interfering with the patients' medication, you will be going to the back rooms!'

As he slammed the cell door, my only reply was, 'What am I doing in your hospital anyway? I shouldn't be here!'

At that particular time I had been housed in the Wendy House for nearly a year and it was an inappropriate allocation for someone of my status and condition. In many respects, it was extra-judicial punishment as I was being persecuted and penalised for the prison van escape several years earlier and I knew that I was right.

One day I remember while I was at the hospital, Dr Cooper came into my cell and sat on my bed with his praetorian guard outside – he had a habit of doing this. He said that he was carrying out a criminological survey and he wanted to know if he could take a scan of my brain for his survey. Politely, I refused his offer, unlike many others who thought that, if you refused, it would compromise access to evening association outside the cell. I did expect to be penalised somehow for refusing to take part in his experiment but, in all fairness, I was not.

It must be said, Dr Cooper was like his chosen profession – quite an enigma. According to prison folklore, Dr Cooper was a man of considerable power and influence and was feared by many hardened criminals.

During mid-September of 1987 the trial of Kendall began for the Kensal Rise robbery at the Old Bailey. Whatever the outcome, I was to be sentenced at the conclusion of the trial. I would not be human if I was to say that I was a little apprehensive about the eventual outcome. I don't know whether it was to scare me or to make things seem much worse than they really were, but there were mutterings in the bushes that the judiciary were thinking about giving me a sentence of life imprisonment due the repeat offence of armed robbery while unlawfully at large from prison custody. Basically, I knew that I was in line to receive a very long custodial sentence, but I was hoping that it would be somewhere below the 20-year mark.

On Tuesday, 29 September 1987, I was summoned to the Old Bailey for sentencing. Upon reaching the court and being escorted to the cells, for some inexplicable reason, the screws at the court would not put me in the same cell as Kendall as they had done before. As a result, we both started making a commotion and the screws finally gave in and put us together. It was then that I was told the reason why.

Part of Kendall's defence was that the third person in the case, the one who ran away from the scene of the crash, was my brother Lenny. Kendall claimed in court that he was now being called 'a grass' by East End villains and that some villains had even smashed down his front door at his wife's address and squirted ammonia all over the hallway. As a result of this, the court screws would not put me in the cells with Kendall until it was considered safe to do so. I did not mind that Kendall was using this scam, but he should have at least told me about it so that I could have been prepared for it. Again, I should have seen the signs.

More significantly, Kendall added that the police were claiming that someone had attempted to nobble the jury and the judge wanted to know whether or not Kendall wanted to proceed with the same jury or seek a retrial. Kendall asked for my opinion. First, I said that I thought that he had not done me any favours as I was due to go up for sentencing today and, if the judge was in a foul mood, then it was possible that he would take it out on me. I could not hold it against Kendall for trying to nobble the jury, if indeed he had, but once again there was only one lifejacket and he wanted it at all costs. I should have seen the signs! My advice to Kendall, as always, came straight from the hip. I said that it would be suicidal if he continued with the jury, as it was obvious that the other jurors were aware of the situation and it may be held against him. Although this would mean another lengthy adjournment for me, I advised him to dismiss the jury and start afresh. This he did, and the case was adjourned pending a new trial date.

After a brief consultation with my legal team, William Denny QC reassured me that the jury-nobbling accusation would not affect me as I had pleaded guilty six months earlier and that this in no way could be held against me. Additionally, despite Kendall's adjournment, His Honour Judge Lymbery QC was not prepared to postpone sentence on me any longer as I had waited some 15 months since the initial arrest. My counsel was particularly impressed with a Social Enquiry Report that had been compiled by my Probation Officer Mr Nick Paul. I have always got on well with Nick and when he came to Wandsworth Prison in order to speak to me about the Report, I inadvertently offended him by claiming it did not matter what type of report was written about me as I was going to be sentenced to umpteen years' imprisonment anyway. How wrong could I have been? William Denny QC argued that I deserved some credit for pleading guilty, that some consideration had to be given to the irreversible leg injuries that I had sustained and, particularly, that the glowing Social Enquiry Report should be taken into account.

In sentencing, His Honour Judge Lymbery stated, 'This was no amateur expedition. Two of you were involved, it was pre-meditated and carefully planned … but you were certainly caught red-handed … So far as the other indictment is concerned, which was a carefully planned escape, maybe you took advantage of what was happening rather than enter yourself into any serious planning, but it was a carefully planned escape on the part of somebody, and off you went.'

On the positive side, the judge proclaimed, 'There is a lot of good to be said for you, strangely enough. People may think of a bank robber as simply being a bank robber and nothing else, but there is a lot which has been said of you which is on the credit side. It is hoped that, in due course, when you eventually obtain your liberty, you will allow that aspect to take over and indeed get into practice for that now and see that you do not land yourself into this trouble again, but that time must be far off … and I think that the appropriate term in all circumstances for the robbery is one of 14 years' imprisonment … and for the escape, a sentence of two years to run consecutively, making 16 years in all, but concurrent to your existing term.'

On hearing the sentence, I looked up at my loyal and devoted wife Tracey and relatives in the gallery and smiled. Outside the courtroom, I jumped about with delight at what appeared to be a fair sentence. On reaching the cells, Kendall saw that I was smiling and asked what I had received. I said 16 years concurrent, which basically meant that I had to start the sentence afresh from that very day. Kendall was crestfallen. He said, 'How can you be so happy with a sentence like that?' Indeed, he had a valid point as the climate of sentencing, more specifically for armed professional robbers, had gone through the roof and we had been judicially conditioned to expect such severe and swingeing sentences. Prematurely, I suppose, I was happy to receive a determinate sentence, a sentence with a fixed discharge date that would enable me to work towards getting home again to my loyal and loving family.

After the sentencing, I was allowed a brief visit through a glass partition with Tracey, who said that she could not hear exactly what the judge had said and it was only when she saw me smiling that she realised that it was not an outrageously long prison sentence.

All things considered, the prison sentence meant that I had already served three-and-a-half years out of the original 15-year sentence, which was now to run concurrently with the 16-year sentence. I had still to serve with remission, ten years and eight months out of the fresh 16-year sentence. All in all, taking the sentence in total, I had to serve 14 years and 2 months, which in prison parlance was equivalent to a 20-stretch.

More importantly, it meant that Tracey and I had got what we had wanted, a future together. We were still only in our late twenties and, all being well, I could be home by my late thirties. By then, hopefully, it was possible to carve a tunnel of hope through the dark mountain of disappointment together, when I would finally be able to put this nightmare behind me.

14

Knuckling Down at Frankland

As expected, there was a radical change of plan and I was not going back to the island with the Category 'A' escort that had brought me to court. I was going to Wormwood Scrubs which, at first, seemed slightly odd to me. One of the first things that I had learnt from veteran, long-term prisoners was never to trust the Home Office as there is no rhyme or reason to their decision-making. The faceless apparatchiks at Queen Anne's Gate behaved with all the unpredictability, ruthlessness and cunning of a Third World dictatorship. The Home Office had experienced over a century of man-management, so I am sure that they knew exactly what they were going to do with me.

As we drove along the West Way viaduct towards Acton in a large armoured prison truck with the obligatory police escort, I looked out of the small TV-screen-type window in my cubicle and I was immediately overcome by a strong sense of disorientation and nausea. I knew that it was not the side-effects of the sentence that I had just received, as, rightly or wrongly, I perceived it as a result. It was motion sickness due to looking out of the prison van window. Somehow, I had to overcome it. I had to focus on an object in front of the moving vehicle and follow it until it left my field of vision and then repeat the process all over again. It was a terrible sensation and, if the journey had been longer than the five miles from the Old Bailey to the Scrubs, I would have been violently sick. Alas, this did happen to Johnny Massey, who unfortunately had to endure the 350-mile trek from London to Durham in the same truck. He declared, 'They will never get me in that truck again!' And he meant it 100 per cent.

As I entered the reception area at Wormwood Scrubs to be processed and allocated to a cell in its voluminous wings, I realised that I had been through the reception palaver at the Scrubs numerous times before. Name, number, sentence, strip off, put on the ill-fitting prison clothing, see the prison quack, collect your bed kit and trundle off to a human kennel. On this occasion, though, I had a heated argument with the prison doctor as I refused to wear prison-issue shoes because of my leg impediment. I pointed out that I could not wear the shoes and that I wanted my trainers. The screws tried the old trick of 'just wear the prison shoes for now and you can see the prison doctor in the morning'. By then, it would be too late. Once I had the shoes on, they would renege on the promise. I decided to make a stand or else the battle, however trivial to them, would be lost. I refused to wear the prison shoes and walked bare-foot, carrying my personal property and prison kit all the way to 'A' Wing. As far as I can recall, it had been a very long day and I crashed out almost immediately.

In the morning, the cell door opened and a familiar face entered the cell, a fellow escapee, Mickey Turner of South London. Mickey was serving 12 years for armed robbery when he received permission to marry his childhood sweetheart from the Governor at Wandsworth Prison. As he was being escorted to the front doors of Wandsworth Register Office, several armed masked men leapt from a stolen British Telecom van and snatched him from the prison guards. Mickey was only at large for about six weeks, when he and a passenger were stopped by the police on a motorcycle. A struggle ensued and a policeman was shot in the arm. Mickey and his co-defendant John 'Noodles' Newman were now waiting to face serious attempted murder charges.

As I was chatting to Mickey, I was called away to see the Prison Chaplain and doctor. At this time, I did not have any strong religious beliefs and considered myself to be an atheist. On the other hand, I have always believed in a superior form of intelligence over and above that of human existence. But the God thing was too shallow for my liking. If there was a God, or superior being, he or she was not necessarily of the Christian variety, but some marvellous divine entity yet to be exposed or revealed.

After another short chat with Mickey, I was informed that I was on my way out of the jail to an undisclosed destination. As any Category 'A' prisoner will tell you, it is wise never to ask the screws where you are going as they will not tell you, and the last thing one wants to do is to give the screws the perverse privilege of refusing to answer your legitimate requests. It is a bit like a game. First, you tune into the screws' accents, vernacular or quirky sayings; then you read one of the screws' newspapers to see where it was printed or the identity of the local TV channel; then you work out what direction the prison van is taking. After some evaluation of these factors, it should be quite clear what piss-hole prison you are going to.

Almost immediately, the gruff Geordie dialect of the screws forewarned me that I was heading north. The only top-security dispersal prison in the North was the recently built Frankland Prison on the outskirts of Durham. Naturally, I was concerned about the jail that I was going to as my family had to visit me, and it is always healthy to be amongst your own social group, the Londoners in my case, as the chances are the passage of time will pass much more comfortably. Moreover, if there was any serious aggravation with the screws, nonces or rivals, the Londoners normally closed ranks and stuck together.

As we powered our way up the motorway to Geordie-land, I sensed that this was the beginning of a new chapter in my life. I had discussed the issue of escape with Tracey and we both decided that, if I received a fair prison sentence, I would knuckle down and see it through, as a life on the run was not favourable to leading a 'normal' family life. We had been through all that before and milked it for what it was worth. For instance, if I had been arrested after only a short period at large, the punitive aspects would have outweighed the advantages but, as things stood, the prison authorities may have had me back inside but they could not seize the proceeds, the miraculous gift of our beautiful baby daughter Jade. Therefore, the psychological conflict of serving a prison sentence or escaping had now evaporated. We had been there and done it with an element of success and it was now time to move forward.

More importantly, there was a new challenge in my life and that was to work my body and achieve a decent level of physical fitness in order to stabilise the leg injury. For the last 18 months, I had been imprisoned in the stagnant world of prison hospitals where there had been very little purposeful exercise.

On my arrival at Frankland Prison, I was placed on an induction wing and told that I was no longer an 'Escape Risk' prisoner as the high-security conditions at Frankland had made the category unnecessary. Instead, I was to be classified as a 'double "A"' prisoner. Basically, all prisoners held inside British prisons are assigned an alphabetical security classification of 'A', 'B', 'C' or 'D', the highest security status being Category 'A' and the lowest being 'D'. More interestingly, the Category 'A' classification is subdivided into three separate and distinct subgroups, such as Standard Category 'A' or single 'A'; High-Risk Category 'A' or double 'AA'; or Exceptional Risk Category 'A' or triple 'AAA'. Standard Category 'A' refers to the fact that, should the prisoner escape, he or she would be considered to be a danger to the police and public. High-Risk Category 'A' refers to prisoners who are considered to be more dangerous, as they are part of an organised gang and could possibly mount an escape with outside help. And finally, Exceptional Risk Category 'A' refers to prisoners who are highly dangerous and motivated individuals and who are part of highly organised gangs and terrorist groups which have access to large financial resources and, as a consequence, these prisoners are usually housed in Special Secure Units (SSUs) or special prisons within top-security prisons.

One of the many shortcomings of being a Category 'A' prisoner is that all visitors have to be vetted by the police before they are allowed to visit. In addition, High-Risk Category 'A' prisoners, such as myself, have to have two screws within earshot of the visitor's conversation. In some jails, this restrictive and oppressive prison rule is enforced to the hilt, such as those that I experienced in Wandsworth and Albany Prisons. But in some jails, such as Frankland, the screws would exercise a little discretion and not sit right at the visit table but a reasonable distance away.

After a week on the induction wing, I was placed on 'C' Wing within the main block of four identical, two-storey, square-shaped wings. The screws detested the angular design of the main wings as they could not see around the corners and therefore they had to man every landing most of the time. When I reached Frankland Prison in late September 1987, it held approximately 450 long-term prisoners, but there were only five Londoners there. These were big Billy Adams, Jeff Petherick, Brian Thoroughgood, Terry Bradford and Daniel Reece, aka Danny Woods from Custom House, who had turned supergrass in the late 1970s. To compensate for the lamentable dearth of Cockney prisoners, there were a healthy contingent of IRA prisoners, such as the very talented scratch board artist Paul Holmes and Brendan O'Dowd.

Among the other sensible lads on 'C' Wing were Rab Caruthers and Frank Wilkinson, a genial Northerner. Because Frankland was a relatively new prison, it was inevitable that there would be some teething problems, such as the usual tug-of-war between the screws and prisoners over restrictive rules and regulations and promised privileges. It seems that the original five Cockneys were the start of a new policy by the Home Office to allocate London-based villains to Frankland. Over the next six months, hordes of Cockneys began to arrive at the jail. Among them were Johnny Read, Johnny Massey, Kenny Noye, John Newnman, Ronnie Pewter, Johnny Dunford, David Judd, David Croke, Ronnie Easterbrook, Paul Cleland and Peter Welch.

In many respects, we all had a lot in common as we were all serving excessively long prison sentences and our visitors had to endure the monotonous four-hour train journey from King's Cross, London. Access to economic means alone could not in itself guarantee a visit. The close family and friends who made the energy-sapping journey week in, week out did it out of sheer love, loyalty and respect for their loved ones. Money alone could not buy this type of dedication and commitment. Visitors had to rise at 6.00am, and many, like Tracey, had to wash, dress and feed young children before setting off for King's Cross to catch the 9.00am Inter-City train to Durham. I have often said that there should be a 'Prison Visitor of the Year Award' for visitors who endure incredible emotional, economic and psychological hardship and yet love their husbands, boyfriends and relations so much that they secretly suffer in silence the travails of visiting remote and hostile prisons the length and breadth the land.

One of the most rigid prison rules at Frankland was that everyone had to work or partake in some form of labour. Work usually consisted of menial labour in the prison workshops, such as the laundry, upholstery or wood mill workshops. In order to work in these workshops, all prisoners had to wear prison-issue protective footwear for health and safety reasons. Because I had a leg and foot deformity, I was exempt from wearing these big crusty boots and I asked for a cleaner's job on the wing. But, because Frankland had another policy that prevented Category 'A' prisoners from working on the wings for security reasons, it left one remaining option, my old friend the Education Block. After being granted access there, the screws managed to get me off the wing and I got to do something creative.

As you may be aware, I have always had an appetite for education and it seemed so natural to be steered towards learning. I felt that I needed to educate myself to broaden my horizons, as the noble art of robbery was no longer going to be my career choice. I wanted to embark upon a long and enjoyable journey of self-development and self-fulfilment, and the only possible road leading to this ambitious goal was through education.

Just as I was settling down at Frankland, completely out of the blue an amazing event occurred. After being at the jail for about ten weeks, on 10 December 1987 I was unlocked for evening association. I was watching the evening news on TV when I heard that there had been a helicopter escape from a top-security prison in Leicestershire. The only prison I knew in Leicestershire was HM

Prison Gartree, where my co-defendant was being held. As I watched the national news programme, they showed CCTV video footage of two prisoners escaping from the sports field in a hijacked helicopter. They named the two escaping prisoners as John Kendall, awaiting trial for serious robbery and firearm offences, and Sidney Draper, serving a life sentence for murder. I couldn't believe it – Kendall had done it again! Outwardly, I was ecstatic, sharing the dramatic news with a few close friends and acquaintances, but inwardly, I was concerned for Kendall as, knowing the intense media coverage we had during the prison van escape, this was going to be a lot heavier. I was hoping that he had organised the use of a safe house and that he had a strong network of loyal friends around him as he was definitely in for a bumpy ride. Too many desperate prisoners had carried out amazing feats of improvisation and invention in order to escape, only to be badly let down by no real back-up once they were over the wall. Surely Kendall had done his homework.

Not surprisingly, the voracious and sensationalist tabloid media were quick to report on the first airborne escape in British penal history. Once again, Kendall and his partner were portrayed as Britain's most dangerous and wanted villains. Evidently, the helicopter had been hijacked by a lone gunman who then produced a shotgun while en route to a golf course in Leicestershire. The gunman had carried out a trial run some weeks earlier and decided to go for it. On this occasion, however, the gunman ordered the helicopter pilot to land on the sports field at Gartree Prison and take off again and fly to a nearby get-away vehicle. But due to thick fog, which made flying conditions perilous, the pilot and his three passengers had to put down before getting to the pre-planned rendezvous. The gunman and the two escaped prisoners then hijacked an elderly motorist and headed towards Sheffield and made good their escape.

As for me, within 24 hours of the escape, I was removed from normal prison accommodation and placed in the prison's Segregation Unit. When I complained about this arbitrary and extra-judicial punishment, stating, 'If someone breaks a prison rule in Gartree Prison, it is wholly unfair and unreasonable to penalise an innocent party in a jail some 250 miles away!' The Prison Governor, Mr Papps, did visit me in the Segregation Unit and said he was 'removing me from normal location for the security of the prison'.

After several days of complaining about this treatment, the Governor said that he would send the Principal Officer of Security to see me to explain the reasons for the lengthy segregation. When the Security PO did come and visit me, he said that the police had told him that, when the prisoners hijacked the elderly man in his vehicle, he had overheard the escaped prisoners claiming that they were coming to Frankland Prison to bust me out. I was therefore to remain in the Segregation Unit until they felt that it was safe to let me back in the main prison.

On a personal level, I viewed this as bewildering, because, if this was so, in order to safeguard his own arse, the Governor would have upgraded my security classification to Exceptional Risk status, or triple 'AAA', and I would have been lodged in a Special Secure Unit somewhere else in the country. In the interim at Frankland, all Category 'A' prisoners were refused their daily exercise period with other prisoners until the Works Department of the Prison had erected anti-helicopter wires across all open spaces within the jail.

When the facts about the planning and organisation of the helicopter escape were reported by the media, it was stated that it cost a mere £700 to hire the helicopter and some IRA prisoners at the jail felt aggrieved that no one in their organisation had thought of the idea first. One rogue Loyalist prisoner even went so far as to proclaim that, if a helicopter landed in the sports field at Frankland, no one would stop him from jumping on it. The sad fact was that many long-term prisoners, albeit members of well-organised criminal networks or terrorist groups, were, to some extent, expendable. The main ingredient required to help someone escape from prison was a bone-deep loyalty and friendship to that person, not the professional detachment of a large organisation that could replace their recruits at will.

I recall that after I had escaped from the prison van in 1984, a message filtered through to me from a respected villain in Wandsworth Prison who was willing to part with up to £100,000 to help him escape from a prison van taking him to the island. As much as I would have loved breaking someone out of prison custody, I would not do it for money. It would have to be because I cared for the person and, in that case, I would do it for free.

One of the humorous aspects of the helicopter break-out was that the Prison Service had anticipated such an escape and, in the event of one occurring, Gartree Prison had to phone the local RAF base and use the codename 'Rogue Elephant' to scramble aircraft to the scene. When the prison did contact the airbase, however, the air controllers at the other end were unaware of the codename or what it meant. More alarmingly, it came out later during the trial that a handwritten note had been put inside the prison mail box the night before the pre-planned escape by a prison snitch that there was going to be a helicopter escape at the jail the following day. The security prison officer who read the note discounted it as nonsense and threw it in the rubbish bin. After the escape had taken place, the embarrassed screw made a frantic scramble to retrieve the note. By the time of the trial, the snitch had been released and moved outside London.

As the festive and New Year period of 1987 approached, all aspects of the news-reporting media kept the helicopter escape high on the agenda. The obligatory *Crimewatch* programme covered the story and plastered mugshots of Kendall and Draper all over the national TV screens. I was hoping that they were keeping a very low profile, as there is nothing worse for a prisoner's morale than to see the police and Prison Service resolve an incident after such a resounding embarrassment.

Unfortunately, listening to a news bulletin on my radio late one night barely four weeks after the helicopter escape, I heard that Kendall had been arrested in an armed operation in the King's Road in Chelsea, London. As the news filtered through about Kendall's arrest, it transpired that he had broken several cardinal rules as a fugitive. First, the term 'low profile' should have become his guiding principle and he should have buried himself in a safe house until the media coverage had died down. Second, he should not have seen his wife who, no doubt, had been placed under 24-hour police surveillance. Third, the person who'd helped him escape from prison should have stayed well away from him; and fourth, the idea of committing further crimes so shortly after the escape should have been put on the back burner for at least several months.

When armed police raided Kendall's Chelsea address, they arrested both Mr and Mrs Kendall and the very game and audacious gunman who'd hijacked the helicopter, Andy Russell. More damaging were the two handguns that were found at the address which could be forensically linked to a recent armed robbery on a Brinks Mat security van at Archway in North London, in which one of the robbers had shot a security guard in the abdomen and escaped with £25,000. If the diagnosis was sore, the prognosis was bleak. Almost every golden rule that we had adhered to when we escaped from the prison van had been broken and, in effect, Kendall had made it far too easy for the police to do their work. If there was one consolation, at least the other escaped prisoner, Sidney Draper, did all the right things by staying low and remained at large for over two years.

As for Kendall, if only he had listened to the old maxim – 'When you are in a hole, stop digging!' On 29 July 1988, at the Central Criminal Court, Kendall faced four counts of robbery, robbery with a firearm, using a firearm to resist arrest on the gasman and escape from lawful custody – the prison van escape. During the sentencing procedure, His Honour Judge Lymbery QC stated, 'Currency is being given to the notion that, if armed robbers are in danger of apprehension, they have little to lose if they show violence and resistance against lawful arrest. Those who hold that view must be disabused and members of the public and, indeed, the police must be protected from such activity ... I am left with the realisation that you are a resourceful and determined man for which you may have admiration, but you are at the same time a dangerous man which cannot be a source of admiration.'

Kendall was then sentenced to a period of 21 years' imprisonment.

Then on 19 June 1989 at Leicester Crown Court, Kendall faced a total of nine counts relating to the helicopter escape at HMP Gartree and the hijack and kidnap of the elderly man in his car. He was further sentenced to seven years' imprisonment to run consecutively to the 21 years imposed earlier, making a total of 28 years' imprisonment.

If that was not bad enough, on 1 June 1990 at Leicester Crown Court, Kendall faced another four counts relating to the Archway robbery which included robbery, carrying a firearm with intent, wounding with intent and possession of a firearm without a certificate. He pleaded guilty and was further sentenced to another seven years to run consecutively to the earlier 28 years imposed. This made a grand total of 35 years' imprisonment.

Taken all together, Kendall did face some serious charges and, as most law-abiding people would concur, after pleading guilty to all the charges it indeed merited a long custodial sentence. But to sentence any person to such a soul-destroying and unconscionable prison sentence when Kendall had not murdered anyone was madness. Some critics later asserted that Kendall's excessive sentence was political in that the highly publicised helicopter escape had far-reaching effects in the corridors of power and influence at the Home Office. Others could claim that the long and ludicrous sentence was a deliberate act of deterrence, a warning to other committed career criminals that beyond the road of short-term gratification lies a super-highway of retribution, suffering and pain. Either way, the Court of Appeal acknowledged that the judiciary had got it wrong and it cut Kendall's sentence by six years to 29 years' imprisonment. This would mean that Kendall would have to serve 19 years and 4 months before he would be released.

As for the bold and audacious Andy Russell, he initially met Kendall in Wormwood Scrubs while Kendall was awaiting trial for the Kensal Rise robbery. Apparently, their friendship was forged through adversity when Russell was in the Segregation Unit and Kendall was walking around an adjacent exercise yard. Evidently, Russell was talking to Kendall through his cell window when an overzealous screw pressed the alarm bell and called the cavalry to intervene. Thereafter, an incident occurred that resulted in Kendall joining Russell in the Segregation Block. A strong bond of friendship was formed. An escape plan was formulated and put into action once Russell was released several weeks later.

As a direct result of the helicopter escape at HMP Gartree, Andy Russell was convicted and sentenced to ten years' imprisonment. Also, after a trial for the Archway robbery, for which Russell was found guilty, he received a further ten years' imprisonment to run consecutive to the original ten, making a total of 20 years' imprisonment in which was not reduced on appeal. The argument goes that, if Kendall had helped Russell with the Archway robbery case and had taken full responsibility for the handguns found inside the flat at Chelsea, Russell may have been acquitted, but as usual he did not and Russell was convicted … I should have seen the signs!

One of the most remarkable aspects of Frankland Prison in 1988 was that it contained a cornucopia of diverse and distinct characters from a rainbow of cultures, creeds and social backgrounds. There were the Geordies, Scots, Irish, Scousers, Mancunians, West Indians, Arabs and, of course, the ubiquitous Cockneys, all piled together in one long-term tinderbox. When I initially arrived at the prison, I had to ask people to repeat themselves due to the wide-ranging styles of speech and dialects. At first, I found the Northerners – those from Newcastle, Middlesbrough and Sunderland – gruff and uncouth, but after living with them for nearly two years I found that they had many endearing qualities, one of which was their healthy disdain for authority. Not only was it customary to detest and fight the police, screws and officialdom, it was their *raison d'être*.

The native Geordies, combined with the defiant Scousers, Mancunians and all the other distinct cultural groups, made Frankland a powder keg of rage and resentment waiting to explode. It was not long before the screws went too far. Every Governor grade and prison officer with a modicum of common sense knows that a prisoner's visits are deemed sacrosanct and that a great deal of care and consideration should be exercised when dealing with complaints and grievances in this area. On one particular occasion, the screws decided to strip-search prisoners' visitors before the visits in order to search for drugs, and once this filtered back to the main wings the touch paper was lit and hordes of prisoners decided to take some action. At least 30 prisoners decided to stage a rooftop protest over the treatment of the prisoners' visitors, some of whom had travelled hundreds of miles to visit their loved ones.

What exacerbated the problem was that there was no constructive dialogue between the prisoners and the Prison Governor, Mr Papps, and he was dismissive of the prisoners' grievances. The rooftop protest lasted for several days, during which the prison underwent a 'lock-down', and we would pass clothing, blankets and food up to the protesters. After a day or two of the protesters singing football songs from the roof, the Governor and Board of Visitors were willing to listen to the prisoners' grievances and they nominated me as their spokesman. But, shortly before I was to speak to the BoV, a bunch of screws in full riot gear came to my cell and carted me off to the Segregation Block. Then the BoV claimed that they were not allowed to negotiate with prisoners held in the punishment block.

At the least, I thought that the screws would regard to me as an *eminence grise*, someone instigating and controlling events from behind the scenes, and ship me out to another long-term jail nearer luscious London. But no, the bastards moved the rooftop protesters and put me back on normal location. The rooftop protest was not all in vain, however, as the very insensitive and clumsy approach towards the visitors eased off and, some years later, I heard on the radio that civil action regarding the illegal strip-searches of visitors had resulted in a £10,000 compensatory pay-out for some visitors caught up in the incident. This pleased me immensely as prisons are not the most hospitable places to visit at the best of times, and many new and vulnerable prison visitors, often women, are not aware of the law and their basic rights when visiting these frequently hostile and stressful institutions. To some degree, the victory in the civil court vindicated the actions of those who took part in the rooftop protest. It was a small victory, but a victory that declared that prisoners also have a duty to stand up for their beloved visitors and support them with positive action.

At about this time, in the spring of 1988, my brother Lenny had been arrested after a chase in a stolen vehicle and it was alleged that several cozzers had been squirted with ammonia in the process. Moreover, he still had to face the Murder Squad detectives over the fatal stabbing at the Stratford nightclub. Lenny was charged with both offences and remanded in custody at Brixton Prison. There he was made a Category 'A' prisoner and was housed in the infamous 'A' Wing Special Segregation Unit. It was during my brother's stay in the unit that the Prison Service decided to abolish the prison rule of allowing unconvicted prisoners to have their own food handed into them on daily visits. The Prison Service argued that the rule was an anachronism in modern penal policy as prison food was now at an acceptable standard for consumption. Paradoxically, it was the faceless bureaucrats at the Home Office who did not have to eat the prison-issue offerings. When the privilege was initially rescinded, it was a major source of contention and the Governor of the jail was prepared to make an example of any protesters.

Along comes my brother Lenny on the first day of the new ruling, and chucks a tray of old boiler chicken up in the air at the servery. As punishment, Lenny was put on a 10/74 lay-down, and transferred to the furthest prison from London in the land, Durham in the North of England. On arrival at the ancient local prison, he was placed in the punishment block where the Security Principal Officer unlocked his cell door and said to Lenny, 'We have not received your prison file yet ... could you tell me a little about yourself? What are your charges? And why were you brought here?'

Lenny went into a long monologue about the way he had been wrongly charged with murder and how he had been dug out by the prison authorities over the prison food palaver, and the Security PO went away and came back to see him two days later and had obviously digested pages and pages of police propaganda as the PO claimed that Lenny was one of the 'Mr Bigs' of London who had orchestrated and masterminded the Kendall helicopter escape and was a very dangerous villain with considerable resources and influence amongst other villains. I could imagine my brother sitting in the cell absorbing and savouring every syllable of this outrageous accolade of misrepresentation and thinking to himself, At least someone appreciates my criminal worth. I do not mean this in a derogatory sense, but there are some villains in this universe who believe everything that is written about them. In Lenny's case, the police have always sought to overexaggerate his potential for danger as a career criminal. For it stands to reason, if the police do not portray and publicise their quarry as Premier League villains, it will not consolidate or enhance their own careers and prestige within the police force. To some extent, my brother Lenny has always been a victim of police persecution, a 'collar' every ambitious cozzer wants to add to his CV.

While Lenny was at Durham Prison and, seeing as it was only two miles from Frankland, I submitted a petition for an inter-prison visit. Six weeks later, we were granted the visit and we spent two glorious hours together at Frankland. The only downside was, in true fraternal style, my savings were several grand short by the time he left. *Plus ça change* ...!

Over the period of a long prison sentence, prisoners confront and experience a whole gamut of human emotions and feelings, ranging from heart-rending despair and helplessness to times of unrestricted joy and serenity. As far as the feelings of helplessness and uncertainty go, none can mirror the occasion when, after a beautiful visit with Tracey, her sister Patsy and my three children, at about ten o'clock that same evening a friend of mine shouted out of the cell window to me that there had been a massive fire at King's Cross train station, the destination of my beautiful family. I immediately banged on my cell door and accosted the night screw and, upon hearing my story, he phoned my family and confirmed that they were all safe and well. Even now, 14 years later, I find it very hard to write about it. Apparently, the British Rail Inter-City train that they were travelling on stopped at Finsbury Park Station and let all the passengers off. Thank God they were safe!

Although I was back in the mainstream prison system and not the cloistered world of prison hospitals, I did not give up on finding a possible remedy for the leg injury. I had written to a laudable local orthopaedic surgeon and asked him if he would be prepared at my expense to come to Frankland Prison and give me a second independent opinion on the leg injury. He replied to my letter and suggested a date for the consultation. The prison doctor, however, refused to let the independent consultant into the prison to examine the leg. The prison doctor authoritatively insisted that, first, I must be examined by a prison-appointed orthopaedic surgeon. I pointed out that I would be willing to see anyone with a constructive opinion about the leg injury, but I had already seen several prison-appointed surgeons at Parkhurst Prison hospital and they had all said that I should accept the leg as it is! The prison doctor added that once I had seen his consultant, I could then petition the Home Office to seek permission about seeing an independent specialist.

One Saturday morning, we were out on the sports field and my pal said to me, 'I've got an Ecstasy tablet here ... do you want to take half with me?' Ecstasy pills had not been on the market that long. Their origin, as far as I am aware, can be traced back to the Leicester Square club scene in 1987, where I had heard about the so-called love-drug's feel-good factor, so I thought, Why not? as long as it didn't transform me into a raving prison queen for the day, so I said I'd have ago.

After about a hour on the sports field, the euphoric effects of the love-drug began to kick in. I then heard a strident, booming voice, calling, 'Smith, Smith, you are wanted for a hospital call-up!'

'No, it's not me, are you sure?' I replied.

'Yes,' said the screw 'It's a consultant to see you about your leg!'

Thus, with eyes looking like saucers and feeling like I loved the world, I skipped off to be examined by the prison consultant. I had planned to fire a million questions at the consultant, as well as possible ideas about the leg, but the effects of the Ecstasy pill made me feel the very personification of contentment and relaxation. The consultant could have even suggested amputation, and I might have considered it. I remember that I had to avoid eye contact with the surgeon as, being an experienced doctor, one look at my mince pies and he would have gathered that I was on something. As things stood, he examined the leg and practically parrot fashion declared that the leg was best left alone. On that day, as I left the prison hospital, I could not have cared less.

It was at Frankland Prison that I began to rebuild myself both physically and intellectually, with regular visits to the gymnasium and Education Block. In the gym, I would play badminton and enjoy strenuous sessions pushing the weights and circuit training, while in the Education Block I was part of a special class of 15 pupils who agreed to take part in a year-long GCSE course in English, English Literature, History and Mathematics. In my view, seeing as I was removed from school with no academic achievements, this would provide me with a superb springboard into advanced education. I completed the GCSE course and came away with two As, a B and a C grade respectively. The next step for me was either to dive straight into the Open University or take an A-level in English Literature with the local college in Durham. This was a correspondence course with occasional tutorials from the college tutor. This suited me as, in the event of being transferred to another jail, I could still carry on with the course. The course itself featured the in-depth study and analysis of several great cornerstones of English literature, such as Geoffrey Chaucer and Shakespeare, as well as F Scott Fitzgerald, Phillip Larkin and Edward Lear from the modern era. The only misgivings I had about the course was that it was two years in duration, a long-distance slog rather than a short, sharp sprint. Nonetheless, I was determined to come away from this prison sentence with something, and it was not going to be a pernicious drug addiction like some of my contemporaries. As far as I was concerned, it was valuable time not to be squandered by sitting in cells talking about crime amidst a cloud of cannabis-induced amnesia.

While at Frankland, I used to socialise mainly with my old friend Johnny Massey and Kenny Noye. We all used to walk around the exercise yard together, discussing topical events peppered with the occasional burst of banter and humour. More specifically, our friendship was based upon mutual respect for each other and our love for the beautiful game of badminton. John was an excellent player, undeniably the best player of the dispersal prison system, and he could easily have become a county player had circumstances permitted. Ironically, I used to beat John at Parkhurst prior to the leg injury in the early 1980s. This rankled with John because, being a perfectionist, a match based upon 'equality of arms' could never be repeated.

On the other hand, Ken was a novice, but took to the game like a wasp to jam. In his own inimitable and methodical style, Ken applied himself to the art of badminton with all the finesse and gusto of a cheerleader at the Super Bowl. Quickly, he was winning games against John and me. In fact, over the time we were at Frankland together, we played a total of 84 games against each other with Ken winning 52 and 32 games going to me.

Contrary to all that has been written about Kenny Noye by the character-assassination machine that we call the news media, I found Ken to be a thoroughly decent guy. In many respects, I felt sorry for him, as he was a very efficient and effective businessman who'd been sucked into the murky world of premiership crime and intrigue through the fatal stabbing of a masked man in the secure garden of his house. Naturally, we spoke about this many times while walking around the exercise yard at Frankland, and I am convinced that Ken thought that he was attacking a dangerous villain in his garden with ill intent, and not a masked-up surveillance policeman as he turned out to be. It was because of the tragic circumstances of the policeman's death that Ken received the maximum prison sentence of 14 years for handling the stolen gold ingots taken from the Brinks Mat robbery at Heathrow in 1984. Ken was very aggrieved at this, but he knew, just as we all knew, that once the police propaganda machine is set in motion it is very difficult, almost impossible, to promulgate successfully an alternative side of the story. Put bluntly, Ken was more a tragic villain of fate and circumstance than an arch villain of evil intent.

As you can imagine, with many hundreds of distinct and diverse prisoners living together in such a confined space, it is inevitable that there will be inter-prisoner disputes and disagreements that develop into violent confrontations and conflicts. I have had my fair share of disagreements and fights in prison, but I have always prided myself on not being a liberty-taker or a bully. No one likes bullies, not even in the seemingly lawless arena of a prison. While at Frankland, I got involved in a dispute with a liberty-taker called Joe the Greek. For some inexplicable reason, this despicable geezer serving a life sentence for shooting a bank cashier through a reinforced glass partition used to gravitate towards the Cockney prisoners. Apparently, Joe the Greek was a fearless knifeman who had cut a screw across the face and stabbed several prisoners. In many respects, he used to milk his notoriety and used it to infiltrate the gullible Cockney groups.

I have always considered myself a good judge of character and can sense an odd mark a mile off. This was confirmed when, on the sports field at Frankland, I saw Joe the Greek strike a match and burn a spider to death while in its web, laughing in the process. It was then I knew that if ever I fell out with this arsehole, I would have to hurt him or be hurt. It was not long before we had a dispute over the prison black market exchange rate. In short, the mush tried to strong-arm me for extra cash. When I said that I did not have it and would he accept £2 a week from me, he said yes! No doubt, he mistook me for a sucker! The next day, I spoke to several close friends to secure a blade as I was gonna serve him up good and proper the same way he would me, but I could not lay my hands on one. In the end, I battered him with a snooker cue and he required stitches at the prison hospital. As a bonus, I was hoping that the high-profile dispute would be enough to initiate a transfer to a jail in the South of England. The Prison Governor decided, however, to transfer the Greek and keep me at Frankland.

When I was eventually released from the prison chokey, all the other Cockneys came up to me and congratulated me on bashing the liberty-taker. Apparently, this was not the first time the Greek had tried to intimidate a Cockney, as he had had a long-standing feud with another London robber called Ronnie Cook, which degenerated into a slagging match throughout the prison system. The last I heard about the Greek, he was repatriated to his native Greece as a life-sentence prisoner and was subsequently released.

For the last six months I was at Frankland, I was placed on 'D' Wing with an amicable group of Londoners, such as big Billy Adams, David Judd, Jimmy Brown, Paul Cleland, Peter Welch and Kevin Brown. The screws did not like to see such a formidable group of Londoners together as, if ever there was a serious protest or dispute, they knew that they would have their work cut out with us. More specifically, many of us had been at Frankland a long time and we were growing increasingly disconcerted and disaffected with the bullshit reasons why we could not be transferred to a jail nearer to London. The overriding negativity and cynicism amongst us was so compelling that we nicknamed the Principal Officer's wing office 'The Bullshit Factory' due to the continuous bollocks that emanated from it. We were hated so much by the Wing PO that he used to tell the Northerners to stay away from the Cockneys otherwise they would not be recommended for prison privileges and perks, such as progressive transfers to lower-category jails, home leave or parole.

One devious screw even left a handwritten note under the cover on the wing snooker table for the nightshift screws to find, claiming that the Cockneys on the wing were orchestrating an escape. But the nightshift screws did not play snooker that night and we found the handwritten note, and marched en masse to the wing PO's office to protest at the attempt to discredit us. Admittedly, as dedicated non-conformists, we were openly hostile towards the screws and we felt wholly justified in being so, as some of us, such as Billy Adams and myself, had been incarcerated at Frankland, some 350 miles away from our homes, for over two years. It was putting an unbearable strain upon our families who would visit us regardless of the distance involved, but we felt that it was our duty as husbands, fathers and sons to do something positive or radical to change things. In this way, we expressed our discontent and indignation by venting our anger at the screws every day, in the hope that we would wear the screws down and force them to transfer us.

Additionally, I had composed a detailed Home Office petition requesting a transfer to a prison in the southern region of England, as, in effect, Paris was nearer to London than Frankland. All in all, I had been at Frankland for two years and my wife and three children had visited me every fortnight throughout that period without one grumble, groan or grizzle. What can one say about such a devoted, loyal and loving wife? Her natural loveliness and loyalty just goes on and on.

15

Acid Reign

I n September 1989, my cell door was flung open at Frankland Prison and a screw ordered, 'Pack your kit, Smith, you are on the move!' It was pointless asking where I was going as the escorting screws were under strict instructions not to tell Category 'A' prisoners where they were being transferred, in case it compromised prison security. Once again, I said a heartfelt *adieu* to all my old muckers on the frontline at Frankland and made my way to the reception area of the prison. There we boarded a Category 'A' prison van and were joined by an armed police escort for the 200-mile trek to Gartree dispersal prison, near Market Harborough in Leicestershire.

The dispersal prison system was first introduced in 1967 after the *Report of the Inquiry into Prison Escapes and Security* by Earl Mountbatten of Burma was considered by the Home Office. Mountbatten's suggestion that all top-security prisoners should be allocated to one or two super-prisons was rejected in favour of dispersing prisoners amongst a select group of top-security prisons spread around the country. The top-security dispersal jails selected were Parkhurst and Albany on the Isle of Wight, Gartree in

Leicestershire, Long Lartin in Worcestershire, Wakefield in Yorkshire, Full Sutton in York, Frankland in Durham and, lastly, the flagship of the dispersal system called Whitemoor in Cambridgeshire. In theory, the dispersal prison regimes, association periods and privileges lists were supposed to be consistent and uniform but, in reality, each prison had its own benefits, shortcomings and problems.

From a long-term prisoner's viewpoint, as far as Gartree was concerned, it was not viewed as the worst dispersal prison, an honour shared by Albany and Wakefield, neither was it the most relaxed or liberal establishment, for which the award went to Long Lartin. For me, Gartree was somewhere in the middle, neither oppressive nor liberal, neither purgatory nor heaven, it was quite plainly a long-term receptacle for offenders of the law. As an anonymous poet once proclaimed, 'There are no handsome prisons nor ugly lovers.'

HM Prison Gartree was opened in 1966 in response to the growing need to upgrade the prison system which was firmly rooted in the Victorian era. It consisted of four main wings that were attached to a central service block that incorporated the education and medical centre, a chapel, gymnasium and Segregation Unit. All in all, it held approximately 408 long-term prisoners, many of which were serving life imprisonment. I was allocated to 'B' Wing. The main wings had four levels, the ground floor being used for offices and association areas and the upper three storeys were used for the cells. Despite my severe leg impediment – a rigid right leg – I was placed on the top landing or third floor.

Almost immediately, I sensed that I was not wanted at Gartree as my co-defendant had escaped from the jail in the helicopter two years earlier. I knew that, if I complained about being allocated to a cell up six flights of stairs, the prison management would probably claim that there were no 'locate flat facilities' at Gartree and I would be moved on to another piss-hole. I decided to keep *schtum* and view the six flights of stairs as a beneficial challenge, like all ambitious people proclaim, 'Life is tough at the top!'

Moreover, I was with an exceptional bunch of guys on 'B' Wing.

They included Charlie McGhee, who had been sentenced to life imprisonment with a recommendation to serve a minimum of 25 years for shooting dead an off-duty policeman during a bungled raid on a security van in Hemel Hempstead; Dickie Trump, serving life for robbery; Jimmy Saunders, serving 15 years for robbery; Patsy Murray, serving 12 years for shooting dead a police dog during a robbery; and John 'Noodles' Newnman, serving a ten stretch for shooting a cozzer. They all knew the predicament that I was in regarding the leg injury and they would all, especially Noodles, fetch my breakfast, dinner and tea whenever they could.

One of the benefits of serving time in a dispersal prison is the access to cooking facilities during association time. Although prison food did enough to keep you alive throughout a prison sentence, your health would definitely deteriorate if you had to depend solely on the prison diet. To counterbalance these dietary and gastronomic deficiencies, prisoners would form something called 'foodboats,' where two or more prisoners would pool their meagre prison wages and purchase foodstuffs from the prison canteen. For a 'foodboat' to stay afloat and function properly, all members had to contribute on more than a monetary level. For example, one person would cook the meal, one would act as the gopher for the cook, one would wash the plates and utensils, or the 'foodboat' would employ a washer-upper who would receive a daily meal or tobacco as payment.

Our main cook at Frankland was Billy Adams, who dished up proper mountainous Cat 'A' meals. At Gartree, it was Noodles, who was an exceptional chef. It was an amazing feat of social diplomacy how a whole wing of prisoners who had access to one electric cooker with four rings could all cook their meals with no serious confrontations and conflicts. It was at Gartree that I decided to enhance my culinary skills and learn to cook. I enrolled on the cooking classes and it was not long before I was entertaining the taste buds of a cohort of Cockneys with Madras curries, meatballs, chilli con carne and Sunday roasts.

Once again, at Gartree I continued with the tried and tested philosophy of mastering a long-term prison sentence with frequent visits to the gymnasium, pumping heavy weights and playing badminton with Paul Sammit and Harry Roberts, who was serving a life sentence with a minimum recommendation to serve 30 years for fatally shooting three policemen in West London in 1966. By this time, Harry had served 23 years and he could still bench press 100k with ease and keep up with the younger prisoners. I found Harry to be a very polite and unassuming person who had obviously read a lot while in prison and was intelligent with it. I found him to be excellent company; when Harry had something to say, it was well worth listening to, unlike a lot of long-term prisoners who had become caught up in a perpetual cycle of regurgitating prison news and gossip, ad nauseum.

Similarly, I was allowed to continue the English literature A-level course at the Education Centre. I was neck-deep into studying Shakespeare's tragedy *King Lear*, but I had already set my eye on possibly joining the Open University. My old IRA companion Ronnie McCartney was also on 'B' Wing and he would encourage me to enrol with the OU by providing me with a stack of his old Tutor-Marked Assignments. I was surprised at Ronnie's high level of intellect and how he managed to frame his arguments so well. I recall that I kept Ronnie's assignments for years and I used to read them from time to time to remind myself of the academic standard that I wanted to achieve.

In order to alleviate the insidious levels of personal stress and tension, we used to make buckets of prison hooch, leave them to ferment for two to three weeks and then enjoy a proper Vikingesque party full of convivial laughter and merriment. Prison hooch, or 'Viking juice' as we called it, was made with the basic ingredients of yeast, sugar and orange juice, and once it had been left to do its stuff it would be as potent as Vodka.

The screws would turn a blind eye towards those smoking cannabis, as it appeared to placate and soothe prisoners, but they were double-dubious about the home-made warrior juice as it frequently transformed model prisoners into riotous agitators hell-bent on mutiny and mayhem. And why not? A bit of disorganised chaos was good for the soul, particularly in a long-term pressure cooker where years upon years of enforced observation and oppression required a long-overdue outlet. Thankfully, the sensible company I guzzled with knew how to handle their drink and we left the time-bomb antics to the patients.

I had a certain amount of sympathy for Charlie McGhee, a Luton-born villain of Scottish descent. Charlie was a very game and fearless man with a healthy streak of good humour and a remarkable ability to tell exceptionally funny and outrageous stories about his life. As I said before, Charlie was serving a life sentence with very little possibility of release. When I arrived at Gartree, because of my pedigree as a successful escapee, he asked me to 'make one', or escape with him. If I had to escape with anyone, it would have been with Charlie, but I had to refuse his offer as I had already carved a tunnel of hope through the dark mountain of long-term imprisonment and I did not want to jeopardise it through another gun-toting period as a dangerous fugitive. In my view, Charlie should have been born 200–300 years earlier as he was far too game for the modern world. Every time I watched the film *Braveheart* about the Scottish revolutionary William Wallace, I thought of Charlie, as that was his era. He was a man any team would want on his side, a genuine diamond.

During one funny incident at Gartree, the screws use to refer to Category 'A' prisoners as 'packages' when they were being escorted from the main prison block to the workshops or the visits area. This used to annoy us as we did not view ourselves as a parcel or commodity in the world of man-management, but a unique vessel of humanity like everybody else. One day, Charlie came up to me and said that the screws had gone too far this time. While on his way to a visit, a screw had referred to him on the prison radio as a 'vegetable'. Together with Charlie, we went to see the Wing Governor about this new level of insult being used by the screws, and the Governor sincerely apologised and said that he would look into it.

Some weeks later, while being escorted to a visit myself, I heard a screw trumpet on his personal radio, 'Permission to move one package from the vestibule to the visits area!' Charlie hadn't, in fact, heard the screw call him a 'vegetable' – it was a small alcove area that the screws called a 'vestibule'. When I got back to the wing and told Charlie what he had heard, we burst out laughing, as at one stage we were a fag-paper close to organising a riot over it.

On another occasion, early one evening I was in the canteen queue when Charlie came up to me and asked me if I fancied an acid trip. He said, 'Several of us are having one!' and, before I knew it, he had put it in my mouth. I always remember the trips we had at Parkhurst in the early 1980s and they were brilliant experiences. This one started off in the same way, as I recall four of us playing table tennis and it was the funniest game of ping-pong that I have ever had in my life. It was as though we had bottled up all our laughter for this mad, bad and hilarious moment. The table tennis ball was being hit on the volley from one person to the next without anyone missing their turn for about 50 shots, and the more we continued with the rally, the more hilarious it got. Then as the evening came to a close and we had to bang up, I recall walking along the landing aware that the other prisoners were whizzing pasts me as though I was on a congested motorway. I realised that I was hallucinating and it was fierce.

Having enjoyed the preliminaries of the acid trip, it was then that it all started to go 'bad'. On evening bang-up, I recall standing up at the cell window and chatting to the others, when I felt a sharp pain in my dodgy leg. I then said to myself, 'I hope the pain don't go to my heart.' It was the worst thing I could have said, as the pain went straight to my heart. All night long I fought the physical and psychological effects of this powerful hallucinogenic. It was the worse night of my life. My heartbeat was racing out of control. It was going at least 200 beats per minute. I kept saying to myself, 'I am not going to die, I am not going to die!' and I made a solemn oath that I would never take hard drugs again while in prison.

I kept the promise as it had scared the life out of me. I put the bad experience down to having negative thoughts or feelings at the time, or that it was really only younger people who should take drugs of that potency, and I vowed that I would call it a day for hard drugs. In that sense, the 'bad trip' was a good thing as I never wanted to experience something as disturbing or as horrific as that night in Gartree ever again. I had heard of people having 'bad trips' before; as a teenager, I recall a school friend who took a trip and was running down a subway in the evening with the lights on and he thought the subway went on for ever until he ran slap-bang into the wall at the end and broke his nose.

One of the principal side-effects of long-term imprisonment, particularly as a Category 'A' prisoner, is the psychological torture and torment of being under continuous observation and supervision. Whether a prisoner is on a visit, in the gym, on the wing or sports field, or even in his cell, he is invariably being watched. To complement this endless observation and surveillance, the screws are ordered to compile wing reports that monitor and record a prisoner's behaviour and associates.

For instance, while I was at Frankland Prison, during the association period I used to play snooker with the Northern prisoners. One of them was called Dean Smith. Dean was not a close friend of mine, or even an ordinary friend. He was just an acquaintance whom I'd met at the snooker table – nothing more, nothing less. While I was at Gartree, the local Essex Police called at my wife's address and said that they were looking for Dean Smith who was wanted for a robbery in Sheffield. 'What has this got to do with me?' enquired my wife.

'We know from reports in prison that your husband Terry used to be friends with Dean Smith and we thought that he may have been putting him up!' replied the cozzer.

On hearing this, I confronted the Wing Governor, stating that it was hard enough trying to keep a marital relationship going as a long-term prisoner without having the police calling at my wife's address looking for wanted suspects based upon a misleading report written by a screw. To compensate for the distress caused, the Governor reissued the Visiting Order ... big deal!

While at Gartree, I got to meet two of the Birmingham Six prisoners – Paddy Hill and Gerry Hunter – who had been wrongly convicted with four others in 1975 for the murder of 22 people in two pubs in Birmingham city centre the previous year. No one can comprehend what these individuals went through as men convicted of such a heinous crime.

I recall Paddy, who was on my wing, as being a volatile firebrand with an understandable hatred for the judiciary and its perverse sense of justice. Gerry was a very good midfield footballer whom I liked to watch during inter-wing fixtures at the weekend. I remember wishing them well in March 1990 as they set off for the Court of Appeal to have their convictions quashed. It was one of the highlights of my stay at Gartree to watch these unfortunate people go home. To be morally and legally guilty of a crime and to be imprisoned for it is bad enough, but to view the brutal world of long-term imprisonment from the viewpoint of an innocent man must be the ultimate in human suffering and distress. It was not until many years later that I would come to realise the gravity of their plight and the heart-rending nature of their experience.

In late March 1990, I had only been at Gartree for about six months when an incident occurred at another jail that had far-reaching effects for the prisoners banged up in our prison. A prisoner at Leicester Prison had managed to walk out of the jail with a group of visitors and escape. The significant aspect of the escape was that the prisoner was not even on a visit. He was with a group of prisoners who had been using the prison gymnasium and somehow had managed to slip among the visitors leaving the prison. The official upshot of the escape was that all the prisoners at Gartree were ordered to wear blue-striped prison shirts when having a visit. The wearing of personal clothing on social visits was a much appreciated and treasured privilege by the long-term prisoners at Gartree, a privilege that had been paid for by prisoners with solitary confinement and loss of remission over the years, only now to witness it being taken away.

More to the point, the prisoners at Gartree felt that they were losing some of their individuality and were being penalised by proxy for the incompetence of prison staff at another jail. This evoked a strong sense of injustice and grievance among the prisoners and, on a metaphorical level, the new prison rule had awoken a sleeping giant. I considered myself to be quite an easy-going and manageable prisoner, but when the sparks of injustice and grievance began to fly, I was attracted to it like a moth to a naked flame. The new prison rule was nonsense and we had to make a stand and organise a protest.

The only problem is that whenever there is serious protest among the prisoners, the spokesman is identified by the screws as the ringleader and is, more often than not, transferred to a remote and hostile Segregation Block somewhere else in the country. Normally, the spokesmen are Category 'A' prisoners and, if they aren't, the screws would generally claim that the Category 'A' prisoners were pulling the strings of insurrection and agitation behind the scenes. Therefore, in the aftermath of a prison protest, the first port of call for punishment by the screws are the Category 'A' scapegoats.

Shortly after this absurd and unfair new prison rule came into play, I was walking around the prison exercise yard with Charlie McGhee when two prisoners came up to us and asked if we would distract or divert the screws' attention while they climbed on to the prison roof to protest about the prison rule. We agreed and, as we pushed the protesters on to the roof, the other prisoners with us were throwing stones at the dog-handlers with their dogs who tried to intervene. As the two daring rooftop protesters began their three-day protest, I turned to Charlie and said, 'I am off to my cell to pack my kit!' as I knew that we had been caught red-handed helping the protesters. Experience dictated that Charlie and I would be identified as the ringleaders and 'ghosted' or transferred without prior notice.

Almost immediately, the prison went on a lock-down with controlled unlocking, during which only six prisoners at a time were allowed out of their cells to collect their food at mealtimes. Basically, I knew that I had shot myself in the foot and that I would be transferred, probably back to the North of England, but I could not sit by and watch the parochial Governor grades seize long-standing privileges at will without reply.

During the three-day lock-down, while waiting for the inevitable transfer, I sent a letter to my old mucker David Judd at Strangeways Prison in Manchester. He was there in the Segregation Block on a punishment 'lay-down', a period of 28 days in isolation. I recall writing to Dave, 'I hope that you have got a spare cell there, as I could be there with you soon!' He received the letter shortly before 1 April 1990 when HMP Strangeways met its nemesis in the form of a massive prison riot.

As expected, the screws in full riot regalia began the process of shipping out the perceived trouble-makers at the heart of the protest at Gartree. As each prisoner was removed from 'B' Wing, everyone banged on their cell doors in honour of their departure. When my turn came, the screws opened the cell door and blurted, 'Grab a few things together, Smith, you are on the move!' I put my hand behind the cell door and grabbed a small bag of goodies, otherwise known as the survival kit and replied, 'What kept ya? I been waiting for ya the last three days!'

As I walked down the stairs of the wing, the shout went up – 'Terry's going, Terry's off!' – and the cell doors began to bang. It was a cacophony of pounding metal upon metal. As I tried to speak to the screws escorting me down the stairs, they could not hear me for the deafening noise. It was like the film clip in *The Italian Job* where the Mr Big is walking down the stairwell of the jail and all the prisoners are banging on the railings with their metal cups and plates. It was so poignant that a lump came to my throat and goose pimples the size of golf balls travelled up and down the back of my neck. It was a great send-off and, even as I reached the ground-floor office, the noise was still unbelievable. I must confess I did not realise that I had made such an impact on the prisoners of 'B' Wing. Obviously, the cannon-like thuds and crashes on the cell doors said it all.

I was escorted to the prison hospital by a phalanx of screws and given a mandatory strip-search before being placed inside a Category 'A' prison van for the transfer wherever. Also inside the van was another High-Risk Category 'A' prisoner from another wing, an IRA sympathiser called Nat Vella. As we left the gates of Gartree Prison, we partook in the familiar game of guessing our destination. As soon as we hit the road, the motorway signs of 'M1 – The North' said it all. Where would it be? Frankland, Wakefield or Full Sutton? Or would it be a local prison piss-hole like HMP Durham, Strangeways in Manchester or Walton in Liverpool?

We were all wrong, because we pulled into Armley Prison in Leeds, a veritable piss-hole, notorious for its austere regime. As I went to get off the prison van, the screw said, 'Not you, Smith, it's Vella!'

Phew, that was a close one. I would take what was coming to me on the chin, but if I could body-swerve the Kafka-esque dungeons of Rule Britannia, all the better. After dropping Vella off, we hit the road again, and finally arrived at Full Sutton dispersal prison near York. Through the prison grapevine, I had heard conflicting reports about Full Sutton. Some said that it was a sufferable jail, while others declared it a real karzy. Either way, we would soon find out!

16

At Full Stretch

By the time we reached Full Sutton Prison, it was late in the evening and the screws rushed me through the reception area and had allocated me to 'D' Wing. To a great degree, Full Sutton was designed according to the same courtyard principle as Frankland Prison in Durham. It had four identical, square-shaped wings with inner quadrangles, a large sports field and attendant gymnasium, Education Block, chapel and Segregation Unit.

In terms of penal history, Full Sutton was built on a former RAF site and opened in 1987. As a modern dispersal prison it was intended to hold in excess of 400 long-term prisoners in top-security conditions. Due to the unsettled nature of the prison system, more especially within the dispersal system, it did not matter what dispersal prison I was allocated to because, as sure as night follows day, I would be bound to know someone within the upper pecking order of the jail.

To some extent, the Category 'A' security system had unwittingly created and developed a peer group or hierarchy among long-term prisoners. More often than not, Category 'A' prisoners exhibited leadership qualities and were accorded the most respect and deference in accordance with the serious nature of their crimes, their very long prison sentences and the moral way most of them served their sentences. Not all Category 'A' prisoners, however, were worthy of respect. Some serial rapists and predatory paedophiles were absolute beasts and were accorded top-security status due to their unequivocal danger to the public should they be unlawfully at large.

In the main, however, most Category 'A' prisoners knew each other and knew what their peers were in prison for. As soon as a new Category 'A' prisoner reached a jail – providing he was a 'decent guy' and was not in for sexual or other abhorrent crimes, was not a liberty-taker and had served his sentence in accordance with the unwritten code of moral and respectful behaviour – he would be shown a warm welcome with immediate offers of food and advice about the benefits and shortcomings of his new residence.

As soon as I was allocated to 'D' Wing and banged away for the night, I went straight up to the cell window and began to talk to the other prisoners who knew me. An amicable Scouser who knew me from Frankland gave me the run-down on what 'D' Wing was like and what wing my friends were on. One of the first aspects I noticed about my new home was that the garden area inside the quadrangle was in pristine condition with its manicured rose beds and flower arrangements. Immediately, experience warned me that this was a dodgy wing as its spick and span garden was usually indicative of a dictatorial senior screw running the wing according to petty rules and regulations. I knew that I would not last long on that wing. One of the golden rules of imprisonment that I'd devised while I was away was that, if I was unhappy about my prison surroundings, the regime, the petty rules or the type of convicts around me, I would not suffer in silence, but I would do something about it. Invariably, this would mean some form of non-co-operative or subversive activity, such as stoking up the fires of discontent and dissatisfaction among the prisoners, usually with me up front giving it to the screws so that when the 'ghostings' were being dished out, I would be at the top of their list. I stood by this self-imposed rule and it always paid dividends.

Unbeknown to me, however, as I chatted out of the cell window to other prisoners on 'D' Wing, an old school acquaintance who was born and bred a street away from my address in Canning Town was listening to and dreading the fact that I had arrived on 'his' wing. I say 'his wing', as apparently he had managed to play down the terrible nature of his crime – the senseless slaughter of a mother and child in Lincoln – and settled down at Full Sutton relatively unnoticed. Now that I was on the wing, all would be revealed and he would have to endure a radical drop in his status.

Evidently, as soon as the cell doors were unlocked the following morning, he rushed straight to the wing office and let loose all of his fears and frustrations about my menacing presence on the wing. To give his grievance added impetus, he proclaimed that if I remained on the wing he would kill me. This account was later confirmed when I acquired official access to my medical file and I read the report in red ink. Absurd as it seems, whether the perverse mother and child killer would have got the chance to kill me is a moot point. But the screws are duty bound not to take any chances and offered to reallocate me to another wing almost immediately. Not knowing the reason for the swift reallocation at the time, I jumped at the opportunity, particularly as I was going to 'B' Wing where several good Cockney pals were residing. It was ironic that this demented butcherer had done me a favour as I was off to be with my buddies.

On reaching 'B' Wing, I was greeted by a healthy and humorous trio of loveable Cockneys – Peter Mitchell who was serving 22 years' imprisonment for 'The Great Crane Robbery' in Essex that I mentioned earlier; Mickey Ishmael, serving 13 years for the production of amphetamine sulphate at an improvised factory; and the very bubbly Kenny Redbourne, serving 15 years for robbery. I was put straight on the 'foodboat' and fell bang on my feet. Unlike the prim and proper decor of 'D' Wing, with its painstakingly precise Garden of Eden, the atmosphere on 'B' Wing was alive and vibrant with an underground vibe of skulduggery and camaraderie amongst its inhabitants. One got the feeling that, if there were any disgusting sex cases on this wing, their first port of call would be the outside hospital.

Not long after my arrival at Full Sutton, the prison riot of the century kicked off at Strangeways Prison in Manchester. The prison itself was the screws' POA union stronghold in the North. The very bricks and mortar of this Victorian monstrosity were steeped in years and years of human misery, oppression and brutality. For decades, the prison officers' omnipotent union subverted and stultified all manner of reform and improvement at the jail. The only way that the Governors of the prison were going to regain total control and power in the jail was to shut it down completely and start again. But for economic, geographical and logistical reasons, this was impossible. So when the full-scale riot took place in the prison chapel and the mass destruction and burning began, secretly we could imagine the faceless apparatchiks at Queen Anne's Gate rubbing their hands together. This was a golden opportunity to regain control of Strangeways and decimate and debilitate the stranglehold the POA had in the North.

Later, I spoke to several of the prison rioters who were involved in the mutiny, such as Kevin Brown and Dave Judd, who'd been released from the Segregation Block by fellow prisoners during the riot. They said that the well-trained and specially prepared prison riot squads, called the 'Mufti', tried to storm and recapture 'E' Wing three times but, as they reached the formidable barricades on the ground floor, the rioters repelled the crash-helmeted screws with long scaffold poles through the wire mesh directly above them.

The official version of the Strangeways Prison and other related riots around the country can be seen in the *Woolf Report 1991*. But for primary source material and eye-witness accounts, the legendary rioters who were there tell the real story. It was a victory for humanity and the humane treatment and care of those incarcerated by the State. If it was not for the high-profile rioters at Strangeways Prison, prisoners in urban, local prisons and dispersal jails would still be writing letters and waiting a week or two for a reply, instead of jumping on the prison payphone and talking directly to their families and loved ones. Therefore, but for the riots, the *Woolf Report* and its far-reaching recommendations and concessions, British prisons would still be languishing in the austere hinterlands of the Dark Ages.

As news of the Strangeways riot filtered through to the prisoners on 'B' Wing at Full Sutton, there was a simmering undercurrent of revolt and destruction ready to explode. The Scousers, Geordies and Mancunians – a resolute bunch of insurgents – felt that they had to do something in support of their fellow companions on the burning rooftop of Strangeways. They came to the Cockneys on the wing and asked if it was all right to stage a protest. We were not against a protest, but we knew that, if and when the protest started, it would be us, the perceived Londoners, pulling the strings behind the scenes who'd would be persecuted and punished with a move to another jail further away from our families. Nonetheless, we also realised that trying to hold back the potential rioters was tantamount to holding back the sea. A protest of sorts was inevitable and we might as well get involved. As Martin Luther King proclaimed in one of his evocative speeches against black segregation and racism in the 1960s, 'There is no greater power on earth than an idea whose time has come.' It was time for action!

Although the prisoners on 'B' Wing needed no excuse to start a protest, ironically it was the screws who lit the fuse themselves by serving up one of the most outrageous meals that I have ever seen in a British prison. At tea, the cooks dished up – and I speak with my hand on my heart – 'vegetable crumble' and jelly for dessert.

The prisoners who could not afford to cook for themselves had come back from a long, boring and monotonous day in the prison workshops to face a disgusting vegetable crumble. Naturally, the prisoners steadfastly refused to eat the slops and the Wing Governor was summoned to oversee the commotion. This man was dealing with a potential powder keg. It was then that I intervened – which I knew was suicidal – and suggested to the Governor that perhaps the prisoners might go behind their cell doors if he got the kitchen to cook and supply egg, chips and baked beans for them. 'Do you think that they will bang up if I do that?' said the Governor meekly.

'Yes, of course they will!' I said, as the prisoners were now flicking jelly all over his two-bob suit. By the time the egg, chips and beans were brought over to the wing, it was time for evening association and we refused to go behind our cell doors. The screws on the wing were fuming and I knew, once again, that it was time to pack my kit as I would not be there that long.

At about 7.00am the next morning, a shout went up around the inner courtyard of the wing that the riot screws were outside Peter Mitchell's cell and that he was being 'ghosted'. Not long afterwards, the Mufti came for me. I was ordered by a screw to grab a few things as I was going to the Segregation Block and then I would be transferred to another jail. On reaching the prison block, I was placed in a holding cell and ordered to strip. Because of the heavy presence of hostile screws and the intimidation and humiliation involved, I refused and asked to see the Governor. The blocks screws went outside the cell door, then less than a minute later the riot squad burst into the cell with their riot shields and tried to beat me up, but because of the weight training I had been doing, the screws could not unclench my hands or bend my wrists. Eventually, despite my protests of 'Why are you doing this to me? I have done nothing wrong!' I was bent double and frog-marched to the punishment block's strongbox. If a prisoner refuses a Governor's Order, the correct procedure is to place the prisoner on Governor's Report and face a Governor's adjudication, not to disregard my basic rights completely by bending me over and humiliating me.

Once in the strongbox with a concrete kerbstone as a mattress and a camera fixed in the ceiling for observation, the screws forced me to lie face-down on the floor and then ripped all my clothes off me until I was naked and then they put a medium-sized body-belt on me with handcuffs at the side. The patently small body-belt compressed my stomach so much so that I looked like an oversized Wonder Woman. It was a diabolical liberty as I had not issued any threats of violence or aggression and they gave me conflicting information about being placed in the punishment block as I was not being transferred at all.

As I sat there completely naked in the lung-constricting body-belt, as a matter of procedure the prison doctor came to the strongbox to examine me for any physical injuries. I pointed out that the body-belt was too tight. Then the number-one Prison Governor Smith came to the strongbox and asked if I was OK. I said, 'I have been in your prison for three weeks ... I have participated in your sports programme,' – I had won the prison badminton tournament – 'and I have participated in your education facilities and this is the way you treat me ... no wonder you've got problems in your jail!'

'Is that all?' he said or some such words.

'No,' I replied, 'can you do something about this body-belt?'

He then ordered the block screws to give me a shower and put me in a normal cell.

In spite of it being over a decade since the incident, I can still recall the humiliating event very well as it occurred on Shakespeare's birthday, 23 April 1990. This was of some significance to me as I was studying Shakespeare's colourful comedy *The Tempest* as part of the A-level course at the time. With extreme irony, I recall sitting in the strongbox in the ludicrous body-belt and quoting a poignant passage uttered by Miranda in the play: 'O brave new world, That has such people in't!' In fact, days later, while I was still in the punishment block, I composed a poem to commemorate the brutal occasion:

UNLIMITED REALITY

Audacious fly, why are you here?
Buzzing around in this queer atmosphere.
Fate brought me to thee, reason I do not know,
Door opened at eight; at nine I said 'hello'.

Pack your kit, you are on the move,
It's Shakespeare's birthday, things will go smooth.
The twenty-third of April, not forget that day
Orwellian storm-troopers treated me like hay.

Bundled, contorted, all limbs a'twist,
'What's going on,' thought I, 'Ouch, watch that wrist!'
From drowsy slumber, to body-belt nightmare,
Yet the sun is beaming bright and fair.

The alleged transfer was all a lie,
Chaperoned to the block in a concrete sty.
Confounded, bemuddled, refused to strip-search,
Like Christ I was pinioned, as seen in a church.

'Let me see the Governor,' my request was met,
By the dark and sinister Mufti in like a jet.
Stripped bollock naked, no pants, top nor socks,
This was my first visit to a penal strongbox.

Manacled, degraded, all dignity remiss
A liberty was took, I didn't deserve this.
Resentment will ensue, a natural course of events,
Block up the passage to bitter malevolent vents.

For many a good man has pandered to canker's ruin.
Imprisoned souls, gurgling hatred a-chewing.
This is not the answer to remedy the ordeal,
Maturity must prevail, like a wine-drunken meal.

'O brave new world', 'How beauteous mankind is!'
Drop me out, Willy, don't take the bloody piss.
And to all who read this, empathise with what I say,
This over-reaction was illegal, I'm not a piece of hay.

Full Sutton Chokey
25 April 1990

17

The Homecoming

I was in isolation for another two weeks in the prison block and was then finally transferred with the usual armed police escort to the sun-blessed Bermuda of the south coast, Parkhurst Prison on the Isle of Wight.

On an analytical level, I had noticed, whenever I was being transferred to another prison it was always to a top-security dispersal prison and not to an urban local prison like most other rebellious and subversive prisoners. I put this down to the fact that the Category 'A' Section at the Home Office was aware that I had loyal and dedicated help and resources outside and the prison department would not take a chance and house me in a semi-secure local prison in case I decided to organise another escape. This did not unduly concern me, however, as Segregation Units in dispersal prisons were invariably more civilised and humane than those at urban local prisons. The heavy-handedness and over-reaction by the Mufti at Full Sutton punishment block, however, was indicative of the abuse of power when it is allowed to run unchecked and unsupervised by an appropriate observer or watchdog organisation.

It was typical, bloody typical – just when all the prisons up North were on the verge of unrestrained anarchy and destruction, the Category 'A' section at the Home Office decided to ship me back down South. The only difference was, after spending over three lonesome years with the prisoners up North, being back among the good gravy guys of London at Parkhurst was like coming home.

I was allocated to a cell on 'B' Wing among hordes of friends and acquaintants, the most prominent being Tony (Top Cat) Colson, Paul Gray, Barry Hayes, Teddy French, Billy Gentry and Andrew and Nicky Dunford. It was a laugh a minute. The humour was as thick as treacle and twice as sweet. We all mucked in with the 'foodboat' duties and chores, trained like turbo-charged athletes and savoured the occasional hooch party. There is nothing better for the morale and camaraderie among prisoners than cracking open a bucket or two of Viking juice and having a rip-roaring, belly-laughing party. These were convivial moments when all the pent-up tension and stress of long-term torment and pressure slid off one's shoulders like a lead overcoat. Some of the parties were legendary, like the toga party that was held before I arrived and the time a well-known South London villain got legless and was escorted to his cell and crashed out on his bed in an intoxicated coma. The South Londoner's trousers and pants were yanked around his knees and hot chilli powder was smeared around his anus. The next morning, obviously worse for wear, he rushed out of his cell and immediately made enquiries about who had put him to bed the previous evening. Everyone said that it was a humorous East London villain who sometimes pretended to be a homosexual. On hearing this, with a look of utter fright on his face, the South Londoner sped off in search of his quarry, only to find out later that it had all been a hilarious ruse.

It was not all fun and games at Parkhurst this time round, however, as the placid culture of peaceful acceptance and resignation exercised by the older warders had given way to a new breed of younger fascist screws. Gone were the days of healthy respect and rapport between the screws and prisoners. The staple diet was now continuous demands, orders, confrontations and conflicts. As the prison rules and regulation became pettier and pettier, the acts of retaliation and revenge became progressively intense and volatile.

For instance, prisoners were filling Thermos flasks with mature human excrement and it was thrown from the upper tiers of the wing at the screws hovering outside the main wing office on the ground floor. The malodorous stench was horrendous. Then a disgruntled prisoner smashed the treasured fish tank opposite the same office on the ground floor with a metal mop bucket, sending its contents all over the floor. It was hilarious watching hardened villains running around picking up tropical fish flapping around on the floor. Then an incendiary device was placed inside the hotplate timed to explode shortly before evening bang-up.

These blatant acts of sedition and sabotage were all being committed by different and diverse groups of disgruntled prisoners. Then there was a protest on the sports field over a new rule to curtail its use. The screws had transformed the jail into a veritable powder keg and, on a personal level, due to the screws' militant attitude, I also wanted it to explode, big time.

On top of all this, I acknowledged an appreciable undercurrent of animosity and resentment directed towards me due to the prison van escape six years earlier. An example of this occurred when Tony Colson chinned one of his arch rivals in the prison gymnasium. Both parties were placed on Governor's Report and taken to the Segregation Unit. Meanwhile, I sidled up to the Wing PO and in a polite and respectful fashion I asked if he could put a good word in for my friend, as I did not want to see him transferred out of the jail. Then at the conclusion of lunch, I heard stealthy footsteps outside my cell door and immediately recognised it as an ominous sign. Then the cell door swung open and the Wing PO entered my cell seemingly alone, but obviously with his henchmen at the ready, each side of the opened cell door. He blurted out, 'Don't you tell me what to do, Smith, I run this wing, not you!'

I looked at the PO in complete astonishment, as he obviously felt intimidated by my having made a polite request. 'Of course you run the wing!' I said. 'You are the Wing PO ... that is why I spoke to you!'

'As long as you know it!' he added as he shut the cell door.

Despite being in tougher prisons up North, I had never

experienced this type of provocation and intimidation before. It was personal, but fuck them, like I said before, they may have recaptured me and returned me to prison, but they could not take the proceeds, my beautiful daughter Jade, who was now five years old.

Another salient example of the anti-convict mentality at Parkhurst can be seen when I had my social visits. As a High-Risk Category 'A' prisoner, I had to strip off the clothes that I was wearing both before and after a visit. One particular day, I had a visit in the morning and afternoon, which dictated that I had to endure four strip-searches in the space of six hours. When I complained to the escorting screws that the Prison Service's 'Statement of Purpose' on placards outside every prison establishment proclaimed that it is their duty to look after prisoners with 'humanity', one screw – who we called 'The Living Dead' due to his cadaver-like appearance – countered, 'Well, you want to be the hard man, Smith.'

'No!' I replied. 'It's not that I want to be the hard man, it is the prison authorities who label us as hard men with their Category "A", double "A" and triple "A" security status and then they expect us to fulfil the stereotypical role or image of these so-called super-crooks!'

As far as experience and education was concerned, if I'd had the 'hard man' comment thrown at me earlier on in my prison sentence, I would have become very angry at the screw for his sarcastic comment and would, most probably, have let loose a machine-gun-like assault of choice expletives in his direction and ended up on Governor's Report down the chokey. Having learnt over time how to construct concise and coherent arguments as a response, rather than resorting to verbal abuse, allowed me to seize the moral high ground of an argument and dispute with the screws without losing face. In my view, this was empowerment through persuasive debate and diplomacy. We know the Prison Service has experienced decades and decades of sedition and revolt in prisons over the years and that they have lapped it up, as it reinforces their role as a public service by keeping violent and dangerous villains locked away.

On the other hand, while the screws can always confront violence with violence, they cannot always meet persuasive and compelling argument with the same. The genesis of the Prison Ombudsman in the mid-1990s, the 'abuse of process' concept and access to legal aid through the law courts has done much more damage to the Prison Service than a fist in a screw's face. Although the latter may produce short-term gratification, the former engenders long-term empowerment and redress for prisoners.

Around the summer of 1990, my co-accused, Kendall, arrived at the Special Secure Unit (SSU) at Parkhurst that housed Category triple 'A' prisoners. The type of prisoners that were kept in these claustrophobic units – or 'submarines', as they were called – were the Irish and Middle Eastern terrorists, armed robbers who were perceived as control problems and the occasional determined escaper such as Kendall and Nicky Webber from South London. Naturally, being cooped up in these small and suffocating special units for decades at a time caused those inside them occasionally to turn on each other. Within these close-knit social groups, someone's little, persistent but irritable habit would be magnified out of all proportion and it could cause friction and conflict.

Kendall had a fall-out with the IRA prisoners at the SSU at Leicester and was transferred to the Parkhurst equivalent. The only problem was the sheer number of the IRA contingent, who controlled the balance of power in the SSUs, so when Kendall arrived at the SSU on the island, the IRA prisoners refused to accept him on the unit. The London lads on the main wings had heard about this and told the screws in no uncertain terms that, if Kendall would not be allowed to live in the Special Secure Unit, then the IRA prisoners on the main wings had better pack their kit and get off the main wings. The Governor at Parkhurst was quick to see a potential flashpoint over this issue and placed Kendall down the chokey. A few days later, he was transferred to the SSU at Full Sutton Prison and the matter was forgotten about.

Other Cockney prisoners have had serious disputes and rows with the IRA prisoners before in the SSUs and, usually, like honourable men, once the row was over it was forgotten. But for some reason, the IRA prisoners had formed a particular dislike of Kendall and … I should have seen the signs!

If there is a love of my life, over and above the natural love and affection that I have for Tracey and my children, it is my love of football. It has always played a powerful part in my life, which no doubt explains the absurd thing I said when I was lying in the gutter with my leg missing after being rammed by the dark green Ford Granada: 'I won't be playing football any more ...'

With this thought in mind, when I was transferred to Frankland Prison in late 1987, I used to watch the inter-wing football matches on the sports field, and I compared the deep sadness of not being able to play football again with the feeling of having been 'jilted by a lover'.

Most of the Cockney lads knew of my love of football and, despite the leg injury, encouraged me to start playing again. After that, it was like being reunited with a lover, and they could not get me off the football pitch. We even took part in the annual summer five-a-side competition. Our team was called Terry's Tigers and there were also The Red Hot Chilli Peppers, The Islington Thunderbirds, The BV (Bank Van) Raiders and The Iron Lung Gang (named after their robust ability to pipe cannabis). The five-a-side games were fast and furious and very competitive with a tranche of humour as seen when The Iron Lung Gang played their fixtures in their prison-issue white Y-fronts.

Conversely, the most costly game of football I ever played occurred during evening association on the sports compound at Parkhurst. We were playing six-a-side on the tarmac area when, at the conclusion of the game, I noticed that my 'parcel' (about two ounces of cannabis, which was the prison currency at the time) was missing from my shorts. I immediately stopped everyone from leaving the tarmac area and asked them all, about six white and six black players, to help me look for it. It would have been quite easy to spot, because, if it had fallen out of my shorts during the match, it would have been visible to everyone. I therefore said someone must have picked it up.

Everyone denied having found it, so I said, 'In that case, we will all have to strip off our clothes in order to find it, because someone here has got it!' The black guys found this rather humiliating, until a big black guy of African origin, a descendant of a chief or something, said, 'I would not strip off for anyone, but the stigma of having the finger of suspicion pointed at me is far greater than stripping off!'

As he started to take his kit off, all the other black guys followed suit. After everyone had stripped off or dropped their shorts to prove that they did not have the parcel, I tried to fathom out which person had it. I made a point of looking at everyone's eyes rather than their clothing or nakedness. I had my deep suspicions about one small black guy, but I knew that, if I accused him, it would look like I was persecuting him because he was black and because he was also small! Without concrete evidence, this would have made me appear to be a racist bully.

As we walked back to the main wing, my mind was racing; who had it? I knew once we all got inside the wing my chances of retrieving the parcel would be non-existent. It was then that Barry Hayes said to me, 'You know the small black guy ... did you notice, when he dropped his shorts, he only flashed his prick, his shorts did not go all the way down!'

This was the confirmation I needed. I saw the black guy walking up the metal stairwell to his landing. I immediately chased after him and caught up with him on my landing. I pushed him into a nearby cell and ordered him to strip off, telling him, 'All I want is my puff back!' I added, 'If I am wrong, I will give you the most sincere apology you will ever have!'

On hearing that, he put his hand down the back of his pants and tried to 'bottle' or secrete my prized parcel up his anus. I quickly grappled with him and seized the chunky parcel and clumped him a couple of times. I kicked him out of the cell and sent a message to the African chief that I had retrieved my goods. The chief was extremely upset over the thought that the culprit was a black guy, believing that he had let the black prisoners down. They were truly gutted over the incident.

That night, after evening bang-up, the culprit asked for protection and volunteered to be placed on Governor's Rule 43. In order to do this, the victim of alleged persecution needs to explain the reasons for the request, although he doesn't need to reveal the names of the people involved. The very next morning, the cell door was flung open and there stood a mob of stern-looking screws and a familiar refrain echoed around the interior of the cell: 'Pack your kit, Smith, you are on the move!'

Apparently, the intriguing drama of 11 prisoners of various hues and races stripping their clothes off on the sports compound had been recorded on the prison CCTV system and I was being accused of bullying and threatening other prisoners. It was the perfect excuse the authorities needed to ship me out to another regressive jail. Where would it be this time? I remember the day very well, as it was 2 August 1990, a momentous day in the world of politics and also a significant day for me, too, as I had only been at Parkhurst Prison for three months. Apart from the good gravy guys there, it was a piss-hole anyway and definitely time to move on!

18

Escape from the Strongbox

As I climbed into the Category 'A' prison van for the fourth time in 1990, I was thinking, Another move to another jail ... where and when is it going to end? It was a toxic combination of hostile jails, hard-hearted screws and oppressive regimes that prevented me from settling down and getting on with my sentence. The successful prison van escape and attendant High-Risk double 'A' security status that followed me everywhere like a shadow, labelled me a living target for every screw who resented and detested the special treatment it afforded such prisoners.

As we pulled out of the prison gates of Parkhurst Prison, I a sneaking impression that we would not be travelling very far. In fact, we drove less than a mile to Parkhurst's sister jail, Albany Prison on the Isle of Wight. Albany was built in response to proposals made in the *Mountbatten Report* into prison security and escapes in 1967. It suggested that a top-security prison be built next to Parkhurst and Camphill Prisons and that it be called Vectis, the Roman name for the Isle of Wight. This was rejected, in preference to Alvington and then, finally, Albany. Opened in 1967, it quickly became the proud flagship of the dispersal prison system only to acquire the reputation of being nothing more than a glorified Category 'B' jail with a severely repressive regime in the 1990s.

Word quickly spread among other Category 'A' prisoners in the prison system that Albany was a veritable karzy. One of the major criticisms of the prison was that long-term prisoners were unable to settle down at the jail and get on with their bird; one minute prisoners were on normal location, and the next minute they were swagged away down to the block for a mild transgression of the prison rules. For this primary reason, many Category 'A' prisoners allocated to Albany Prison refused to recognise or accept it as a *bona fide* long-term dispersal prison. Instead of becoming a virtual yo-yo, going up and down from the main wing to the block and vice versa, many prisoners opted to volunteer for the prison block on a permanent basis until they could be allocated to another genuine dispersal prison with facilities to match.

Some critics of this non-co-operative, non-violent protest viewed this action as self-defeating or counter-productive as it was doing the screws' job for them by volunteering for solitary confinement. They claimed that it was much more effective to go on to the main wings and cause as much chaos and mayhem as possible by setting fire to cells, TV rooms or workshops than spending months and months in segregation for nothing.

As always, I weighed up the pros and cons and decided to sit it out with the other Category 'A' prisoners in the chokey.

The Segregation Unit itself was L-shaped in design with cells on each side of the corridor. There were a further seven cells along an adjoining corridor. I was allocated to one of these isolated cells in the corridor. The overall capacity of the block was about 25–30 single cells with the Category 'A' prisoners taking up as much as 15–20 of these spaces at any given time. Often, the block screws would moan to me about the fact that Albany block was being used as an unauthorised Special Control Unit with its high concentration of dangerous Category 'A' prisoners and that they should receive extra danger money for working in such perilous conditions.

One consolation for me was that, by volunteering for the non-violent protest in the block, the psychological torture and torment would be offset by the knowledge that another Category 'A' prisoner would be transferred out of the block to better climes in order to make way for me. There was a fine body of staunch and resolute men in the block while I was there, including Alex Sears, Steve Jonas, Mark Foley, Mickey Adams, George Stokes, Kevin Gregory, Charlie Bronson and a whole host of other game Category 'B' prisoners.

The cells in the block were minimalist in the extreme; we had a concrete kerbstone as a bed, a four-inch thick mattress, a piss-pot, a cardboard table and chair and a small, heavily barred window that let in the essentials of light and ventilation. In short, it was 'back to basics' 23 hours a day behind your cell door, fighting to do your time without harassment and persecution from the screws on the main wings who pushed prisoners to the brink of eruption.

Initially, prisoners involved in the block protest were placed on Governor's Report for refusing to go on to the main wing, resulting in the loss of two weeks' remission, pay and privileges. This would be repeated every fortnight for two months until, out of the kindness of his heart, the number one Prison Governor Kitteridge would supplant the punishment measures with Governor's Rule 43(a) in order to maintain the 'good order and discipline of the prison'. Basically, this meant the Governor would keep the prisoner in the block until he decided to transfer them out of the jail without additional punishment.

Fortunately for me, opposite my cell in the isolated corridor was an old Towner friend called Peter Mitchell, who claimed that there was a possible loophole in the prison rules that could circumvent a lengthy sojourn in the block that, on average, lasted for about five to six months. Peter claimed that, if I made out that I had a personal enemy on the main wings and that I feared for his or my life, then I might get transferred to another prison quicker. To give the stratagem added credence, however, I would have to volunteer to be placed on Governor's Rule 43(a) that might expedite the transfer. The only problem was the stigma of being on Rule 43(a), which was usually a bolt-hole for the nonces and debtors. I had no need to worry about that, because everyone who was anyone knew my pedigree and knew that it was a genuine ruse to circumvent the prison rules.

The next morning, I was produced on Governor's adjudication armed with my plan. I claimed that I could not accept a cell on normal location because there was a threat on my life and that it was better that I did not confront the person in order to prevent serious injury to that person or myself. Moreover, I claimed that I could not divulge the person's name as I was not a grass. The Governor granted my request and said that the Board of Visitors would come to see me to endorse his action.

The beauty of the plan was that the Governor could not seize any remission, privileges or pay from me and, additionally, it might expedite the transfer. More importantly, I had £150 saved up in my prison canteen that I could spend on the poverty-stricken lads down the block. So every week I would spend £20 on matches, Rizlas, tobacco, Alpen, milk and teabags, etc. and hide them in the recess for the other prisoners to collect when it was their turn to slop out.

It goes without saying that, the dreary routine of 23 hours a day behind the cell door was tedious in the extreme. The remaining hour was set aside for the mandatory exercise period, walking around a small wire mesh compound like a polar bear in the zoo. The argument goes that, if the prisoners held in Albany punishment block were dogs and the RSPCA were called in to investigate and monitor the circumstances and conditions of their confinement, it is highly probable that they would shut the prison block down due to it being deemed wholly inadequate and unacceptable for the wellbeing of animals.

Paradoxically, the very watchdog organisation that was employed to monitor and supervise the abuse of power by the Prison Governor and his staff – The Board of Visitors – actually sanctioned the long-term isolation of prisoners in the block, as it was their role and function to authorise or refuse to authorise the segregation of prisoners on a monthly basis.

One prisoner in particular, called Alex Sears, who was involved in a near-successful escape at Long Lartin Prison the previous year, was kept in the block by the angry Governor for ten months. When the Governor sought to extend his isolation for another month, the BoV refused, claiming that he had been in solitary confinement long enough and it was time to transfer him to another prison. Under closer examination, it took a seemingly impartial watchdog agency ten months before it would speak up on a prisoner's behalf.

In order to combat the endless boredom of 23-hours-a-day bang-up, I devised a coping mechanism of reading, studying for the A-level, writing letters, composing poetry and doing circuit training during the daily hour exercise period. I recall one wet and rainy day, I was in the exercise compound opposite Charlie Bronson. We could not see each other because of a solid wall partition, so we decided to get the screw's nuts by having a game of tennis with a medicine ball. Charlie would throw the ball over the wall and if it touched the ground before I caught it, it would be a point to him and vice versa. It was hilariously funny. It was the first time that I had met Charlie and I found him – contrary to propaganda and reputation – an excellent guy.

On a political level, there was plenty of action in the broadsheet newspapers to keep my mind active while I was in the block. On the day I arrived at the prison, Iraqi armed forces had invaded Kuwait and the battle between the Scud missiles and exocets began. Then we had the long-awaited political demise of Maggie Thatcher, whose irrepressible disdain and hubris over the poll tax issue helped to bring about her comeuppance.

To combat the long hours of boredom, I even had a pet spider called Caesar who had made his home on my windowsill. I recall once I had written over 20 pages of work on Geoffrey Chaucer's *The Franklin's Tale* and handed it to the screws to forward to the Education Department, but it never reached my tutor. The study and analysis of English literature was a great help to me in writing poetry, especially with themes exploring the negative experiences of life, which I found were much easier to compose than those poems of an uplifting or joyous nature. One poem I composed, however, based upon a true account, tries to combine the positive and negative aspects of long-term isolation:

CHUCKLING

As I ponder in my cell
Thinking about this place,
Abnormal chuckling
Echoes from an unknown face.

He is in the pad opposite
His name is not known,
Yet strangely his chuckling
Makes him feel quite at home.

The shrinks will have their day
Translating his insane tone,
Pumping him with crazy drugs
Driving his dribbly drone.

But he sounds incredibly happy,
In his quaint way,
Chuckling, chuckling, chuckling,
Take heed, I pray!

For his maniacal mirth
Contrast with lucid reason,
Who's to say sanity
Outweighs the barmy season.

So keep on chuckling, simple mind
I envy your style,
Who gives a fuck what they put
In your medical file.

Albany Prison
14 November 1990

Throughout this long period of solitary confinement and sensory deprivation, my family were as strong and resolute as ever, visiting me every fortnight and even visiting our local Member of Parliament, Nigel Spearing, in order for him to put some pressure on the Home Office to transfer me to another jail. When my mother- and father-in-law took my handwritten Home Office petition to the MP at his surgery, he read it and asked rather suspiciously if someone else had written it for me as it was written so well. Although Mr Spearing wrote a letter to the Home Office on my behalf, it all came to nothing.

The High-Risk category visiting conditions themselves were very oppressive and intimidatory. They were held in a short, thin room with a doorway at each end. Tracey and I would sit in the middle of the room facing each other over a table, while a screw would sit directly behind each of us looking and listening to our conversation intently. How we were meant to maintain and sustain a strong family bond in such bleak conditions and circumstances is beyond me. If it were not for the intense way that we felt for each other, our relationship would have buckled under the pressure of such obscene observation and scrutiny.

This type of persecution and intimidation extended way beyond the realms of wide-eyed consciousness. One perverse screw on night duty would come to our cells in the block and check us, switch on the subdued red light and kick the cell door and wait until the prisoner in the cell woke up and then he'd walk away. So, even when we could escape the brutal world of imprisonment by sleeping and dreaming, this sick screw would wilfully wake us up on the pretence of checking that we were in the cell. The perpetrator of this torture thought that he was safe and secure doing this at night behind closed cell doors. He underestimated the lads in the block, because the next time he did it, we woke up at 3.00am and began the biggest and loudest racket we could, waking the nonces sleeping snugly in the cells above us. The next morning, the nonces complained to the screws and we were all placed on Governor's Report. Bingo! The screw who'd been on night duty put his surname on the nicking form and, fortunately for us, it was an unusual name. A few quid parted hands and, lo and behold, the lads in the block had the screw's home address and phone number. One evening, when our pals were out clubbing in London, they gave our 'door-kicking screw' a phone call and warned him that, if he kept up his antics, he would be getting a visit! Not surprisingly, the kicking of the cell doors in the night stopped.

On another occasion, I was out on the exercise yard with Andy Russell who had helped Kendall to escape from prison in the helicopter three years earlier. Andy had become embroiled in a verbal confrontation with a loquacious Scouser who was serving life for burning a poor old granny to a cinder. During the verbal row, the Scouser spat in Andy's face through the wire mesh separating us. It was a despicable act and one that would be avenged in the dispersal prison system, no matter how many years it took.

It was customary for the Governor to walk around the cells in the chokey every day to check on and speak to his charges. Some prisoners would return the pleasantries with 'Good morning, Guv'nor', some would simply ignore him, some would let fire at him with a blunderbuss of volatile invective and some would go so far as to prepare a bucket of fecal waste and urine for him. Over the months, I would invariably ignore the Governor, which obviously grated with him. It was well known in the punishment block that the Governor had a list of Category 'A' prisoners who were next to be shipped out. It was like a league table based upon the length of time you'd been in the block, where once you reached the top of the league you would be promoted or transferred to another jail.

One day, while on the exercise yard, the prisoner in the next yard to me asked the Governor where he was on the list. Seizing the moment and seeing as I had been in the block the longest, some seven-and-a-half months, I asked the Governor where I was on the list. He said, 'I have got a list, Smith, but you are not on it!'

The screws on the exercise yard had overheard this remark, as they often had to deal with the violent consequences of such remarks when prisoners exploded and attacked them because they could not reach the offending Governor grade. I knew that the prison block had two strongboxes which were remote, isolated cells with double-skinned doors to prevent anyone being heard in them. These strongboxes were used for allegedly violent prisoners who were seized on the main wings by the so-called control and restraint teams. These cells were in constant use all the time at Albany Prison. The lads in the block would hear the alarm bell go off and hear the block screws prepare to accept a new, allegedly volatile prisoner. The constant use of the strongboxes was indicative of the type of prison Albany had become; the repressive regime would create and develop excessive levels of stress and tension and this would lead to a higher-than-average level of assaults on prisoners and staff alike. It did not take an Einstein to work out that the excessively repressive regime was the root cause of this grief and mayhem, but the screws appeared to like to run the jail in this manner, as it was pay-back time for the major riot in May 1983 when they nearly lost the jail completely. It was like being part of some perverse social experiment, where those confined in the block cells were compelled to listen to and endure the screams of pain and suffering as the control and restraint teams dragged their next victim into the strongbox and forced him into the indestructible space suit. In fact, I will always remember the piercing screams of Tony Steel who was thrown in the strongbox. I was earmarked to give evidence at an inquest into the incident but, as yet, it has not been resolved.

Seeing as the strongboxes were being used all the time, I knew that, if I was in one of them and refused to come out until I was transferred, not only would it cause location problems for the perceived violent and disruptive prisoners, but the Governor would also have to notify the Home Office that a High-Risk Category 'A' prisoner was in the strongbox and outline the reasons for this drastic action. As a result of this deductive reasoning, I refused to go behind my cell door on returning from the exercise yard and volunteered for the strongbox. As a rule, prisoners had to be bent double and frog-marched to the strongbox but, to some degree, the block screws were sympathetic to my cause.

The screws chaperoned me to the strongbox where I voluntarily changed into the space suit and they all left the cell. I knew that I had to make a stand on this issue as, all things considered, I was not in the Segregation Block for punishment. In effect, I had refused to go on normal location to avoid a potential violent situation or incident. I was in the strongbox for two hours when the block Principal Officer and a member of the Board of Visitors entered the cell. The PO said, 'I have been on the phone to the Governor and there has been a mistake. There is a transfer list for prisoners in the Segregation Unit and you are at the top of it. I have been told to tell you,' he added, 'if you come out of the strongbox now, this will not be recorded and you will be transferred within the next two weeks.'

I considered the proposition for a short while and I knew that if I stayed inside the strongbox I would be transferred most probably the very next day to some other piss-hole and spend a month in the block there. Alternatively, if I returned to my cell, I would be moved in two weeks anyway. I said that I was willing to come out of the strongbox but, now that I'd had to embark upon such a radical course of action, how would it reflect upon my transfer to a progressive jail?

The PO replied that it would not change those plans one iota. Outwardly, I knew that I had made my point but, inwardly, I knew who would have the last laugh.

Ten days later, someone shouted from the lower section of the block that Vicky Dark had arrived from the chokey at Frankland in Durham and I knew that I would be on the prison van to Frankland the next day. The slags had rumped me. They knew that I had already spent two years at Frankland, which had put my wife and children under immense strain, and the Governor grades were sending me 400 miles to Geordie-land once again.

There is no disputing that the transfer to Frankland was initiated as a 'punishment move' and one that was moulded or shaped to crush the strong family bond that I had with my loved ones. The next day, I was taken to the reception area at Albany Prison where, as I was about to be loaded on to the prison van, I was involved in a pointless disagreement with a screw who insisted that the handcuffs were ratcheted to the tightest notch. I pointed out to the screw that we were not going on a Sunday jaunt to the local park, but 400 miles to the other end of England with an armed police escort. The debate developed into an argument which, in turn, became a major confrontation. Eventually, the alarm bell was pushed by some gormless screw and I was bent double and forced to the floor by a score of screws and then threatened with being placed in a body-belt all the way to Frankland. If it were not for the intervention of the PO in charge of the escort, who clocked the wishes of the Albany screws, I would have been placed in the body-belt. He took over the handcuff dispute and placed them on me in the correct fashion. Good riddance to Albany!

As we motored our way up the M1 towards Frankland, I wondered how Tracey would take the blow that I was back at Frankland. In many respects, I felt like the sea-faring adventurer who had set sail from the shore in search for the New World only to return with terrible tales of woe and despondency.

19

So Long, Farewell ...

In simple, straightforward language, my reallocation to Frankland Prison was pure bollocks. Despite feeling very aggrieved at being returned to the North of England, I was relieved to escape the claustrophobic effects of the chokey. I had spent over seven-and-a-half months behind the cell door and now I had to readjust to the social and psychological pleasantries and nuances of normal location. I say 'psychological' because, for some inexplicable reason, I felt strange, weird, even paranoid. One of the symptoms that I experienced was not being able to cope with lots of people. Obviously, this was a debilitating side-effect of being in solitary confinement for so long and I was hoping that it would go away. I wanted to speak to someone about it, but I was mindful that it could be perceived as a weakness and that could be dangerous in such a macho environment as prison.

I was allocated to 'B' Wing and immediately fell into the open arms of my old prison mentor and buddy John Massey. I opened up a little bit to John about how strange I felt and he said that it was normal to feel in such a way. John told me about the time that he was in Wakefield Prison in the mid-1970s, where the Yorkshire screws absolutely detested the Cockney prisoners, especially the ostentatious, so-called 'London Gangsters' such as John. He was involved in a fracas and the screws overpowered him and injected him in the buttocks with the 'liquid cosh', rendering John unconscious for what seemed like days. When John finally came round, he found himself in a body-belt in a cell on an empty and isolated wing. The menacing screws would come into his cell to feed him, goad and taunt him, saying things like, 'Who's the tough Cockney boy now ...?' In plain and unequivocal terms, John claimed that he thought that he was going to die.

Compared to John's nightmarish experiences in prison chokies, my complaints were mild. John soon had me playing badminton and walking around the exercise yard every day talking to my other buddy Kenny Noye.

It was during one of these leisurely meanderings that our topic of conversation came round to sentencing. We was speaking about a friend of ours who had just had his sentence reduced on appeal and Ken asked me what the mathematical formula was that had been used to determine my sentence of 16 years. When I went through it with him, and pointed out that I had received 14 years for robbery and two years consecutive for the prison van escape, he asked what Kendall had received for the prison van escape. I replied, 'Two years, to run concurrent with his sentence for robbery.'

Ken immediately said, 'That's not right ... that's called "disparity of sentence".' In effect, His Honour Judge Lymbery admitted that he had not decided which defendant was culpable for the organisation of the escape, and yet he had sentenced me to two years consecutive and Kendall to two years concurrent. This equates to a fundamental legal error.

Immediately, I wrote to the Registrar at the Court of Appeal at the Strand and applied to ask for an appeal against sentence 'out of time', as the disparity between our sentences had not been apparent until now because, although we had been sentenced by the same judge, at the same venue, it was at different times. Eventually, I was granted the appeal and I asked my family to travel to the Court of Appeal in the Strand and visit the law library and obtain all the relevant case law with regard to 'disparity of sentence'. This they did, and I compared and contrasted all the appropriate cases and compiled my own grounds of appeal. Admittedly, the grounds of appeal were not as polished or as refined as they would be by counsel, but the principle of the argument was there.

Many years earlier, I had appealed against the excessive nature of the original 15-year sentence that I had received at Chelmsford Crown Court, only to be fobbed off by the judges with the refrain, 'This court is not renowned for being a court of mercy!' On this occasion, however, I was not asking for mercy or clemency, I was pointing out a glaring inconsistency that evoked in me a strong sense of injustice and grievance. This was a legal challenge, not a moral one.

My family employed the services of Stephen Batten QC, and we were forewarned that we had a strong case but, for various reasons, he felt that we would not win. When the day of the appeal hearing came round, we were not optimistic, but we had hope.

Put bluntly, the appeal judges refused the appeal, claiming that the sentencing judge at the time took into consideration the overlap of the original sentences between Kendall and myself, i.e. I was originally serving 15 years and Kendall was serving eight years, therefore I had received much more benefit than Kendall. But this was hard to believe. Kendall had been sentenced over a year after me, and there was no mention in his sentencing transcript about the benefits of overlapping sentences.

Moreover, at a deeper level, it came to light that Kendall had sent a personal letter to the His Honour Judge Lymbery during his sentencing, which prompted the judge to state, 'I am left – or, having read your letter – I am still left with the realisation that you are a resourceful and determined man for which you have some admiration ...' I have no idea what was in the letter, but the inference is, taking into account the judge's sentencing comment, that Kendall was trying to deny that he was a man of resources and that it must have been someone else who'd planned the prison van escape. Did the letter claim something along the lines of, 'If it had not been for Smith and his friends who organised the prison van escape, I may not be in this sad position today'? I don't know what was in the letter, but it might have scuppered my appeal and, as the saying goes ... I should have seen the signs!

While I was at Frankland this time round, I felt a compelling sense of injustice at forcing my family to travel all the way up to Durham for visits. I had had enough of lobbying Wing POs and Governors and writing petitions to the Home Office, to Members of Parliament and prison reform groups. The only thing I felt that the prison authorities listened to was 'direct action'! As a result, I was up and down the prison block like a yo-yo.

A massive bone of contention were the phone calls to my family. Access to the phones was handled in a very arbitrary and dismissive manner, particularly as far as I was concerned as there was a ready-made case for refusal always available to the screws – I was still a High-Risk Category 'A' prisoner. One day, I was so incensed at a refusal to use the phone, I kicked the Wing PO's office door in and gave him a volley of choice invective about the blatant injustices over using the phone.

Later that afternoon, in July 1991, I went to the visiting room for a social visit with Tracey and my staunch mother-in-law, and they had a worried look on their faces and I immediately sensed that something was wrong. Initially, I thought that something was wrong with my immediate family, but this wasn't the case. It was my best friend, the Best Man at my wedding ceremony, the man who helped me break out of the prison van in 1984, young Tommy Hole had hanged himself in Parkhurst Prison.

I was devastated. Why, why, why ... what had happened? What had driven this happy-go-lucky, mischievous villain to such a desperate act? Apparently, he was within the last two months of release from an eight-year prison sentence for the manufacture of amphetamine sulphate. He was even eligible for pre-release home leave. He had a lovely devoted wife, Tracey, and two gorgeous children, Thomas and Lauren. To take his life was so unbelievable and inexplicable that it defied all logic and reason. To compound matters, young Tommy Hole had been fitted up by a cozzer, who'd planted a kilo of amphetamine sulphate under the front seat of his vehicle. Many years later, the Court of Appeal posthumously cleared young Tom, along with his co-defendants, of being involved in the amphetamine sulphate case and they received a substantial financial settlement.

An interesting feature of the case was the involvement of another rogue, Detective Witchelo, who was later convicted and sentenced to 17 years' imprisonment for the contamination of tins of baked beans at supermarkets in order to extort large amounts of money. Ultimately, the sad fact of this tragic episode was that it was all too late for my friend young Tom; and now he was dead. Even the omnipotent legal powers of the venerable Court of Appeal could not rectify this miscarriage of justice. Young Tom was dead as a direct result of police malpractice and the fabrication of evidence to secure a conviction. Who knows what psychological torment and torture my mate went through as he served his sentence as an innocent man? One thing is for sure; young Tom did not have faith in the issue ever being resolved. The only way out for him was to take his own life.

We lost dear a friend that day. It is axiomatic that we only live once, and that, in our lifetime, it is not often that you can have a friend like young Tom, who put his own life and liberty at risk to rescue a friend from a long prison sentence. In many respects, I felt that young Tom had betrayed me by taking his life, in that he never gave others and me a chance to return the brilliant sunshine that he brought into our hearts. One thing is certain, if I can emulate the excellent standards of friendship, loyalty and love that he gave to others in my life, then I will leave this weird and wonderful planet a happy man.

After the social visit that brought the sad news of young Tom's departure from us, the screws escorted me to the Segregation Unit for kicking in the Wing PO's office door earlier that morning. I was placed on adjudication and sentenced to three days' CC (cellular confinement). It was the best thing that could have happened to me as it allowed me to grieve in solitude. Grief is a strange bedfellow as it searches your mind like a computer to replay all the good times and then it leaves you on a desolate island of loss and despair. It was easy for me to go with the grain over those three days in solitary confinement, but I decided not to let the tragedy dilute my resolve in beating my own prison sentence. I decided to press on and let the tragedy make me stronger. I know young Tom would have wanted it that way.

On release from the block, I was returned to 'B' Wing and I knew that I would not last long there. I had to put my golden rule into action – if I was not happy, do something about it. My pal John Massey was being transferred to Long Lartin and Kenny Noye was being moved down South, so it was time for me to move on, too. I spoke to the number one Governor Mr Buxton, one of only two Prison Governors during my sentence that I had respect for, and asked him if he could get me a move to Long Lartin with my friend John Massey. He said the next time he was at Head Office in London, he would bring the idea up with Category 'A' Board.

In the meantime, my patience was at a low ebb. I decided to stage a protest with a resolute group of Londoners – Mickey Reilly serving 12 years for bank robbery, Dezzy Cunningham serving 15 years for robbery, Kevin (The Soldier) Gregory and Tony Steel, a very audacious little lifer whose loyalty was second to none. The plan was to seize the screws' keys just before bang-up on Sunday night, barricade each end of the landing, crash through the TV room external windows and climb up to the roof and stage a protest about being many hundreds of miles away from our families and loved ones.

On the Saturday morning, we decided to ask the IRA prisoners if they wanted to make one with us. We made it plain that they should not let one particular non-IRA prisoner on the periphery of their group know about the plan, as we had him down as the wing grass.

The plan worked a treat. By teatime on the Saturday, a team of riot screws came to Mickey Reilly's cell two doors away from mine and swagged him down the block. I was next. I knew that we had been well lollied, good and proper. The screws could not get inside my cell as I had barricaded the cell door. I then smashed the cell to smithereens, the porcelain toilet, sink, windows, everything. I said that I was fed up being placed in the block for nothing, so I'd decided to smash up the cell. After I'd destroyed the cell, I volunteered to walk down to the block. Dezzy Cunningham followed us down there later that day, along with Tony Steel, who felt so aggrieved at being overlooked by riot screws he sploshed a screw the next day, just so that he could be in the block with us.

I settled down for a long stay in the block, because when a normally placid and influential prisoner like me decides to stage a rooftop protest and becomes a time-bomb, it unsettles the rest of the prison population. On the following Monday, the screws shipped Kevin Gregory out to Durham Prison block. Sadly, that was the last time I was to see him alive as, many years later, he was cornered after an armed robbery on a jeweller's shop in Putney where it is alleged that he fatally shot himself rather than return to prison.

When the prison van returned from the short trip to Durham Jail, it was my turn to be moved. I was loaded into the van with screws that I did not recognise. The usual game of guessing the destination through the complex weighing up of the screw's dialect, the route, the newspapers and so on was going through my mind when, to my utter amazement, as we pulled out of the prison gates a screw proclaimed, 'You know where you are going?'

'No,' I replied.

'Long Lartin.' he said.

'Yeah, I'm sure I am!' I countered sarcastically; I was not about to fall for that trick ... how dumb did they think I was?

After my departure, over the next few days Mickey Reilly was moved to Albany block and Dezzy Cunningham was transferred to Parkhurst on the Isle of Wight, so one way or another we all got our transfers South. Sadly, again, that was the last time I would also see Dezzy Cunningham; for reasons I do not understand, he also committed suicide in Whitemoor Prison several years later. What drove Dezzy to take his life I do not know, but it annoys me when law and order activists and hardliners claim that prison sentences are too short and that the prisons are too soft. Tell that to the families of young Tommy Hole and Dezzy Cunningham, and I am sure you will get an appropriate reply. God bless them.

20

Party Games

As we know, the most disturbing aspect of climbing into a prison van as a Category 'A' prisoner is that the destination is unknown. In effect, your next stop could be any one of a number of penal dustbins in the British prison system. Providing it had giant walls, a self-contained segregation unit and enough screws to oil its monotonous daily routine, any Category 'A' prisoner could end up there. Therefore, it was with great relief, during the gorgeous Indian summer of 1991, that the prison van I found myself in was carving its way through the picturesque countryside of Shakespeare-land – Warwickshire – to Long Lartin Prison in nearby Worcestershire. The screw hadn't been pissing me about after all!

According to the prison grapevine, I had received positive feedback about Long Lartin with its liberal and relaxed regime, spacious sports field and electronic cell doors which could be unlocked throughout the night to enable prisoners to use the toilets and showers. How Long Lartin had eluded me for so long is a mystery. I now needed to settle down and get a couple of trouble-free years under my belt because, the way I was going, I was living out of a suitcase, too frightened to put up the curtains in my cell as, every time I did, the cell door would burst open and those ominous words would bounce off the walls, 'Pack your kit, Smith, you are on the move!'

It may well be that I did not get on with the Prison Governors or the screws – which is no hardship – or that they were intimidated or fearful of my prison record and presence. All I knew was that, I wanted to be treated like an adult and not like a child with an oppressive security label which kept me on the back roads of trouble and regression. In short, it was time to get on the motorways of progress and accelerate towards the prison gate and freedom.

In essence, Long Lartin was a large, modern dispersal prison located in the Vale of Evesham. Built in the late 1960s and early 1970s, it was finally opened in January 1971. From the outside, however, it looked like what it was – a sprawling, three-tiered council estate for prisoners surrounded by massive reinforced walls and motorway floodlights. From the very outset, I had good feelings about coming to Long Lartin. Rumour had it, because of the mature and responsible way the prison staff treated their charges, it reputedly transformed lions into lambs. There was a general consensus at the time that many ultra-subversive prison rebels had come to Long Lartin and, over the months and years of residence, they had faded away into painless obscurity and oblivion. There could be only one compelling reason for this – the screws left you alone.

There was no overt animosity, no exocet vindictiveness and no excessive coercion or pressure to do anything that you did want to do, except that you had to work. This was a bane for most prisoners but, in general, most prisoners could find a sensible niche on the labour board. If the prison workshops or laundry were not suitable modes of employment, then cleaning the wing or even full-time education were available. In my view, if you could not do your time at Long Lartin in the early 1990s, then it could only be down to a basic problem with prison or one's own prison sentence.

Initially, I was allocated to one of six identical T-shaped wings, 'E' Wing, and was made very welcome by a trio of convivial Cockneys: Johnny Read, who was serving 22 years for ramming a Brinks Mat security truck with a mobile crane; Cyril Birkett, a corpulent and extremely affable robber, serving 20 years for a daring robbery of a Post Office depot; and Ronnie Easterbrook, who was serving life imprisonment.

Apparently, Ronnie and his accomplices had been ambushed by armed police after a robbery at a vehicle change-over point. As Ronnie and his accomplice were about to switch cars, the police opened fire and killed Tony Ash. It is alleged that if Ronnie had not returned fire, he would have been killed, too. Later, while awaiting trial, Ronnie tried to blast his way out of a secure cubicle in a prison truck by smearing Semtex explosives around the emergency escape hatch overhead while being taken to court. Despite the dramatic escape attempt being unsuccessful, Ronnie showed exceptional audacity and gameness in his bid for freedom and he deserves all the respect coming to him.

In spite of this amiable trio making me feel very welcome, my close friends John Massey and Rooky Lee were on 'A' Wing and urged me to join them. Also on 'A' Wing were a great bunch of lads from London, including Bubba Turner, Bobby Knapp, Lionel Jefferies, Chrissy Hague, Alan Byrne and Nicky Webber. We all got on together exceedingly well, especially when the Viking juice was retrieved from its hiding place and Rooky Lee and Lionel Jefferies commenced their hilarious debagging act, which usually involved a liberal application of raw eggs, flour, jam, boot polish and other spicy condiments.

In between these stress-relieving bouts of wild saturnalia, I was revising for the long-awaited English A-level examination which, despite all the trouble and upheaval I had endured, I finally sat in November 1991. Most teachers and academics will proclaim that the A-level is the most difficult exam a student will ever have to face, as it relies upon two years of advanced study being regurgitated from memory in three separate three-hour exam papers. Preparation and revision for the exam gave me a personal insight into the psychological hell many A-level students have to endure when they are studying for two or sometimes more A-levels at once. Although I was studying in unconventional surroundings, one A-level was enough for me.

When the results came back and I was awarded an A-grade, I was ecstatic as it was a personal achievement and victory for me as I had been booted out of school at 13 and placed into care with no qualifications. In my view, this underscored and confirmed that I had the academic wherewithal to take on an Open University course.

As far as serving time in a top-security prison goes, it does not get any better than 'A' Wing at Long Lartin. I threw myself headlong into education, keeping fit and having the occasional guzzle down the 'Dog & Duck' at weekends, the mythical name of our watering hole. It must be said, the screws were dead against prisoners getting intoxicated as invariably you always had one drunken doughnut who thought that he could fight the world and conquer the globe.

As the festive season was approaching in 1991, I came up with an ambitious plan to secure a brand-new plastic dustbin, sterilise it and fill it up with the wondrous ingredients of hooch, copious amounts of yeast, malt, sugar and tepid water. The idea was to put the dustbin on a small platform with wheels so that it could be pushed with ease from cell to cell to avoid being seized by the 'burglars', otherwise known as a designated team of official cell-searchers. When we filled up the dustbin with all the necessary ingredients, it held a mouth-watering 96 litres of pure, unadulterated Viking juice. The idea was that no one would touch it until New Year's Eve. Little did we know that it would be a day we would never forget.

At Long Lartin, we were allowed out of our cells for evening association between 6.00–9.00pm, and then we had to bang up for the night. On New Year's Eve 1991, we cracked open the dustbin and started guzzling at 6.00pm and, by 8.00pm, we had practically the whole wing on our landing getting more and more inebriated. By 9.00pm, we were firing on all cylinders with rave music blaring from my sound system outside my cell. The screws wanted us to bang up but Rooky – our spokesman and therefore perceived leader – told the screws that we were not banging up until ten minutes past midnight. The riot squad was told to kit up and wanted to steam into us, but we were equally ready with countless makeshift weapons and missiles. A Governor grade who was in charge of the incident obviously foresaw the possibility of a bloodbath and let us party until we all banged away at 12.10am. The duty Governor was well aware that we may have won a small battle, but he would win the war in the long run. The irony was we only wanted to hear the poignant chimes of Big Ben, sing 'Auld Lang Syne' and then bang up, but we were so boozed we completely missed the chimes due to the blaring music.

The next morning, we all woke up with enormous hangovers and realised that we had to face the music. The screws and Governors had their meeting and briefings and it was decided that we would all be placed on adjudication and face the Governor for sentencing. I tinkered with the idea of pleading not guilty as the music was coming from my cell and my defence would have been, how could I turn the music off and bang up with 30 drunken villains on the threshold of my cell door intent on enjoying themselves? I decided against the not guilty plea as, whatever punishment I received, it was worth every day of it.

On the subsequent adjudications, 31 prisoners involved in the New Year's celebration each received 21 days' loss of remission. One Governor said rather beseechingly to Johnny Massey, 'Don't you feel ashamed of yourself? Eighty-five prisoner officers' wives were waiting for their husbands last night and had paid £15 a ticket to celebrate the New Year with them and, because of you, they could not make it!'

John poignantly replied, 'I am sorry, Governor, I don't feel sorry for them as that is the first time in 17 years that I have been able to wish some happy New Year to their face on New Year's Eve!'

Not surprisingly, John was transferred the next day to Gartree Prison in Leicestershire. Over the next few days, it was payback time for the screws as they shipped out nearly all the party-goers. Rooky ended up in the punishment block at Dartmoor Prison where they had a peculiar block rule that prisoners were only allowed to walk on the black squares of a chequered floor. All in all, our little New Year's party cost the Prison Service over £500,000 in the loss of remission, the transfer of prisoners and overtime pay for the screws. The party even made the national press. The *Sun* newspaper ran the story with the heading OLD LAGS SYNE, stating that 31 hard men at a top-security prison kept screws at bay during a New Year party. We don't have many New Year parties in our short and sweet lifetimes, but this one, despite its strange surroundings, will go down as one of the most remarkable yet.

Over the following days, everyone who was at the party had been transferred, except Nicky Webber, Chris Hague and myself. My personal survival kit had been packed and ready for days as I knew from experience that the screws would come for me eventually. The next day, they came for Nicky Webber and then I went to see the Wing PO and asked him outright if I was going to be transferred as my kit was packed and I was ready to go. The PO said, 'All those responsible for the incident have been transferred ... seeing as you only just got here before the incident, you are staying!'

I couldn't believe it. Unbeknown to the Wing PO, it was my idea to make a dustbin full of hooch and have the party, and I had come through it unscathed. What a result! It was time to celebrate. 'Anyone got any hooch?'

21

Taking the Rep

After the 'Old Lags Syne' exodus of January 1992, I decided to have a break from the hectic social life of Long Lartin and immerse myself in my studies. Oddly, I have always found reading novels, especially fiction, hard work, but give me an Open University text and I would absorb its contents like a sponge. I found the OU immensely satisfying, more particularly with its modular system of progress through writing one essay a month from February until October, which makes up 50 per cent of the course, and then a final examination which constituted the other 50 per cent.

Initially, I went for the Art Foundation Course A103, which embraced six core subjects taken from the Victorian era 1840–1900. These included English literature, music, poetry, religion, architecture and art history. After the examination in October 1992, I decided to change topics and opted to study the Social Sciences. Although I had found the Arts very interesting and rewarding, I could not see the practical value of visiting an art gallery and pointing out the elevated social and economic position of an aristocratic exploiter of the working classes to my wife. I wanted to understand why a high proportion of professional armed robbers came from predominantly working-class backgrounds and were invariably raised in and around large tenement council accommodation of South, East and North London. I wanted to know what makes people commit crime, what are the causes of crime, who commits crime and why. Put succinctly, I wanted to know about myself!

All my life, I had been in and out of care homes, Detention Centres, Borstals, juvenile institutions and adult prisons and I rationalised that, if I knew the reason why I committed serious crime, it could go some way to halting the vicious circle of imprisonment. Obviously, the salient reason for committing crime or armed robberies was money, but what did money get you? It brought you freedom to do what you wanted to do. Money and lots of it dictated that you did not have to get up in the mornings; you did not have to work. You did not have to have fried egg and chips twice a week as you could afford lobster thermidor, spinach and sauté potatoes, washed down with expensive wine. Money dictated that you could provide clothes and presents for your children without running up huge debts. In short, money brought you respect in the modern world and, if you were 'a good money-getter', like I was in the world of crime, prestige and respect followed automatically.

At a micro level, the same principles applied to prison life. If all prisoners had to rely upon the carefully planned diet of prison food, they would, over a decade or so, gradually degenerate or cave in through nutritional deficiency. Therefore, those who could afford it sold drugs, usually cannabis, to other prisoners, in order to secure enough money to survive in prison without having to rely on prison food. What is the point or value of serving over a decade in British prisons only to be released as a decrepit, dispirited and degenerated has-been who would be nothing but a burden to their family and loved ones?

No, long-term imprisonment was all about survival, in every sense of the term, that is, psychologically through mental stimulation, physically through a healthy diet and exercise, and socially through keeping – absurd as it seems – decent moral company. I would not say that I was unsympathetic or a cold-hearted person, but sometimes in prison you have to protect yourself against the professional or insidious whingers and groaners. Some prisoners even put up a sign in their cell: 'No tea and sympathy here!' In many ways, you had to insulate yourself from these emotional and psychological parasites who worked away at your resolve in the most surreptitious of ways.

For example, I had a close friend at Long Lartin and he had a companion tagging along with him. I accepted his presence in our company purely due to his friendship with the other guy. Over the course of three weeks, this person had broken through my outer force field of insulation and gradually, bit by bit, began to nibble away at my inner core like a voracious termite. After weeks and weeks of continuous grumbling, groaning and grizzling, I unceremoniously booted him out of my cell and told him not to come back. It was like lifting a soaking wet overcoat off my shoulders, the pest had to go! If this was not proof enough, my friend who'd introduced the termite to me suffered a mental breakdown and had to seek sanctuary in the prison hospital and, later, the block. It took me three weeks to tumble this high-speed hammer drill on the brain, while under normal circumstances he would not have even been allowed to enter my company. It was a lesson to be learnt – don't suffer whingers lightly.

Towards the end of my sojourn at Long Lartin, the prison introduced a Listeners Scheme run by the local Samaritans agency. I was approached to become a Listener, involving several short lessons on how to become a sympathetic listener to people with serious personal and mental problems. Primarily, I volunteered for this because up to 50 prisoners a years commit suicide in prison and one of them had been my best friend. I felt that, if I could save one prisoner from such a desperate and tragic act, then it would all be worthwhile.

Obviously, you have the perpetual cynics in prison who claim prisoners only become Listeners for their own selfish reasons but, as I was to find out, prison can become a veritable hotbed of malicious gossip, rumour and disinformation. A spiteful and vindictive whisper can be halfway round the jail before the truth has time to get its boots on! By definition, most prisoners are professional liars, as they need to be to wheedle their way out of official accusations of crime.

A prime example of this occurred on 'B' Wing at Long Lartin when a friend of mine, Perry Wharrie, rather stupidly left a brown paper bag with five ounces of tobacco on the side of the kitchen area while he was cooking. I am not being disrespectful when I say Perry is clumsy or forgetful. He is a tremendous guy with an equally tremendous disposition towards others. In any event, the 'snout' went missing. Naturally, there was a big inquiry about who'd nicked it. Acquaintances and associates were summoned, witnesses pursued, passers-by collared, anyone and everyone near to the last-known whereabouts of the snout were quizzed and eliminated. Then a white guy came to me and said that he saw a black guy take the snout. I took the white guy to Perry, who then went up to the black guy and had a fight with him in the cell. But there was a major dispute as, although the white guy pointed the finger at the black guy, the accused was adamant that it was not him. There was only one solution; we put the black and white guy in a cell and we let them argue their case.

Without any qualms, the black guy chinned the white guy and the white guy, guilty as sin, bolted for safety down the block. The problem was far from over, as it had become a race issue. A small group of concerned black guys on the other wings then started stirring up the race issue. It looked like all-out war as weapons were extracted from secret hiding places and the fear factor began to rise. Being a thorough gentleman, Perry sincerely apologised to the black guy for accusing him of the theft and, in a dignified manner, the black guy accepted his apology and reassured the galvanised brothers. The point is, prisons are full of mischievous, malevolent and mendacious people who are quick to blame others when the blame lies squarely upon their own shoulders. Many are salvageable. Many retain their moral and upstanding values and principles, but some sell their souls to the devil, as I was to find out at great cost.

Rumours, gossip and lies are not the sole domain of prisoners either. One incident comes to mind when the legendary prison hellraiser Charlie Bronson came to Long Lartin. I had met Charlie before in Albany Prison block several years earlier, but this time we were able to share a potent gallon of hooch together. As you can imagine, he had us Cockneys in hysterics as he recounted the time he sang 'Amazing Grace' for Ronnie Kray on a stage at Broadmoor Hospital.

On arrival at Long Lartin, however, there were some screws who detested the fact that Charlie was able to enjoy the relatively relaxed regime at the jail when he had successfully attacked many screws over the years and had become a perennial menace throughout the prison system. Obviously in an effort to encourage Charlie to settle down, the Hush-Puppied mandarins at the Home Office had decided to give Charlie a chance. Every prison rebel deserves a chance some time or other, but some screws with long memories were determined to sabotage this plan. But it was at this point that an allegation of rape was made against Charlie.

When we heard that Charlie had been removed from normal location and placed in the prison block because of this baseless allegation, we all voiced our concerns. Charlie may have been the ultimate prison time-bomb with, as he sometimes claims, 'too much electricity in his head', but he was not a male rapist. The Governor ordered a swift investigation and Charlie was returned to normal location and, on a glowing summer's evening, Charlie did a remarkable Shakespeare-like speech on the sports field expounding his undisputed innocence. As Charlie spewed forth his heartfelt vindication, we were all cheering him on. The fine booming speech was not needed, as we all knew the truth, but it made for excellent theatre.

If there is one overriding aspect the screws and prisoners dislike in prison it is unpredictability. Prisons are generally run on the premise of security and stability and, when someone like Charlie Bronson comes to the jail, weak and insecure people who feel intimidated become apprehensive and concerned. They need to be reassured that everything is all right and therefore, every morning in every prison all over the British Isles, prisoners embark, either wittingly or unwittingly, on a perverse ritual of reassurance – 'Good morning, Tel!' which is followed by 'All right, Charlie!' and so on. If one party to this verbal transaction of reassurance fails to acknowledge the other, a chain reaction of anxiety, suspicion and paranoia ensues. As a result, total reassurance can only be re-established by renewed greetings and pleasantries.

A prime example of this can be seen when Charlie Bronson was digging at his allotment in Parkhurst Prison when he said 'hello' to fellow armed robber, Dezzy Cunningham. Whether Dezzy heard Charlie's greeting is a moot point, but Dezzy ignored Charlie. On the next circuit of the exercise compound, an argument developed and later, no doubt due to Charlie's fearsome presence that worked against him on this occasion, a fight occurred and Charlie was stabbed.

This type of artificial social behaviour exemplifies the fragile balance of inter-prisoner relationships throughout the chattering landings of top-security prisons. All it takes is one sleepy-eyed morning, a lack of concentration or a mental blockage which could trigger an insecure neighbour to slide into deep and dark paranoia and plot all sorts of harm. I have had prisoners come up to me and state that they said 'hello' to me on Thursday last week and I did not acknowledge it and they ask whether everything's OK, as unbeknown to me they have obviously been dwelling on it. This is what makes prisons so odd and intriguing; the prisoner in the cell across the landing could be thinking deeply about something that concerns you for days and days, and you are the last person to know about it. It is scary, but it is true.

Physical training and sport were high on the agenda at Long Lartin, and particularly football. Every weekend, there were one or two football matches and sometimes, during the evening sports field association in the summer, we would arrange an impromptu match. We would play our 'nonce-free' football matches on Sunday mornings where, despite my leg impediment, I would stretch my legs and play in the midfield.

Over the years, all the games were played with the dedication and determination of athletes and, to give the games an extra competitive edge, we would arrange theme matches that usually had a geographical and vernacular slant. I was the player-manager of our team called 'The Lions of London'. The unwritten rules were that I could select a team of Londoners from the prison population to play against a team from the remainder of the jail. This consisted of some extremely good players from Liverpool, Manchester, Birmingham, Wales, Ireland, Iraq or wherever. We had some great games in which invariably the 'Cockney bastards' came away triumphant, that is until two nondescript players arrived at the jail and my rival manager, Mr Mabrouke, had a deeply embedded smile etched across his face. The new players, Vinny and Branco, were allegedly serving long prison sentences for smuggling cocaine inside footballs. They were professional footballers who'd played for Red Star Belgrade. That weekend, The Lions of London suffered their worse defeat when we lost 12–2. We were the laughing stock of the prison. We had got our comeuppance, as everyone wanted to see the flash 'Cockney bastards' get thrashed.

It was back to the drawing board for me. Much to his chagrin, I had to relegate our lethal striker Perry Wharrie to the defence to man-mark the deadly front man Vinny, and we had to shut down his supply from Branco in their defence by pressurising him at every opportunity. The following week, we lost 6–1, the next week 6–5 and then we won 4–3. The tide had turned and we started to win again in thrilling matches. It even got to the stage where I would encourage the players to abstain from drink and drugs on Saturday nights. On Sunday afternoons, however, there was always a celebratory party for The Lions of London.

Due to the great demand and enthusiasm for football in the jail, we sent a letter to the local football league and asked them if we could join their league on the condition that we could play all our home and away matches inside the confines of the jail. This had been arranged once before but, due to violence on the pitch, the prison team had been booted out of the league. Several years had elapsed since the previous banishment and we decided to try again.

As an *hors d'oeuvre*, we arranged a friendly game with a local side and had the referee and linesmen come in from the league to officiate the match. The game was going smoothly until our ginger full-back from Wales attempted a hospital ball back pass to our very athletic goalkeeper Steve Davis. A volatile argument developed between them, which resulted in Steve biting off our full-back's ear.

With blood dripping from Steve's mouth, our chances of rejoining the league were well and truly ruined for another decade or so.

Equally momentous was the charity football match that I organised at Long Lartin along with the Principal Officer of the gym department in support of the local handicapped children who visited the jail on a weekly basis. I contacted my friends Tony and Martin Bowers and Steve Clark of The Peacock Gymnasium in Canning Town, East London, and they arranged to bring a celebrity football team into the jail to play us. Among the celebrity players was the legendary Millwall and Glasgow Rangers maestro Terry Horlock. We had to submit all the players' names and addresses to the prison security department and, once they were cleared, the game could go ahead. I know that the prison Governor Mr Atherton and the gym PO were up for the charity match, but there was a weasel-looking screw who had the ear of a Governor grade, both of whom were not in favour of the match. The Peacock All-Stars team arrived at the jail in their appropriately named 'Battle Bus' and the game went ahead.

It was played in very difficult, windy conditions and the game was all square at 1–1 when one of my players, an embittered mixed-race guy, senselessly attacked a Peacock player. As a result, the game was abandoned and all the post-match pleasantries and photographs were aborted by the smug-looking screw. Later, I heard that the mixed-race guy was bouncing along the prison corridors with a large knife in his hand issuing expletives in all directions when another black friend of mine, Mark Blake, could take no more of his behaviour and sparked him, and then used him as a football along the corridor. To compensate for this person's infantile 'look at me, I am so hard' behaviour, we raised over £1,000 for the handicapped children, which when all's said and done, is what really mattered.

After nearly 18 months at Long Lartin, I was invited to become a 'wing representative' for the prisoners. Basically, two prisoners were chosen from each of the six wings to represent the prisoners on their wing at monthly meetings with the number one Governor. In this way, we were able to air prisoners' grievances and complaints and initiate change and improvement in the prison through proactive dialogue and negotiation. The sort of topics that were brought up at these monthly meetings ranged from the trivial to the serious. For example, the vegans among us might not have got their extra apple for a few weeks, or we might look at the heavy-handed strip-searching of visitors coming into the jail.

Like my predecessors, the litigious Chris Hague and urbane advocate Peter Welch, I only spoke about matters that I considered worthy of mention or matters that would improve living conditions or the prison regime.

One of the prominent things that I have noticed about prisons is that, whenever prisoners ask for an improvement of any kind, it is usually rejected on the basis of the perennial shortage of staff or for security reasons. In the early 1990s, however, Long Lartin was slightly different in that the number one Governor was in favour of progress and the improvement of the jail. Sensing this sea-change in attitude and approach, I pushed for and achieved the introduction of family visits. Once a month, you could pre-book a family visit which would be held in the prison gymnasium. This enabled families to use the gym's sporting facilities, such as football, basketball, badminton and even visit the 'punch-bag room', where little boxers could exhibit their pugilistic prowess in front of their proud mothers and fathers. I was quite proud of this achievement, which turned out to be a resounding success. But these groundbreaking improvements could only be successful if it had the full support of the Governor and his professional advisers in the psychology, probation and education departments. With the Governor's backing, I even managed to initiate a pilot-scheme for prisoners doing educational courses to have an in-cell laptop computer. Providing the wing reps presented a logical and compelling argument to the Governor at Long Lartin, he would rarely refuse a viable idea or suggestion.

One of the major problems for prisoners and prisons in general, more specifically at Long Lartin, was the pernicious relationship between drugs and violence. We are all aware that not all drugs lead to violence and, likewise, not all violence is drug-related. But through personal experience and observation, I believe there appears to be a strong correlation between serious acts of violence and drugs.

For instance, the toxic sequence of events usually went as follows: a debtor gets out of his depth and becomes paranoid; paranoia engenders fear of attack or persecution; this fear then invokes a need for a weapon, usually a blade; the paranoia and fear then prompt a pre-emptive strike because the fear has been allowed to calcify into direct action. If you add a little prison machismo – exaggerated masculine pride – to all these volatile ingredients, what have you got? A screw calling for a body bag.

On my wing, that is 'B' Wing at Long Lartin, we had the highest proportion of Cockney prisoners than any other wing. That was because, over the course of time, any new Londoners who came to the jail invariably wanted to come to 'B' Wing. This high concentration of Londoners on one wing was permitted on condition that we did not attack the nonces or sex cases. Sometimes, however, there would be a particularly despicable abduction and murder of a child on the national news and prisoners would sidle up to me in the TV room and ask if it was permissible to attack the resident nonce or sex beast. I would authorise these attacks on condition that they did not occur on the wing. If they occurred along the vast inter-wing corridors, then it did not affect our position on the wing.

Naturally, the high concentration of 'London Gangsters' – or 'LGs' as one Prison Governor liked to call us – made 'B' Wing the focal point of the jail. What did not help our position was that there were two unfortunate murders or fatalities on 'B' Wing during the early 1990s. Remarkably, neither of these deaths involved the Cockneys on the wing.

The first occurred in September 1994, when a verbal row developed between a group of black prisoners and a white guy in the prison chapel. Although the facts are vague, a prisoner from another wing came over to 'B' Wing during evening association and stabbed the black guy in his ground-floor cell. I was cooking on the ground floor when another prisoner came to me and said the black guy had been plunged and he looked in a bad way. He asked me what to do and I said he'd better tell the screws in case he needed urgent medical care. Little did I know the black guy was already dead. Later, the police were called, photographs were taken and a body bag removed. As a result of the incident, two prisoners were prosecuted for the murder and I believe one was acquitted and one was convicted.

Later still, family and friends of the deceased orchestrated a campaign against racism outside the gates of the prison. The *Guardian* newspaper published an article proclaiming that there was a 'white London gangster' on a wing of death at the jail who ran the jail and was behind the racism. The white London gangster was obviously me and it was not true; the Londoners were not involved in the death and, more personally, I was not a racist as I was on a two-man foodboat with a very likeable and endearing black guy called Mark Blake while I was at Long Lartin. Our friendship developed to such an extent that we are lifelong friends now. I did, however, raise the racist tag with the Prison Governor and he assured me that he knew that it was all nonsense. Calling me a racist was like calling Marilyn Monroe a virgin, as I had run away with three black boys when we were 13.

Of equal sadness was the second fatality that occurred in February 1995. It all started when the Welsh prisoners were watching an international rugby match between England and Wales. I ventured into the TV room to watch the game but already I could see the Welsh fans with a bellyful of firewater were boisterous. Not being a lover of watching rugby on television, I retired to my cell with my friend Perry Wharrie.

Inevitably, a fight occurred over the rugby in the TV room between a devout Muslim and a vociferous rugby fan. The non-drinking Muslim called Jamma decked the rugby fan and leathered him in the face, forcing his nose up into his brain. He was taken to the prison hospital unconscious, not a rare sight in prison, but, when the Prison Governor came to my cell later that evening and told me that he had not regained consciousness and had died as a result of his injuries, we were all devastated. The truth was that Jamma and Dia Matthews were very good friends, and now Dia was dead.

There are no winners at times such as these. The family of the deceased have to face and endure devastating grief and the survivor has to face the full rigour of the law. The only people who come away smiling are the police with another conviction under their belts and a chance of promotion. Jamma was charged with murder and appeared at Birmingham Crown Court where the charge was, at the last minute, reduced to manslaughter and he later received five years' imprisonment.

On a purely physical level, I had come a long way since the initial apprehension and arrest at Kensal Green. I had to work hard to overcome the terrible injury. I was at the stage where I was almost a fitness fiend. I would play basketball, football, softball, badminton and complete rigorous sessions of circuit training, sometimes involving the punch-bag, skipping, sit-ups ... you name it. Keeping in tip-top physical condition had become an important part of my life. I don't know whether it was the buzz of endorphins running around my veins, or the discipline and dedication involved in training or the competitive frisson I received from testing my athletic skills against a competitor, but I was hooked.

Throughout the prison sentence, I must have played badminton hundreds of times and one game stands out among the lot, more so because it was against a screw – the screw who was against the Charity Football Match. Most badminton players viewed my leg injury as worth about five or ten points before they started and would concentrate on my backhand as a possible weakness. But because of that reason, I had worked on this aspect of my game and it had become one of my strongest points. Armed with 'Excalibur,' my ultra-light graphite racquet, I would challenge all-comers and slay them as if they were fire-breathing dragons.

In the badminton instruction manuals, they teach you how to use the whole court, dinky net shots, power clearances, back to base, use the tramlines, back to base, but most of all, 'Go for the jugular'!

The screw fancied his chances and he threw down the gauntlet. The game was arranged for one Saturday afternoon and I took along two witnesses, Peter Welch and Keith Jones. The match was to be the best of three games. In the first match, I played my usual powerhouse, aggressive game, going for the kill, but the screw was a very supple and wily player. He had been around a lot longer than me and knew how to outfox the power game. Unbelievably, he took the first game 15–12. The second game – and last game if I lost – was going much the same way as the first. Excalibur was slaying the dragons, but I could not kill the monster. Power and strength like an oak tree are self-defeating in the storm. If I was to survive, I needed to bend a little like the reed by the riverside.

At 13–4 down, the sheer ignominy of letting the screw beat me was unbearable. It was then, in all honesty, that I cheated. I could not beat this screw without outside help. I looked to the roof of the gymnasium and summoned the succour and support of my long-standing and now dead friend, young Tom. I recall saying, 'Tom, give me the skill and strength to beat this screw, otherwise I will let you down!' Immediately, I changed the powerhouse tactics of my game. I no longer smashed, whacked and walloped the shuttle in aggression. I played subtle net shots, pushed my opponent to the back of the court, net shot, back of the court again ... There was more than one way to slay a monster.

I clawed my way back into the game and reached 14–14, which meant we had to play the first to three points to decide the game. I kept up the same subtle tactics and took the game. Physically, my opponent was still viable, but psychologically he was a whooped man. At one game apiece, it went to a final game that I duly won 15–11 or something. As court etiquette dictates, at the conclusion of the match I shook the screw's hand, and my witnesses, one of whom was an ex-county player, said that it was the best comeback performance he had ever seen. I must confess, it astonished me as well. Thanks, Tom, I knew that you were there for me!

In spite of my excellent physical fitness and mobility, I still wanted to try and get the rigid right leg fixed. Metaphorically speaking, it had become my very own 'ball and chain' which would always remind me of the Kensal Rise robbery. I had no bitterness, vindictive thoughts or feelings towards the person who'd rammed me on the motorbike. As far as I was concerned, I was morally and legally culpable of the crime and I took the injury and prison sentence flush on the chin. I have had several good friends sidle up to me in prison and say, 'When we get out, we will go and plug the guy who done that to you!' But I have always said, 'No!' I have absolutely no animosity or wish for vengeance towards the guy. What he did to me was punishment enough, it will be on his conscience as much, if not more, than it is on mine.

Having said that, it did not prevent me from seeking the assistance of revolutionary orthopaedic surgery in order to acquire some more movement from the knee joint. The first obstacle I had, however, was to get de-categorised to Category 'B' security status that would enable me to visit an external, independent consultant to see if he could fix the leg. As things happened, about a year after my arrival at Long Lartin Prison, the Inspectorate of Prisons carried out a security audit of the jail and recommended in his report that Long Lartin should lose its High-Risk security status, as it was not secure enough to house such dangerous and determined prisoners. In any event, all the High-Risk prisoners had their security status reviewed and those who were not de-categorised to standard Category 'A' status were to be reallocated to more secure accommodation.

I distinctly recall the day that I was de-categorised as it was the day that Windsor Castle was going up in flames and Sid Sivewright and myself cracked open a vintage bottle of prison hooch to celebrate. It appeared quite fitting that, as the establishment was burning, we were downgraded to the status of mere mortals. It was a good omen.

One of the main factors in aiding the de-categorisation from High-Risk to Standard Category 'A' status was a favourable report from the psychology department at Long Lartin. I have always been rather cynical and distrustful of authority or State-funded bodies, especially in prisons, and steered well clear of them. But a wise friend of mine, Peter Welch, advised me to visit the psychology department and ask them to compile a report for de-categorisation. In many respects, it makes sense, because a Prison Governor would very rarely support an application for de-categorisation per se, unless it was bolstered by favourable wing, probation, medical or psychology reports.

While at Long Lartin, I was introduced to a senior psychologist, Josephine Trustcott, a young, attractive Scot. I found our conversations very enlightening, particularly the encouragement, support and advice that she gave me with regard to my academic studies. As time progressed, Mrs Trustcott provided me with all the professional support and assistance I required to descend the security ladder. Over several years, her favourable reports, supported by Prison Governor grades, saw me go from High-Risk double Category 'A' to Category 'C' status, which meant that I could apply for all sorts of special privileges. More specifically, her reports helped me to acquire an escorted day release to the London Independent Hospital to see an orthopaedic consultant regarding the leg injury.

I met Tracey at the hospital and was examined by a Dr King, an eminent orthopaedic specialist. He claimed that there was nothing that he could do for me and that the leg was best left alone. To be honest, after eight-and-a-half years in long-term prisons surrounded by gruff, hairy-arsed men, all I wanted was to spend some time alone with my wife. Naturally, the thought did occur to me to give my personal prison officer Ray Hill the slip, but I felt things were going so well for me that, being at the fag end of a long prison sentence, if I acquired a place at university, there was a real possibility of early release on parole. Moreover, being a man of honour – my word is my bond and all that flapdoodle – there was no way that I would betray those who'd supported me. The way I viewed things, if I returned to prison, not only was I in line for possible home leave but it proved that the Governor's and the psychologist's judgement was right in allowing me out for the day and it would not prevent or jeopardise other prisoners from enjoying such accessible privileges.

As for the senior psychologist Mrs Trustcott, her compelling reports for home leave, a progressive transfer to another jail and parole carried great weight. No doubt, without the psychology department's support and assistance, my prison sentence would have been several years longer. Speaking totally candidly, however, I used to feel slightly uneasy and apprehensive about visiting the psychology department, as some of the dubious characters also visiting there were definitely not the type who'd keep *schtum* in the police station. Full credit to Mrs Trustcott, though, not once did she ever try to pump me for information with regard to prison politics or protests. Only once did she broach a particularly contentious issue during a sensitive time at the jail, to which I said, 'As a wing rep, there are no problems on "B" Wing, so please don't ask me about the other wings as they do not concern me!'

Many years later after my release, scandal was to strike at the psychology department at Long Lartin where a new female psychologist became passionately involved with a charismatic armed robber. He was told, whether it was true or not, that all the one-to-one conservations in the department were secretly monitored and recorded. Looking back, it always amazed me how a very attractive female psychologist could sit in a private room at a top-security prison and talk to all types of perverts, rapists and nonces and still feel safe. It made me think that the eavesdropping of seemingly private conservations was probably true; nonetheless, I am deeply indebted to everyone concerned for their professional help. Thanks!

One day, I was sitting in my cell eating my tea with a couple of pals when someone came up to me and said that a new Category 'A' prisoner had arrived on the wing. I asked who it was as we were bound to know the person, and someone said that it was a 'McKenzie'. Immediately, my mind went back to Albany Prison block in 1990 when a scowling, humanity-hating Scouser, who'd burnt a poor granny to a cinder, spat into Andy Russell's face through the wire fence on the exercise yard. That day, we swore revenge upon this scumbag and now he was standing barely 20feet away from the 'Cockney bastards'! Needless to say, he was not on the wing long as he had to go to the outside hospital for treatment.

When it came to assaults on Prison Governors and screws at Long Lartin, it is fair to say that, when they did occur, they were very rare. Normally, they only occurred when a prisoner or prisoners felt that they were being unfairly persecuted or penalised by one specific Governor or screw. In many respects, this is the worst type of problem, where a prisoner feels victimised and bottles up a strong sense of grievance towards the screw as it has become 'personal'. This happened to my black friend Mark Blake who used to get exceedingly passionate with his beautiful girlfriend and future wife Annette on the visit. At this time, a specific screw kept arguing about the size of drink cartons that we were allowed to bring back to the wings after visits. One day, the screw went too far and Mark nutted him on his nose. Later, Mark was convicted at Birmingham Crown Court for grievous bodily harm, and his 14-year sentence for robbery was extended by a year.

Usually, serious assaults on screws only occur as a last resort when all manner of official complaint and redress has broken down and the prisoner still feels that he has nowhere to go but to explode violently. A prime example of this occurred on 'B' Wing when a screw would not leave Charlie McGhee alone over trivial things, such as unblocking the spy hole on his cell door and missing the electronic door-locking system when it was to be locked. This went on for a while until Charlie was placed on Governor's Report. I had already given evidence for Charlie at one of these adjudications before, but this time Charlie gave the order to put a chip-pan on and get it red-hot. Charlie had had enough and it was time to act.

Charlie and another prisoner put on a mask and went down to the wing office and chucked the boiling contents of the chip-pan all over the screws. Later that morning, Charlie McGhee and Tony McCann were removed from the wing and, after a police investigation, they were charged with a new prison offence of 'mutiny'. In October 1993, they both appeared at Birmingham Crown Court and, after ten prisoners had been summoned to court to give evidence, including me, they were both acquitted.

When it comes to the hardest or toughest man in the British penal system, Charlie McGhee – God bless him –was the living embodiment of fearlessness. For instance, Charlie was sent to Birmingham Prison punishment block, which was notorious for its systematic humiliation and degradation. While in the prison block, Charlie was given the customary treatment by the screws over a minor disagreement. Most prisoners, realising that they were in a 'no-win situation', would have licked their wounds and sought revenge another day with the pen, in a court of law or by spotting a disguised screw walking along the street on the outside. Not Charlie. He waited until the screws came round with the evening drink, and threw his hot cup of diesel (prison tea) into the screw's face and chased him down the landing with a fire extinguisher. The prison alarm bell was pressed and Charlie received another beating. But the message got through that this man could not be broken and they moved him for *their* own safety.

Charlie was no stranger to pain. He told me about the time he was driving along in his Ford Transit van and was involved in a terrible crash. The crash itself was not that bad; it was the Calor gas cylinder bottle that came from behind him and smashed him in the face that did the damage. The surgeons at the hospital had to rebuild his face.

As I said before, Charlie McGhee was serving a soul-destroying life sentence with a minimum recommendation to serve at least 25 years before being considered for release. Alas, in the late 1990s, after a short illness, Charlie passed away at Frankland Prison. In many respects, Charlie's sudden death was a blessing in disguise, as the British prison system would have sucked every last drop of spirit from this vibrant and fun-loving person and then waited for him to make peace with his maker. I believe Charlie foresaw this future of suffering and yielded to his illness. God bless, Charlie!

Towards the end of my almost five-year stay at Long Lartin, I had not only become a prominent wing rep, but I was also a Listener, took part in an anti-robbery course for youngsters and was actively opposed to the use and abuse of heroin in prisons. Over the years, I had witnessed Long Lartin transform from a predominantly 'puffers' jail' to a burgeoning snake-pit of scag-heads. I was not in any position to dictate to others what drugs to take, neither did I want to, as I was fully aware that, if heroin was strong enough to break the bond between a mother and child, what chance did I have of helping these unfortunate addicts?

You would be amazed at how many well-respected 'London faces' were users of the drug at Long Lartin. Some were very blasé about its use – and credit to them – they were, on the surface at least, able to cope with its hydra-headed problems and side-effects.

Others, however, were more secretive and liked to keep it in the closet. The central problem for me as a non-user and vocal opponent of it was that it produced an insidious undercurrent of animosity, jealousy and resentment towards me. My OU studies, wing rep-status – which I had used to promote the progress of prisoners' privileges and rights – day release and home leave were all ammunition for the scag-heads to attempt to denigrate my good name and reputation. In some long-term jails, the addictive powers of the drug had led to malicious dealers issuing 'contracts' on the good guys. Put succinctly, the pervasive disease of heroin and its consequences were, in some cases, able to capsize the moral order on some wings. Suddenly, scag-dealing rapists and wrong 'uns had more power than the non-liberty-taking prisoners.

A whispering campaign about me as a wrong 'un that had emanated from several disgruntled miscreants in the prison block was exactly what it was – poppycock. If the most powerful and influential police officers in the land at Scotland Yard could not make me turn turtle, then a Prison Governor or screw has got no chance. This appeared to be a recurring theme in my life; I had attracted bitterness, jealousy and resentment from others who could not live up to my high moral standards. This would not be the last time that I would become a victim of bitter and evil people.

As things turned out, once I had been downgraded from Category 'A' and I had served another compulsory year in the dispersal system, it was time for a progressive move to another jail. I was hoping to get to a Category 'D' establishment, where prisoners were allowed to go to college or work outside the prison as, by now, I had secured a place at university and I was utterly serious about continuing my academic studies. I wanted to, or rather needed to, go to Latchmere House resettlement unit in south-west London, which would give me access to the University, but I was ineligible to go to Latchmere because you could only go there with two years or less of your sentence remaining, and I had three years left to serve. I recall having a conversation with a Governor grade about a place at Ford Open Prison in Sussex, when he blurted out, 'You cannot go there, Smith, as we have serving Prison Governors there!'

Quickly, I replied, 'How can you sit there and say that, when I get on so well with you?'

In short, the only option left open to me was a Category 'C' institution called The Mount Prison in Hertfordshire ... so you can guess where I was sent.

22

Light at the End of the Tunnel

In late February 1995, once again I bade farewell to my closest friends and acquaintances at Long Lartin – Bubba Turner, Tony Martin, Mickey Reilly and Perry Wharrie – and was loaded into a basic white prison van with three screws for the 90-mile trip to The Mount Prison on the outskirts of Hemel Hempstead in Hertfordshire. The jail is a relatively modern prison built in the late 1980s and finally opened in March 1988. It contained several two-tier wings that were linked by a service corridor. Rumour has it that the jail was built near a disused airfield, whose claim to fame was that it was the airfield that the late musician Glenn Miller took off from before he was killed in an air crash.

Despite being a modern penal institution with over 400 prisoners, the liberal regime that is usually associated with Category 'C' establishments was non-existent. New fences had been erected, the discipline was harsh and home leave for prisoners due to adverse public opinion had been severely curtailed. Fortunately for me, I had already had a weekend home leave while at Long Lartin, so there was little reason for the prison authorities to stop further periods of pre-release rehabilitation.

As is the custom, I formally applied to be transferred to Latchmere House resettlement unit on the understanding that I could accept my place that had been reserved for me at the University of East London in September. But, to my utter amazement, my application was refused due the disruptive nature of my 'previous prison record'. When I checked the required criteria needed to be accepted by Latchmere House, I noticed that, of the seven qualifications required, 'previous prison record' did not apply.

From experience, I knew that the knock-back was open to judicial review as the new prison Ombudsman, Stephen Shaw, had visited Long Lartin while I was there and pointed out that these were the types of difficulties and 'abuses of process' that he was there to look into and hopefully solve. When I applied to see the Prison Governor over this strange decision, he ordered Latchmere House to give me another interview. This they did and, amazingly, it was refused yet again!

One of the criteria of acceptance for Latchmere House was that all prisoners had to have a maximum of two years of their prison sentence left to serve. On arrival at The Mount, I still had three years left to serve but, due to the excellent sleuthing skills of my co-defendant Kendall, he had the good fortune to explore and evaluate the complex nature of his prison sentence and, by doing so, he found out through another prisoner that, several years earlier, the prison authorities had adopted and embraced a new system of calculating prison sentences, and specifically those involving concurrent prison sentences where the prisoner had also escaped. Apparently, the prison service had informed all the other prisoners in this category, except Kendall and myself.

In a nutshell, the 'single net concept' of calculating sentences was applied to our sentences and they were both reduced by 12 months – which made me eligible for Latchmere House.

While at The Mount, I enjoyed another glorious home leave, was visited by a representative of the parole board and was still ploughing through voluminous texts and coursework with regard to the OU degree. In essence, the OU had been a veritable lifeline in a stormy sea for me, as not only did it divert hours and hours of pointless introspection over the anguish of imprisonment, but it flexed my long-dormant brain like a muscle and taught me how to question the unquestionable, challenge assumptions and formulate compelling and winning arguments. Quite plainly, it opened new doors of perception and understanding that would help me to overcome other difficulties in my life.

On Thursday, 24 August 1995, I was summoned to the Wing PO's office and formally told that I had been granted early release on parole. I was to be discharged the following Tuesday. I was ecstatic and could not wait to share the fabulous news with Tracey and several friends at the jail. It had been a long, hard and gruelling haul.

Including the two pre-escape years in prison, I had been a reluctant captive of the State for 11 years and 3 months. During that time, Tracey had visited me without fail every fortnight throughout the whole prison sentence, and never once did she grumble or groan about her plight. We had conquered the sentence together. We had confronted and overcome a gargantuan obstacle to our relationship and still emerged as a strong, resolute and unified family. This was emphatic proof of the fact that we should never underestimate the power of love and a good family. I had discovered that, indeed, 'There is always a good woman behind every great man!' I would not venture so far as to describe myself as a 'great man' but, in my heart of hearts, I know that I am a good person with strong moral principles. The overwhelming problem seems to be, as I get older, some wayward friends and acquaintances cannot maintain or sustain these high moral or criminal values and, for some reason, wish to see me suffer in pain and torment. Well, we shall see!

23

Born Free

As you can imagine, the five-day interval between being told that I was going home and actually going home were the longest days of my prison sentence. I had acted out the glorious day of my release over and over in my head countless of times over the years and now it was upon me. In many respects, my release was a leap into the unknown as all I had known over the last decade or so was the clanging of prison doors.

Early on Tuesday, 29 August 1995, I was unlocked and escorted to the reception area of the prison where I signed the appropriate pre-release forms, collected my personal property from the store and was taken to the prison gatehouse where I was greeted by my devoted wife Tracey, my two teenage sons Terence, aged 15, Bradley, aged 14, and my delightful daughter Jade, aged 10.

Although I had been let out of prison several times before for very short periods, this was the big day when I could sleep in my own comfortable bed and not be subconsciously aware of the night watchman screw peeping through the spy hole to check that I had not escaped. This was the big day of my life on which the nightmare chapter of long-term imprisonment would be supplanted by a new chapter of redirection and change. A brand-new chapter, in which I had to take into consideration all the needs and demands of those around me. To some extent, prison fosters selfishness, as you drag yourself out of bed every morning, month after month, year after year, and all you have to focus on is getting through the long monotonous day. The real challenge for me now was how to integrate smoothly back into 'normal society' and attendant family life. I did not view myself as an intruder in my own home, far from it, but the cold facts were that it was my wife and children's home, *their* home, and their social space, and I was the newcomer. Quite clearly, I had to fit into my family's life, and not the other way round. Thankfully, I was conscious of this and did my diplomatic best to be, first and foremost, an authoritative and loving father, but also a potential friend and ally.

I was also aware that it would not be long before the sun-blessed joy of release and celebration would be over and the cold reality of familial duty and responsibility would be upon me. I had to confront the brutal fact that I had to go through the rest of my life avoiding prison. I had reached the mellow and mellifluous age of 36; up to now, in one way or another, I had been incarcerated since I was 13 years old and I was absolutely determined to change and reverse this distressing trend. And the all-important key to this achievable ambition was my beautiful family. They had been without me for so long and to be taken away from them again would be nothing short of a gut-sickening tragedy.

Therefore, I decided to stick to the winning formula and take my place at the University of East London, where I was to take a degree course in Sociology, Politics and Economics.

Alternatively, I could have enrolled at the University of Middlesex, where I had a place to study my favourite subject, Criminology, but due to geographical convenience I chose the Barking campus in Essex. As a student, this was my first mistake, because a student is more likely to get up in the mornings and travel to college or university to study a favourite topic rather than a tolerable one. Nonetheless, I was determined to embark upon this academic journey of self-knowledge and self-enrichment as my liberty depended upon it.

I received excellent encouragement and assistance from my family, Erika Calvo at the University and my Probation Officer, Nick Paul, to carry out this endeavour, as well as from my friends at The Peacock Gymnasium in Canning Town, who provided me with a plush office table and chair on which to study at my home address. Naturally, there were the usual cynics who viewed this venture into academia as a fanciful dream, as it is one thing to study in the monastery-like confines of a prison, but quite another to study in the freedom of the modern world with so many colourful distractions and preoccupations at hand.

Nonetheless, study I did. I travelled everyday for six months to the University at Barking where I attended seminars, lectures and made copious notes in the library. I was deadly serious about the degree course, but then several things occurred at the same time that compelled me to reconsider my position as a mature student.

First, I had become increasingly disgruntled with the 'micro-economics' aspect of the degree course. I absolutely abhorred Economics, so I spoke to the course supervisor and asked if there was any way that I could body-swerve or drop the Economics side of the course and replace it with another topic. Apparently, this was impractical for administrative and organisational reasons and it was refused. Second, it was inconceivable that a growing family of five people could live on the monetary allowance of a mature student's grant. And third, and most important, I used to come home from the campus and go straight up to my desk in the main bedroom, shut the door and write up all my notes before I did anything else. After six months of this, I was becoming desperately unhappy, as I had realised that all I was doing was infusing my outside existence with prison traits and behaviour. In prison lexicon, I said to myself, 'Why am I banged up upstairs in my bedroom in my house, when in reality I want to be down stairs on "association" with my wife and children?' I had had enough bang-up and enforced solitude and, through being brainwashed, I was volunteering for it again. It was then that I decided that I needed a heart-to-heart with Tracey as I was becoming increasingly despondent and depressed with the university course.

Thankfully, going to the University was not a condition of early release on parole. I returned the student grant to Essex Council and dropped out of the degree course. I felt as though I had been set free once again, only this time to do what I wanted. On reflection, if I had chosen the Criminology degree course at the other venue, I may have seen it through.

One of the conditions of early release on licence, however, was that I had to visit my Probation Officer, Nick Paul, on a regular basis. Nick is a well-respected Probation Officer in East London, who keeps himself super-fit by running full and half marathons for charity. I have always had an excellent rapport with Nick and used to view our meetings more like one-to-one discussions with a therapist than an official chore. Over the years, both in custody and outside, I have always valued his personal and professional judgement and advice. I know that he was disappointed when I dropped out of the degree course as the badlands of temptation and crime were never far away back in Canning Town. I assured Nick that I had too much to lose by returning to frontline crime. Admittedly, I was not 'whiter-than-white', but serious 'big-time' crime was anathema to me.

Now that I had lots of time on my hands, I started jogging and going to evening classes at the local gymnasium with Tracey. Then I acquired a serious infection in my dodgy leg. I had had this rampant infection twice before while I was in Long Lartin Prison, and on both occasions it left me seriously ill in bed with a very high temperature, a pounding headache, dizziness and nausea. The infection was so bad that I used to wake up every night with my bedding wringing wet. Quite literally, I used to sleep in puddles of perspiration. I visited the prison doctor, who examined the big lump inside my groin and the violent red blotches on my leg and he would confirm that it was an infection. I was told to take two tetracycline antibiotic tablets four times a day and basically sweat the infection out of me.

Once outside, when the same condition flared up again, I went to the local hospital, where I was admitted and put on an intravenous drip, whereby a big bag of liquid antibiotics was pumped into me four times a day, until after four days the infection was brought under control. In medical terms, the condition was called 'phlebitis', the inflammation of the vein, which is, apparently, a serious condition. It definitely *felt* serious, splashing about in my bed at night in Long Lartin Prison.

Apart from this medical hiccup, my social and family life was progressing splendidly. I am not saying that we wanted to make up for lost time, but Tracey and I used to go out to restaurants and clubbing with a large group of friends and family. Fortunately, we both enjoyed the same taste in spicy Thai food, football, hardcore dance music and, in my case, lashings of alcohol. Being a dedicated mother, Tracey had encouraged our two schoolboy sons to play both school and Sunday football for teams on Canvey Island, where she could be heard screaming at the top of her voice all over the recreation grounds of south Essex. When I first went to watch my sons play football, I was astonished at Tracey's in-depth knowledge and understanding of our national game. She was very familiar with the offside trap, overlapping, dropping back, pushing wide, tightening up, and so on. It was like going to watch a football match with my best buddy. The only problem was that she shouted louder and more often than me.

Upon being released from a prison sentence, especially a very long one, it is customary for close family and friends to rally round and offer what social, moral and economic support and assistance is possible. Generally, close family express this by way of genuine love and warmth, and others, like close friends and new acquaintances who like to partake in the home-coming celebrations, offer gifts of cash and opportunities of future employment.

Unfortunately for me on my release, all my old armed robber friends were either still in prison, dead or had evolved into other more profitable crimes. What I had learnt was that a new generation of sophisticated criminals had taken over and were enjoying the boom years of smuggling cannabis. These people, some of whom I considered friends, gave me cash out of respect and encouraged me to join them in their stylish and exciting social circle. I remember one occasion when I became the subject of some hilarious banter over a particular 1980s-style suede jacket that I was wearing. My friends ruthlessly explained that the jacket gave all the indications that the wearer was trapped in a time warp. Under great emotional pressure, because it was a cherished gift, the suede jacket had to go.

In many respects, the new generation of East End 30-something trendsetters gave me a much-needed crash course in the modern hedonistic delights of club life. At least once a month, sometimes more, Tracey and I would meet up with this exciting crowd of pleasure-seekers, upon which we would lose ourselves in a beautiful world of pulsating dance music, smiling faces, champagne and the occasional chemical stimulant. I recall one night of exotic oblivion, when I came out of a sound-proof toilet in a West End nightclub, and was reduced to atavistic forms of communication on the dance floor by the powerful tribal music. Before long, I had hijacked the mobile saxophone player and was pushing clubbers up on to the podium and found myself enjoying a tidal wave of ecstasy and rapture. The 'taking-me-to-heaven' dance music was completely at a variance with the prison life I had known. It was a universal language where people of all colours, cultures and creeds could forget their differences and live life to the full. This was when I really knew that I was home. This was what freedom of expression was all about; this was undiluted paradise, an amalgamation of happy humanity squeezed together on a sweaty dance floor and united by the anthem of love and friendship. If I could reproduce the feeling of that night and distribute it all over the world, the evils of war and conflict would become obsolete. Yeah, the night was that good!

In between social and family commitments and pressures, I was still revising for a forthcoming OU examination on the topic of crime and punishment. I even drove to the city of Cambridge for tutorials with fellow mature students. Up until that time, I was having one-to-one tutorials in prison, which were excellent, but the tutorials with 15–20 students were much more beneficial as we were able to bounce ideas and suggestions off one another.

What was particularly strange was that the course was attended by policemen and policewomen, many of whom were from the criminal justice world and I was the only one there who had a practical knowledge and experience of its end results. I took the third-level exam and, several months later, I received notification that I had once again passed with a 'distinction'. By the time the next OU course had started, I knew that there were too many social and familial distractions for me to maintain such a high academic standard, so I did not enrol again. *Sic transit gloria mundi* ... one of the glories of my world had, indeed, slipped away.

It was not long before my very first Christmas at home was upon us. There would be no pre-Christmas Eve prison visit this year, as I would savour the delights of family life at our home on Canvey Island. There was nothing unusual about the Smiths' residence; we had the same preoccupations and indulged in the same activities as everyone else. The same salvos of staccato laughter, the same wrestling matches on the lounge floor, where invariably it became everyone against Dad, the same sibling rivalry and the same petty arguments over infinitesimal issues. But most of all it was home, a home that my beloved Tracey had built out of maternal instinct and fortitude. Tracey was our planet and we all revolved around her, absorbing her natural loveliness and affection. Her gravitational pull was appreciated by all in equal measure, where the magical term of 'Mum' appeared to be the preferred remedy to all our problems.

Slotting into the difficult role of fatherhood, I set myself one overriding rule that, unlike my childhood experiences, I would never, ever hit my children. My superior aim in life was to make up for lost time and enjoy 'quality time' with my children. I took an active interest in their schooling, sports and personal interests. More specifically, I had encouraged them to partake in mine, such as dance music, football, snooker, cars and motor sport. On one particular occasion, after a heavy downfall of snow, I took our quad motorbike over to a local playing field and attached a sledge to it and began to tow my children on the sledge through the snow at high speed. It was exhilarating and everyone was overcome with shrieks of delight and joy, until some demented spoil-sport came over to us from some nearby houses and began to complain about us enjoying ourselves.

To me, he symbolised a thousand despotic screws who'd wanted to exert their tin-pot power on the landings in British prisons. I wanted to take his head off with one almighty punch and watch it disappear into the firmament, but I knew this man was a witness-box merchant, so I had to be content with merely decking him.

Living or residing 20-odd miles outside the badlands of East London had its advantages and shortcomings. To some degree, I saw the 20-mile gap as a buffer zone between the dark, inner reaches of crime and trouble and the sun-kissed world of home and comfort. At times, it was a pain to have to travel to London to meet or socialise with someone but, at other times, Canvey Island could be as enchanting as any Mediterranean isle. I noticed the inhabitants of the island were hard workers who loved their little luxuries in life and were always looking to ascend the social and economic ladder to betterment. Like the very tide of the Thames Estuary that lapped against its fortified shores, the workers of Canvey Island, many of whom were in the building trade, would set off for London and the South-East in their fully freighted trucks and vans before first light. Similarly, they would flood back along the main road to the island as the day came to a close. It was like a religious ritual for six long days of the week that was only undermined by the ubiquitous taxman. I liked Canvey Island and the people to whom Tracey had introduced me, but my heart still yearned for the badlands of London.

During the mid-1990s, the criminal art of armed robbery was about as healthy as a brontosaurus. Unless a professional armed robber had inside information and easy access to chunks of cash, it was far better that the robber looked elsewhere for an illicit income. Security companies had evolved along with the technology that protected them, and if the robber had not evolved at as impressive a rate as the new security measures, breaking into a security van would be like trying to shatter a ball bearing with a pin hammer. The security vans had voice-speaking alarms, exploding boxes with red dye, inaccessible locked safes and satellite-tracking devices that could pinpoint the location of the security van to the millimetre. For a novice robber who also had to contend with the growing culture of

CCTV, witness identification techniques and DNA evidence, the chances of success were slim. For a former, experienced armed robber like myself, for whom one stupid mistake could mean the 'two strikes' mandatory life sentence, the risks involved were very real and were not worth it.

Alternatively, the lucrative world of drug-smuggling and dealing appeared to offer large rewards and seemed to offer very little risk. I had seen carpenters, electricians, plumbers and labourers – nobodies, in fact, who simply had the gift of the gab, some style and charm – get involved in the drug-smuggling scene and crack it. Personally, I liked to see this, as years ago if you saw a young person driving a top-of-the-range BMW or Mercedes in the East End, he was stereotyped as either a successful armed robber or involved in a sophisticated fraud or long firm. Back then in the late 1970s and 1980s, young people with ostentatious clothes, cars and lifestyles stood out like a female streaker at a Wembley FA Cup Final. In the mid-1990s, however, the young, ambitious, designer-clothes-wearing smugglers or drug-dealers were everywhere.

On the down side, however, the involvement in the drug scene involved a whole host of sinister problems, particularly if the smuggler or dealer was using his or her merchandise. They had to contend with rip-offs (other criminals who robbed drug-dealers), knockers (criminals who refused to pay for the merchandise), police informers (jealous criminals who betrayed their friends), paranoia (a powerful by-product of taking drugs), the carrying of weapons, usually firearms, for protection, violence and sometimes death because of disagreement and conflict between rival criminals. When things were going well for the *nouveau riche* drug-dealer, life was all strawberries and cream, but when things went pear-shaped, it was creosote and custard all the way.

One of the salient observations I made during this period was the seemingly insatiable appetite both young and old drug-users had for cocaine. Being a fast-living, trendy drug, users would shove it up their nostrils like it was the last day of their lives, and then endure the transition from being interesting and vivacious company into a jaw-munching automaton with attendant slurring and limited vocabulary. It was painfully sad to see, especially when the older party people tried to keep up with the younger cocaine-snorters. Alas, not surprisingly, there were a spate of drug-related deaths due to the over indulgence of cocaine by older users in the mid-1990s. It become a palpable warning to slow down and get out of the fast lane of compulsive drug-taking as all the evidence was there to see, a steady stream of funerals of 'good people' who had pushed the accelerator flat to the boards.

A prominent drug-user and abuser of that time proclaimed that it was 'better to go out with a bang than to fade away'. I am not so sure, as it is the loved ones who they leave behind who have to wear the heavy cloak of bereavement and pain. As the great civil rights activist Martin Luther King declared, 'It's only when it is dark enough, you can see the stars.' The funerals were a stark reminder of the rigours and ravages of drug abuse.

As if to emphasise the bleak and sinister side of drugs, nowhere was safe, not even the rolling, picturesque countryside of Essex as seen in December 1995, when three well-known villains and doormen were blasted to death as they sat in their Range Rover not far from Canvey Island, Essex. It is alleged that the three men – Tony Tucker, Patrick Tate and Craig Rolfe – were lured to a field on the pretence of collecting a consignment of drugs, but their violent reputations preceded them and competitors took them out. Two men were later convicted of this crime and sentenced to life imprisonment despite the evidence of a witness being hotly disputed in court. The two men, Michael Steel and Jack Whomes, are still fighting to prove their innocence today and, one day, hope to be cleared.

Some nine months after I had been released from prison, I had my first encounter with the law. I was driving a motorcycle to my work as a fitness instructor at a well-known gymnasium in the East End when a police car pulled behind me and ordered me to stop. But, because I did not have a full motorcycle licence and I was still on parole, I panicked and went up on the pavement and tried to escape. I broke the continuity of the chase but a security guard at a superstore showed the police where I was parked. Initially, I was arrested for theft but when the police carried out their enquiries they quickly realised that the motorcycle was not stolen. I was reported for dangerous driving and driving with no insurance. Remarkably, I was given police bail and there was no mention of the parole situation; I assumed it was because it was only a driving offence. I elected to go for trial and, before I knew it, due to the fast-track system, the trial was set for October 1996. I offered to plead guilty to 'driving with undue care and attention' instead of the much more serious 'dangerous driving' charge which carried a maximum sentence of two years' imprisonment. The judge adjourned the case for 15 minutes to discuss my case with the prosecutor who was not in the least bit interested. The judge obviously wanted to deal with the case there and then. It was almost certain that he was going to send me to prison and, as a consequence, trigger the revocation of the parole licence. Prison, prison, prison ... I had had enough of time behind the cell door.

Normally, I would be produced in the dock of the court from the cells. This time, however, I had the option of voluntarily returning to the dock to incur the wrath of my nemesis, the judge and parole board, or take what was rightfully mine, the sunlit path to freedom and family life.

There was no contest ... inherent loathing and fear of prison gave wings to my feet and I was henceforth a fugitive. A warrant was issued for my arrest. I was of the opinion that I was not going to volunteer for one minute of prisondom. If the police and court authorities wanted me, let them come and find me. Obviously, the warrant for my arrest meant that I could not reside at my home address with my family, which was a bitter blow for us all, but it was better to be a free, fun-loving fugitive than a pensive prisoner and a burden to my nearest and dearest. Quite simply, I would have had to have been neurologically unbalanced to volunteer for prison, as it is a fundamental human instinct to flee from any form of incarceration.

Life on the run or as a fugitive was nothing new to me. It was a pain to have to go 'on my toes' again over such a senseless and stupid driving offence, but there was no alternative. I knew the rules; find a new place to live, new vehicle and stay away from my old haunts and habitat. Because of the lack of seriousness of the situation, I knew that the police were not exactly going to unleash the bloodhounds to rearrest me, so it was a matter of adopting and embracing a low-profile lifestyle for a while.

Inwardly, I was annoyed at myself for having got into this stupid situation, particularly as that is what the more sinister side of the police wanted. An ex-long-term prisoner, former armed robber, a fugitive forced to commit serious crimes in order to eke out an existence.

Unfortunately for them, with age comes wisdom and knowledge. I was fully conscious of the perilous position I was in, and I was determined not to become a gift-wrapped arrest-and-conviction for them. If there was one thing I had learnt in prison, it was not to let enforced circumstances dictate events. Think things through thoroughly and rationally. Avoid taking unnecessary risks. Keep cool, keep calm and, most of all, stay out of prison. They were not having me … or so I thought!

Due to the self-imposition of fugitive status and the publicity it brings, I was, of course, unable to visit my friend and co-defendant John Kendall in prison. Directly on release from prison, I had applied to the prison authorities to be vetted and cleared to visit Kendall, as he was still a High-Risk Category 'A' prisoner. I was surprised when the Home Office and police cleared me, as they kept us apart throughout the duration of our sentence. I recall the first visit I had had with Kendall; he was in Frankland Prison in Durham, where I had been held for over two-and-a-half years.

The long and exhausting train journey took approximately four hours without delays from King's Cross. Tracey and our small children had endured exactly this journey every fortnight for two-and-a-half years without fail. That meant Tracey and my young family had travelled to Frankland prison at least 65 times over that period. I did the journey once and found it incredibly tedious, but necessary to visit a friend.

Kendall was later transferred to Whitemoor Prison in Cambridgeshire, where I visited him once or twice before the warrant for my arrest was activated. Once the warrant was issued, naturally, to Kendall's chagrin, the visits ceased. Kendall had obviously became aware of my predicament and, to make amends, very occasionally I would stop off at his relatives and leave money in an envelope so that his wife was able to visit.

A short time after decamping from Snaresbrook Crown Court, my Probation officer had to notify the Home Office that I was no longer living at my home address and therefore I had broken the conditions of parole. A warrant was issued and I was declared unlawfully at large. At the time of the revocation, I had approximately nine months left of the sentence to complete. But, due to another stroke of good fortune, Kendall had somehow managed to recalculate our prison sentences again and we had them reduced by 196 days. It meant that, on recapture, I'd have 31 days left to serve. I considered giving myself up but ruled against this as, while in custody for the 31 days, I would be produced at court in custody, which would leave little option for the judge but to impose a custodial sentence. It was a catch-22 scenario.

Throughout the next three years from 1997 to 2000, I had two overriding aims in life. First, to remain free; and second, to create, savour and enjoy some quality time with my loyal and devoted wife and family. With the help of my fabulous in-laws, Pat and Iris Etherden, Tracey managed to move from the old house to a new address on Canvey Island. This enabled me to come back home and live with my family. Obviously, I was conscious that any serious investigation by the police to trace and locate my wife's new address would not be too difficult but, after all, it was only a driving offence and 31 days of parole, not exactly worthy of an intensive manhunt.

More interestingly, I was of the opinion that, due to the sterling status that I had in the so-called criminal underworld, the élite surveillance squads of Essex and the Metropolitan Police Forces were most probably monitoring the movements of both my associates and me anyway. It made logical sense to leave me alone and wait until I possibly organised or committed a more serious crime. I was aware of this and therefore accepted that any venture into serious crime would be monitored and logged even before it was committed. I had seen too many old prison pals come out of prison and return to their old criminal haunts and end up back in prison sentenced under the new 'two strikes' mandatory life sentence statute.

A controversial case comes to mind: the apprehension and arrest of Rooky Lee, a very charismatic villain, who had been released from an 18-year prison sentence for robbing a Post Office security van in Chelmsford, Essex, in the mid-1980s. It transpired that, in March 1997, he had been visiting a friend in Edmonton, North London, when he was arrested for a robbery on a Securicor security van that had occurred some five miles away in Whetstone, North London. As is always the case, once Rooky's previous convictions were realised, the wheels of fabrication and corruption were put into motion. Rooky was taken to a police station where as he was leaving a police cell, a uniformed police witness proclaimed to a senior officer, 'Yes, that is the man!' and made a seemingly legitimate identification of the potential robber.

Behind the scenes, to compound Rooky's problems and consolidate evidence in the case, it was alleged in court that black fibres were found on Rooky's white shirt, a discarded coat and the seat of a hijacked vehicle, and yet the source of the black fibre was never found. When Rooky appeared at the Old Bailey, the trial was going so well for the defence team the police claimed that the jury had been nobbled and a fresh trial was ordered. At a retrial, utterly bereft of any faith in British justice, Rooky decided to remain in the cells below the court. Rooky was convicted and sentenced to life imprisonment.

Rooky's case was heard at the Criminal Court of Appeal and dismissed. As I write, Rooky is awaiting the outcome of an internal police investigation into the case before he takes the matter any further. Personally, I have always been concerned because of my past history of armed robbery that I, too, may become a target of depraved and corrupt detectives who'd want to fit me up. After the tragic cases of George Davis in the 1970s, the Birmingham Six, the Guildford Four and, more recently, Stephen Downing, who had served 27 years in prison before being cleared, we would be naïve to believe that the fabrication of evidence does not go on to secure convictions of potential suspects. On average, going by modern reinvestigation methods and procedure, it takes a decade or more before a miscarriage of justice is exposed and rectified by the Court of Appeal. Let's hope the likes of Barry George, who was convicted of the Jill Dando murder, and Rooky Lee don't have to wait that long.

Another poignant reminder of the perilous pitfalls of contemporary armed robbery was the apprehension and arrest of Perry Terroni, a South-East London robber who would openly admit that he was not the most successful armed robber to come out of the badlands of Rotherhithe and Bermondsey. Nonetheless, Perry was a very well-respected villain; he had served successive prison sentences of seven and 12 years for robbery during the 1980s and 1990s and was therefore eligible for the 'two strikes' mandate.

In April 2000, Perry, now in his 40s, took stock of his lugubrious home and economic circumstances, and all he could see was a cycle of poverty and suffering. Perry had had enough, he went out on his own and robbed a security guard in Bromley, South-East London, and was knocked up into the air by a have-a-go witness driving a car. Perry was nicked, processed by the courts and sentenced to life imprisonment, all within six months. It was a tragic waste of a 'good person' who worshipped his elderly parents and his beautiful son. Many of us may have sympathy and respect for a person like Perry Terroni, who acknowledged but refused to accept his dead-end predicament and tried to get out of the gutter with a gun. Undeniably, what Perry did was illegal and now he is paying the price of failure. But, in the annals of modern crime and criminals, Perry is an honourable guy and he has my respect.

As a judicial concept, the 'two strikes' automatic life sentence mandate for armed robbery is a powerful deterrent to all career criminals. For some like Perry Terroni, who committed an impromptu robbery out of economic necessity, it is a tragedy. For others like Rooky Lee, who was convicted under flimsy evidence, it is a living nightmare. For me, there is no alternative. Prison has had its pound of flesh out of me and, however painful and priceless an experience and education, it is time to hang up the six-shots.

As we all get older, it is inevitable that people close to us pass away. These people may be very close family members, mere friends or remote acquaintances; either way, we are reminded of our fragile grip on mortality. When I was a child, I used to sit in bed at night and try to unravel the enormous dark and unfathomable riddle of what happens to us once we die. The problem was so huge and daunting that it used to leave me feeling utterly desolate and despondent. I still have this comfortless feeling when I hear of the death of someone young, and it's particularly poignant if it's a young person I know.

In 1995, I met a very well-respected East London villain, Chris Pearman, while I was at The Mount Prison in Hertfordshire. Chris was a very private person and obviously liked to serve his sentence with as little fuss or brouhaha as possible. While at the jail, Chris would receive regular visits from his wife Lorraine and his two popular sons, Darren and Scott. As any outsider could see, he loved his sons immensely and they made an adorable family unit. Several years after my release, I bumped into Chris at a nightclub and we became close friends. Occasionally, I would pop over to Bethnal Green to visit Chris and his family. On a personal level, I feel that I have always been a good judge of character and, because of past experiences, I have always embraced a healthy splash of cynicism before getting to know someone. I had no such misgivings about the Pearman family, though, as they exuded a genuine warmth and affection that I had not seen for a long while.

One Saturday morning in November 1999, I decided to pay Chris a surprise visit. I had not seen Chris for about three or four months; we had a chat and he invited me to a function at a West End nightclub later that evening. I declined as I was staying indoors. Nonetheless, after speaking to Darren, I swapped our latest phone numbers and set off home. I never take my mobile phone up to my bedroom, but that night, for some inexplicable reason, I did.

At about 3.30am, the mobile phone rang. It was a very distraught Chris; he was phoning from the West End, saying that Darren had been stabbed and he was in Whipp's Cross Hospital. I offered to meet Chris there. I quickly got dressed and set off along the A13 towards London, when I got another call from an inconsolable Chris; he said that his beloved son was dead. Angrily, I told him to disbelieve this and to get to the hospital and find out for himself. I did a quick detour and collected my brother Lenny, as I knew this was going to be a rough ride. When we reached the hospital, it was like the aftermath of a Shakespearean tragedy. Innumerable police, doctors, nurses and an utterly distraught array of family and friends, most of whom could not reconcile the fact that a good night out had been turned into a wretched tragedy.

It was one of the most heart-wrenching moments of my life to witness the dignified and proud parents of a beloved son, a brother and close friends weeping profusely and some talking incoherently. Chris implored me to come with him and to 'warm his son up'. While the police were waiting in the wings to take everyone's names and addresses, Chris would repeat time and time again, 'He is not dead, Tel! He is not dead, Tel!'

Once again, the police were the only ones to profit out of this tragedy. They waited like vultures to investigate the case, arrest someone and perhaps imprison someone for life and cause another unsuspecting family inconsolable grief and suffering.

Alas, several arrests were made by the Murder Squad but, due to the unwillingness of eyewitnesses to the tragedy to provide details, the case never got off the ground. The following year, a former nightclub doorman was shot dead outside his house in Grays, Essex. The Murder Squad detectives did not need a motive, they'd already guessed it, and it was revenge. Another cadaver, another case, another tragedy. No one wins.

I went to Darren's funeral and, for someone so young, vibrant and colourful, he could not have wished for such a poignant and well-attended service and burial. Over 500 close family, friends and acquaintances turned up to pay their respects and, if I am allowed to use the term, 'celebrate' a life that was so brutally cut short by a pointless tragedy. God bless, Darren!

Not long after Darren passed away – in an uncanny coincidence – two of his close friends also died. One of them was the irrepressible and ever-humorous Jarrot whom I had met through Darren. Jarrot was one of those people you meet once in your life and you never forget. Jarrot possessed the ability to make the grumpiest and most inconsolable person in the world laugh and giggle until his or her belly hurt. He was loved and adored by everyone who had the pleasure to meet him. Tragically, he was killed in a road traffic accident on a motor scooter while taking flowers to his mother on Mother's Day.

The other close friend of Darren's was Mark Rutherford. I had only met Mark through Chris Pearman and we became good friends almost immediately. Mark was strong, resolute and radiated all the qualities that I liked in a person. There was no bullshit and he got straight to the point. Again, tragically, Mark passed away while on holiday in Thailand. Due to a lack of communication, I was unaware of both these tragedies until they had both been buried. I would have loved to have paid my respects to these two extraordinary individuals as they were and remain 'good gravy guys'.

As we came to the fag end of 1999, things did not get any better when I heard that my best friend's father and mentor, old Tommy Hole, and another man, 'Joe the Crow', had been shot and killed in the Beckton Arms in East London. Allegedly, two masked gunmen walked into the pub on a Sunday afternoon in December and shot them while they were drinking. Gossip and rumours circulated in the media and the criminal underworld as to the motive for such a callous and cold-blooded crime. The most compelling theory for the murders was that it was pay-back for the equally chilling assassination of Nicky Gerard, who'd been gunned down as he left his house in June 1982. Others speculated that it was the result of a consignment of drugs that went missing months earlier, or a drug deal that went wrong. Either way, it was a sad loss for me as old Tom, along with his best friend Lenny Carter, had taught me the craft of armed robbery.

As a team, they were 'Generals of the Game', using a bold and daring display of imagination and artistry to relieve security vans of their fibrous contents. In their heyday, no security van was safe. If they fancied a bit of work and formulated a plan, it would be put into motion and attacked with the audacity and precision of a military operation. I liked to think that young Tom and I contributed to their reign as 'The Grand Masters of Armed Robbery'. As with most professional armed robbers, unless they were arrested for the crime, they were unable to claim their fame or notoriety. By that, I mean in the 'perfect' crime, like the perfect professional robbery, no one is ever nicked and the super sleuths of the Serious Crime Squads have nothing to go on. As a result, no one will ever know who the perpetrators of that particular crime were. Although, for obvious reasons, I am unable and unwilling to specify or enumerate the successful bits of work that we had over the years. In many respects, it has been left to me, albeit belatedly, to acknowledge and confer on the masters of armed robbery – old Tommy Hole, Lenny Carter and young Tommy Hole – the glory or, as some would say, the notoriety, that they deserve. As a lasting epitaph, all I would to say to them is that it was a pleasure working with you guys.

As the old millennium came to a close and a new bright and vibrant one emerged, I reflected upon how far I had come and how – through wisdom, experience and suffering – I had evolved into a more mature person. They say that life begins at 40 and now I had reached that momentous milestone. On a business or economic level, I felt that I had not yet quite reached my full potential as, having been incarcerated for over a decade between the ages of 23 and 36, my competitors had been given an unfair advantage. On a personal level, however, I felt that in some weird way prison had made me a better person; through a process of self-education, realisation and enrichment, I had finally come to acknowledge who I was and where I was going. I would not go so far as to say that I was satisfied and contented with life, as I still possessed a strong drive and ambition to attain financial security for my family and children.

That aside, however, I felt that I had become aware of a new facet of my life. A feeling that there was more to life than the scientific measurement of phenomena and materialism that I have always been led to aspire to. I found that, for whatever reason, I was undergoing a spiritual awakening and I could sense both goodness and danger. I therefore faced the unknown of the new millennium with a degree of ambivalence. I knew that there were good and bad events lying ahead. I can't explain this, as it was very intuitive and instinctive, but I knew that the new millennium was not going to be all peaches and cream. More like peaches and vinegar.

Unfortunately, the darker side was still with me when, in April 2000, my beloved grandmother-cum-mother Dolly Smith passed away after a long illness. Since being released from prison in 1996, my family and I had become frequent visitors to her little bungalow in the backwaters of Essex. Dolly led a very simple existence and, towards the end like most elderly pensioners, she became dependent upon home helps, meals on wheels, and the unswerving dedication and loyalty of her middle son. Her health deteriorated to such an extent that she was hospitalised until she passed away aged 88. If there is one lasting image or trait that I have of my grandmother, it is that she always saw the best in people. Of course, over the years, some people took advantage of this and it hurt her very much, but her lasting belief – 'Whatever you put into life you will get back' – still persevered. I like to believe, in spite of my problems and attendant hardships in life, that I have adopted and emulated this simple caveat. And, despite being ruthlessly let down by some people myself, it still appears to be the best advice I have ever had!

I have always felt, as far as the Smith family were concerned, that we were a complete functional family unit. Our two teenage boys Terence and Bradley had evolved into fine, strapping young men and our beautiful daughter Jade was at the GCSE end of her schooling. It was then a complete surprise when Tracey announced that she was pregnant. I had been aware of her broodiness when her two younger sisters had recently given birth to their babies. So the notion that we were going to be parents again in our forties was a pleasant surprise. I never ever thought that we would have four children; it just wasn't in the script.

After the initial shock of the pregnancy and the delightful prospect of parenthood, we were made aware of the potential dangers of women giving birth in their forties. Our greatest fear was that of giving birth to a baby with Down's Syndrome. In order to establish the likelihood of this occurring, we decided to volunteer for invasive surgery in which a sample of the placenta is extracted from the womb using a long needle and tested for evidence of the disorder. Apparently, the invasive procedure does incur a small risk of miscarriage but, in our view, it was essential that we were certain that our baby would be healthy and normal.

A week after the operation, we received the results and they indicated that everything was OK. Then, after five long hours of pain-ridden, belly-contracting, lung-panting, knuckle-clenching, faith-reassuring phantasmagorical labour, Sonny George Smith, weighing a healthy 8lb 4oz, entered the world looking both red as a beetroot and white as a turnip. By that, I mean the umbilical cord had been caught over the baby's neck and shoulders. As the sporadic contractions forced the baby down the birth canal, when the contractions receded, the baby would return to its former position. It was like the baby was attached to an elastic band which itself was attached to its lunch pack – the placenta. It was no coincidence that, when Sonny eventually managed to dislodge his backpack, he entered the world as the full-time football results were being broadcast on Saturday, 16 December 2000. As soon as I saw his very compact muscular body and large powerful hands, I knew that he was going to be a footballer – a left-footed footballer who'd eventually solve the perennial problem of the weak left flank in the England team.

Amazingly, within a minute of being born, this phenomenal mass of hormones and chromosomes was gagging for his first feed from his happy and exhausted mother. It was a sight that put everything into perspective for me. It reduced all pre-conceived beliefs and values about life to a minimum. This was why we were put on earth to procreate and recreate the continuous cycle of human life and existence.

Over the following weeks and months and well into the New Year of 2001, our beautiful newborn baby would wake up in my brawny arms with a beautiful smile that would melt the hearts of a million mothers. Due to the occupational hazard of my chosen profession, I had missed out on the parental delights of raising our other children and I was therefore desperate to make amends this time. More than anything, I was looking forward to it. That is, until my erstwhile co-defendant came home with other plans.

Epilogue: Seeing the Signs

In early April 2001, I heard some splendid news – my old robbing partner and former co-defendant John Kendall was finally coming home from prison. Kendall had served 17 long and hard years out of a 29-year prison sentence and it was long overdue that he was coming home. I always felt that Kendall would have been released from prison a lot earlier if he had used his time constructively while in prison as I did, and had not pandered to the media image of himself as a London gangster and a dramatic prison escaper.

Upon hearing that Kendall was being released, I heard that the Police Federation was up in arms over his release as he had nearly five years of his prison sentence left to serve and that he was still viewed as a top-security High-Risk Category 'A' prisoner. This meant, by definition, that he was still considered a danger to the police and public. Normally, top-security prisoners of Kendall's stature have to jump through the 'good behaviour' hoops of de-categorisation, from double 'AA' to single 'A' status, right down the ladder to 'C' or 'D' categorisation before release. Kendall had unusually by-passed this time-consuming process and was to be released almost immediately.

I had discussed the release of Kendall with Tracey and we both decided to give him a good homecoming but to keep him at arm's length, as the last time we were at large together we were both arrested for the Kensal Rise robbery, placed in prison for a decade or more and, perhaps more fundamentally, I had nearly lost my life.

When I finally got to meet Kendall and his wife, we were all hugs and cuddles and I was genuinely pleased to see that, although prison had not been kind to him – he was now a bald, pot-bellied 50-year-old has-been – he still had some of his marbles intact. I made him feel welcome and gave him a £6,000 car that I had for sale on my driveway.

We spent the night together at my house drinking champagne while we came up to speed with each other's lives. Initially, I found him very humorous and talkative, although I could sense an underlying seam of bitterness and resentment over prison issues and the way he had wasted the best part of his life.

Over the coming weeks, Kendall had become a regular visitor to my home address on Canvey Island, Essex, and although I wanted to help him readjust back into 'normal society', I soon realised that a social and cultural gulf had emerged between us. In short, Kendall wanted to party, whereas I wanted to savour the phenomenal delights of family life with our newborn baby boy Sonny Smith.

Two weeks after his release, Kendall came to my house and dropped the bombshell that he wanted to start robbing again. I looked at him in amazement and also looked behind him to see if there were any dinosaurs following him, as what he was saying to me was totally and utterly prehistoric! Without a moment's hesitation, I told him to forget about it as, not only was *I* not robbing, neither was he! He seemed disappointed with this response.

To cut a long story short, Kendall became a constant visitor to my home address and he always wanted some advice or he wanted me to commit some serious crime or other. For instance, he wanted to know whether or not I would be interested in committing a robbery with his close friend Danny Shankshaft. I gave him the same answer as before – I was not robbing, and neither was he!

Kendall came to my house again and again; he asked if I could acquire for him a large consignment of cannabis resin through some associates I knew. He also asked what would happen if he were arrested with a firearm in his possession; would he be liable for the automatic 'two strikes' life sentence in prison? On another occasion, he asked me whether or not I had committed a high-profile armed robbery in East London that had occurred several years earlier, which I hadn't! He also asked me if I could get him a gun as a black guy had allegedly fired two shots at his 21-year-old son who had foolishly tried to chat up the black guy's attractive girlfriend.

Each time Kendall came to my home, he always had a problem or he wanted something from me. It got so bad that Tracey and I nicknamed him 'The Pest'! I did not want to ignore or ostracise Kendall as he was in dire need of guidance, but I wanted to keep him at arm's length as I had been home from prison for six glorious years with my lovely family and I wanted to keep it that way.

A short time after that, in mid-May 2001, Kendall came to my home address and gave me his new mobile phone number. He said that he had had to destroy his original phone because he and Shankshaft were supposed to collect some amphetamine sulphate from an old prison friend but the fellow failed to turn up for the meet because he had been arrested. I knew the guy that Kendall was alluding to. He'd only been home from prison a short time himself. I remember thinking to myself, God, that fellow is awfully unlucky! Months later, I found out this was all lies, as Kendall and his accomplice Shankshaft had returned a kilo of the drug to the unfortunate guy who, minutes later, drove away into a police trap!

Then, in late May 2001, Kendall came to my home with a proposition regarding counterfeit money. He said that he and some prison pals of his were relocating a printing workshop from London to the Midlands and he initially wanted someone reliable to run the 'valuable printing presses' up to the Midlands, and thereafter I could be part of the scam. This sounded like a bit more like it as, although it did not involve frontline crime, there would be a healthy profit margin in it for me. I agreed to become a part of this criminal venture and Kendall said he would give me £500 to deliver the 'valuable printing presses' to the Midlands.

At about 4.00pm on 4 June 2001, Kendall came to my home and asked me to collect the printing presses that evening and deliver them to his friend in Cambridgeshire the following morning. He gave me a map of where I had to go and promised me the money. Unfortunately for him, I was expecting some relatives to come from London who were going to buy my jet-ski from me. I explained to Kendall that it was impossible for me to collect the presses that night, as I wanted to sell the machine. I offered to let a friend collect the presses in London and I would deliver them the following morning but, for some reason, Kendall felt uneasy about this and said that he had to leave and that he would phone me later.

Later that same evening, Kendall rang me and said that Shankshaft was unable to deliver the presses that night as there were 'too many Old Bill about' and Kendall said that he would ring me the next day.

The next morning I dropped my daughter to school, had a jog, showered and dressed and was on my way to London to see a friend nicknamed George Best when Kendall rang me. Kendall wanted to meet me at Upminister Tube Station. I met Kendall outside the station and he asked if I would be willing to collect and deliver the printing presses that day. I said yes. He said that Shankshaft was bringing them there and then. Knowing that Kendall was on parole, I asked Kendall to give me Shankshaft's mobile phone number and he could get on his way but, strangely, Kendall insisted on remaining with me. Meanwhile, I rang Shankshaft, whom I'd only met once before at a football match, and he asked me to meet him at his home address in Hornchurch, Essex. Shankshaft said he was not home yet and could I give him 25 minutes, as he had to stop off somewhere.

What a sucker ... if only I had seen the signs! Unbeknown to me, almost simultaneously at nearby Hornchurch Police Station, a resolute team of very senior and specialist policemen and women had gathered over an hour earlier for an 'impending job' and were about to be briefed. They included the Borough Commander, three detective inspectors, a police sergeant, 13 Armed Response Vehicle police officers and two eminent detectives from SO11, the élite intelligence branch of Scotland Yard. Also at the same time, five undercover surveillance officers were deployed in three unmarked police vehicles around Shankshaft's home address in nearby

Hornchurch. Whatever was going down, this was no Sunday crowd-control operation, this was spot-on information and someone was supplying it big time!

After the call to Shankshaft, I asked Kendall where his partner lived and told him to go and let me get on with it, but he refused, claiming that he would take me to Shankshaft's house personally. We drove in convoy to Eyhurst Avenue, Hornchurch, where we parked our cars and went for a walk in a nearby park. After about 20 minutes, I received a call from Shankshaft; he claimed that he was indoors and that we should come round. We left the entrance of the park and turned right down Warren Drive, Hornchurch. After walking about 250 yards, we came to Shankshaft's house.

As we stood outside the front door, I looked along the street and I had this strong sensation that I was being watched. Before I had time to assimilate these strange thoughts and feelings, the front door was opened and Shankshaft asked us to come in.

According to the police observation log, we entered Shankshaft's house at 12.33pm. We greeted each other and then I asked where the parcel was, as I wanted to get on my way. Oddly, Shankshaft then asked me where my car was parked as he said he'd bring the parcel round to my car. I told him that I was parked around the corner in Eyhurst Avenue. I then asked for the £500 that he'd promised me, and Shankshaft pulled out a wad of banknotes and gave me the £500 in used £20 notes. I was a little concerned that Shankshaft wouldn't let me carry the parcel or examine it. What raised my suspicions even more was Shankshaft wanting to walk the parcel round to my car ... or did he want to see what type of car it was?

The time was now 12.36pm and, going by the official surveillance log, I left Shankshaft's house with Kendall and we walked empty-handed back to our vehicles. Exactly one minute later, Shankshaft left his house carrying a blue bag with the 'valuable printing presses' inside. He walked around to Eyhurst Avenue and placed the 'heavy blue bag' inside the passenger footwell of my vehicle. He tapped on the roof of my vehicle and walked back the way he came and jumped into Kendall's silver Vauxhall Vectra that was registered to his home address.

Meanwhile, I leant over the centre console of my vehicle and partially opened the blue bag using a drawstring. I wanted to check the bag for drugs, because I was suspicious as to why they would not let me carry the bag or check the contents of the bag inside the house. I looked inside the blue bag and saw a yellow cloth or towelling-like material. I put my hands inside the blue bag and I felt something hard and metallic. Happy that I couldn't feel any drugs, such as pills, powder or bush (weed), I pulled the drawstring and got on my way.

Again, unbeknown to me, most of the police personnel who had attended the earlier briefing were now strategically parked up at a nearby rendezvous points. These vehicles consisted of five assorted Armed Response Vehicles and a Dog Section van. Little did I know, at 12.37pm, the same time that Shankshaft left his address, the Detective Inspector in control of the armed operation instructed the other ARVs to 'stop the vehicle coming away from the premises, which is believed to have a weapon in it'. Somehow, the heavily armed police ARVs are aware that there is a 'machine pistol' in my vehicle ... while I believe that I am carrying 'valuable printing presses'.

Who gave the police this information? Was it Shankshaft? Was it Kendall? Or were they both working as a team?

At about 12.40pm, I pulled away from Eyhurst Avenue and set off on my way. I was about 15 minutes into my journey, approximately three miles away from Shankshaft's address, when the DI controller of the armed operation, who maintained direct contact with the Borough Commander, authorised the other ARVs to conduct a non-compliant stop procedure as it was now believed that there was a sub-machine pistol in my car.

I was driving along Wood Lane in Dagenham, Essex, when I came to a busy traffic junction appropriately called 'The Fiddlers'. The traffic lights were red and there was a stationary car in front of me. I looked into my rear-view mirror and I could see two marked Vauxhall Omega police cars behind me. But, even more disturbingly, the policeman in the passenger seat of the lead vehicle (Trojan 211) was wearing body armour and was staring at me intently; so much so, in fact, I thought to myself, Are they for me? I looked down at the blue bag and said to myself, 'Nah, they can't be for me, I'm only carrying printing presses!'

I looked into my rear-view mirror again and I could see the cozzer's piercing eyes burning into me. I could literally feel the intensity of his concentration as if he was really psyched up for something. As the traffic lights changed to green, the car in front began to pull away and, at the same time, an unmarked black Honda police car came up the inside of me and pulled across my path, leaving me an appreciable gap to squeeze through and go round the police vehicle. Once again, I looked into my rear-view mirror and the cozzer was already out of the lead police vehicle with his MP5 carbine machine-gun trained at the driver's side door of my vehicle.

For a split-second, I considered slamming the accelerator of the powerful BMW 328ci to the floor and going for the gap, but sensibly I said to myself, 'I have got nothing to worry about as I have only got printing presses on board. It isn't the end of the world ...' Or so I thought!

Even before the cozzer had time to bark his orders at me – 'ARMED POLICE ... SHOW ME YOUR HANDS!' – I already had my hands out of the open window of the driver's door. Another ARV police officer came to the driver's door and ordered me to get out of the vehicle. He escorted me to the rear of the BMW where another ARV police officer took over and began to handcuff me behind my back. As he was doing this, I noticed that his hands were trembling considerably. Very strange indeed!

As all this was occurring, I was thinking, God, what's happening? This is not some pot luck, off-the-cuff, routine vehicle check ... this is heavy shit! With my hands manacled behind my back, I looked up to the clear, blue summer sky and wondered, What the fuck is going on? Something was definitely not right here and the only way to get to the bottom of it would be through the power of undeniable truth.

To compound my suspicions, as I was being handcuffed at the rear of my vehicle, another police officer ran past us and blurted, 'Who fucking parked that like that?' alluding to the unmarked black Honda police vehicle which was supposed to conduct an authorised non-compliant stop. I can visualise the headlines in the newspapers now: DANGEROUS VILLAIN SHOT DEAD IN POLICE ROAD BLOCK ... POLICE FIND LOADED UZI SUB-MACHINE-GUN AND 376 ROUNDS OF AMMUNITION IN THE VILLAIN'S CAR. My wife might have been planting flowers on my grave, always wondering the extent of Kendall and Shankshaft's roles.

Again, while at the rear of my vehicle, another plain-clothes detective ran past me proclaiming that they were from the Romford Crime Squad and that they were looking for drugs. Minutes earlier it had been circulated over the police airwaves that there was a sub-machine pistol in the car. I was then chaperoned to the driver's door of the vehicle by a member of the Romford Crime Squad while another officer went to the passenger footwell of the car. I was ordered to watch as the detective searched the blue bag. As one detective searched the bag, the other one restraining me was saying, 'What have we got?' His colleague replied, 'A pistol!'

My mind was racing, as I was expecting 'valuable printing presses' to be in the blue bag, and not a gun. In my view, I had undeniably been set up, but who was responsible? Was it Shankshaft or Kendall?

Nah, my pal Kendall wouldn't do that, he was good stuff and I had known him for a long time. Or was he? All the dark anxieties and concerns over the sudden and unusual release of Kendall from prison began to haunt me. I went over the events that had occurred earlier that day. On the whole, Shankshaft appeared to play the part very well. But Kendall did look perturbed by something and it showed. Was it an irrepressible pang of guilt or was it his new perfidious persona? Anyone who knows Kendall knows that it is hard for him to conceal his thoughts or feelings. Why wouldn't Kendall tell me where Shankshaft lived? Why did Kendall want to be at the collection point when he had no need or reason to be there? He did not add up!

As for Shankshaft, I hardly knew him and it was highly probable that he was behind all this, as he insisted on knowing where I had parked my car, possibly in order to register what car I was driving. He insisted on coming out of his house after Kendall and me had left. More damagingly, he personally made sure that the heavy blue bag was placed in my car and that I did not have a proper chance